100
UNDER
100

100 UNDER 100

THE RACE TO SAVE THE WORLD'S RAREST LIVING THINGS

SCOTT LESLIE

FOREWORD BY STUART PIMM

Collins

HarperCollins Publishers Ltd
2 Bloor Street East, 20th Floor
Toronto, Ontario, Canada
M4W 1A8

www.harpercollins.ca

Library and Archives Canada Cataloguing in Publication
information is available upon request

ISBN 978-1-44340-428-0

Printed and bound in Canada
TG 9 8 7 6 5 4 3 2 1

100 Under 100 is printed on Ancient Forest Friendly paper
made with 100% post-consumer waste

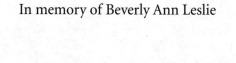

In memory of Beverly Ann Leslie

CONTENTS

FOREWORD

They have such strange names. Wollemi pine. Gilbert's potoroo. Greater bamboo lemur. Iranian Gorgan Mountain salamander. Nene. Bachman's warbler. And they're so unfamiliar, too. These aren't species most of us know. Is anything really at stake as they hang on to survival by only a thread?

The answer is an emphatic yes. Some of the species are intrinsically beautiful. All of them live in special places. Their declines shout out at our carelessness with our planet. And, some show that we can bring species back from the very edge, that we need not, indeed must not, accept extinction as an option.

I saw my first Iberian lynx after midnight at the Coto Doñana in Spain, walking along the edge of a lake in the light of a full moon. The memory is still vivid. It looked at me just as cats do, with complete contempt, for it belonged there and I didn't. Cats appeal to us in deeply interesting ways. It was a lovely animal.

So, too, are Przewalski's horses, though I've only seen them in zoos, where they are everyone's favourites. Lemurs, too, are appealing. Most mammals are, but being cute isn't enough.

What unites the creatures, both large and small, in this book is where they live. The seven billion of us are destroying our forests and grasslands—almost all terrestrial habitats—and making a mess of rivers, lakes, and the ocean. Habitat destruction is the major cause of species extinction. Not all habitats are equal. Some are very much more vulnerable to our actions than others. The species mentioned herein teach us that.

I saw my first nene at Slimbridge, a successful captive breeding facility in England, a world away from their homes in the Hawaiian Islands. The nene I remember most were wild ones—a small flock that descended through the mist as I hiked across Haleakala on Maui. They landed in front of me as grey fog gave way to brilliant blue skies and revealed the surreal purples, yellows, and browns of the caldera. Wild, remote, beautiful—and how can anything live in such a strange place? These birds and more than 100 others, 1,000 species of plants, and countless insects once thrived only in the Hawaiian Islands, adapted to those unique conditions. Note the past tense: so many Hawaiian species are now extinct.

I watched the movie *Avatar* and enjoyed its creativity but spent the next day watching pteropods—snails that literally fly with their feet through the ocean. Biological diversity—"biodiversity" for short—is far stranger than fiction!

Iran conjures up an image of deserts and, when I was there, the memory of days on rough, dusty roads. We crossed northward from the deserts of eastern Iran toward the Caspian Sea. In minutes, wet air replaced dry, and lush moist forests took over. In a cave nearby was the Gorgan Mountain salamander, living in a pool, in a sliver of wet forest south of the Caspian, in the middle of deserts and grasslands that stretch 16,000 kilometres from the Sahara to Mongolia.

Nature has amazing inventiveness and recognizes the places where these species live as being exceptional. Alas, this book's species are rare because we do not. So many of them are on the edge because we have been careless. The Guam rail used to be common. Then a snake accidentally introduced to Guam ate it—and all the other birds on Guam—to extinction. Goats ate the vegetation off Floreana Island in the Galapagos, so the mockingbird that lived there survives only on small offshore islets. This mockingbird was one of four species, each living on a different island, that made Darwin first think about adaptation in the Theory of Evolution.

That so many aquatic species are included in this book testifies to the wretched state of the world's rivers and lakes. Not even the world's oceans are pristine.

Right whales were "right" because they were close to shore, easy to kill, and floated when harpooned. They almost disappeared because we lacked the wisdom to manage them sustainably. Or, for that matter, to anticipate that there is now a flourishing whaling industry where people shoot whales with digital cameras, not harpoons, and it generates more income than the first whaling industry ever did.

That the Amsterdam albatross, living on a remote island in the southern Indian Ocean, is in this book is further testimony to our human abilities to destroy nature in even the most lonely parts of the planet.

Above all, this book is about hope. Yes, there is bad news, for most endangered species don't even get a mention here. Many may be unknown. We may drive many species to extinction before ever giving them names. Yet there are successes. I have seen nene in the wild. With colleagues, I released the first captive-bred Guam rail back into the wild. With other ecotourists, I've watched right whales and whooping cranes, been thrilled by the story of the crested ibis, inspired by the man who saved the cahow, and will get to see Przewalski's horse in the wild one day.

Extinctions at the present rate—my research shows them running at 100 to 1,000 times faster than expected—are unacceptable. This book also shows that they are not inevitable.

—Stuart Pimm

100
UNDER
100

INTRODUCTION

The beauty and genius of a work of art may be reconceived, though its first material expression be destroyed; a vanished harmony may yet again inspire the composer; but when the last individual of a race of living things breathes no more, another heaven and another earth must pass before such a one can be again. —WILLIAM BEEBE

"Dead as a dodo." "Gone the way of the dodo." This giant flightless pigeon has become synonymous with failure. Such clichés imply that the bird couldn't cut it in an evolutionary sense; it was unfit, and didn't deserve to survive, so its extinction is somehow acceptable. But the reality is that the dodo (like all organisms in healthy, natural ecosystems) was anything but unfit. In fact, archeological evidence tells us the one-metre-tall birds were once incredibly abundant on their 600-square-kilometre island of Mauritius in the Indian Ocean.

Evolution had done its job well with the dodo, adapting it beautifully to its environment. It thrived in harmony with its surroundings, reaching a peak population of possibly a half million birds; this is the epitome of a successful species, not a failed one.

1

But time was not on its side. Having lived for millennia without natural predators, dodos had no need of an instinctive fear of anything, so they were very tame. This made them easy pickings for the first humans they had ever encountered, Portuguese sailors who stopped by the island in the early 16th century to gather food for the onward leg of their journeys.

Following on the heels of the Portuguese, who never permanently settled Mauritius, the Dutch arrived in 1638, staying for good. With them came rats, pigs, cats, and dogs, a marauding army of dodo destruction loosed from the holds of ships onto a pristine tropical island that was set with a sumptuous buffet of easy-to-obtain food. The decline of the dodo was swift. By 1680, it was gone for good, done in not by its own shortcomings but by unnatural forces against which it had no defence. Such a fate has befallen many other species in the past and likely will more in the future. But it doesn't have to be this way. Even against tremendous odds, extinctions aren't inevitable, as you will discover in these stories of the world's rarest living things.

Inhabiting every continent and coming in every size, shape, and colour, the 100 species and subspecies in this book range from a bumblebee to a 50-tonne whale, from a diminutive orchid to a tree 40 metres tall. With current populations in the double or even single digits, these mammals, birds, reptiles, amphibians, fish, insects, trees, and flowers teeter on the brink of extinction (as you will see, a few lucky ones have made stunning comebacks—because somebody cared—and now number over 100). Though just a tiny sliver of the millions of species in existence, their loss would diminish the value of life on earth.

The narratives associated with these rarest-of-the-rare beings are often unexpected and bizarre: a Victorian naturalist bronco-busting an ancient reptile; China's Great Leap Forward; Russian piracy on the high seas; a flock of birds guiding Christopher Columbus to a New World; a "mythical" giant marsupial; the criminal madness of a French scientist; a peek over a wall that saved a species—nearly all of them taking place in far-flung, exotic, and often threatened places. Of course, as they have with all the earth's living things, volcanoes, earthquakes, floods, natural climate change, asteroid impacts, and disease, in concert with natural selection, have also played a part in the evolutionary paths of these organisms throughout the ages.

Now a new era of life on earth has begun. It is known as the Anthropocene (the age of *Homo sapiens*), and it indicates our role as the dominant global force, surpassing all natural ones. The seven billion of us are driving the decline of an immense variety of living things through habitat destruction, pollution, overhunting, over-fishing, invasive species, and man-made climate change. So, as with the dodo, let's not blame the species themselves.

Back on Mauritius, the loss of the dodo in 1680 was just the beginning of a spate of extinctions. Other species would soon dis-appear, 13 in all: two giant tortoises, a giant skink, a blind snake, two ducks, a parrot and a parakeet, a night heron, and an owl, among others, would eventually be wiped out as a result of hunting, intro-duced predators, and forest destruction. Things weren't much bet-ter for those species that *did* survive. For example, not so long ago, the populations of the Mauritius kestrel, the pink pigeon, and the echo parakeet could each be counted on one's fingers and toes (on one hand, in the case of the kestrel). Three living treasures were poised to disappear from the world forever.

Speaking of treasures, most of us recognize how precious the ones that have been created by humanity throughout history are. As a civi-lization, we've toiled to preserve and protect many great works, such as the Angkor Wats and the Mona Lisas of the world, not to men-tion countless pieces of art, literature, music, and artifacts which have meaning for us. As grim as the loss of any one of these would be, however, we could recreate it, at least in facsimile, within our life-times. But living things are treasures of a different kind, the result of thousands, millions, or billions of years of evolution (and they are equally precious if you believe they are God's creations). We cannot recreate even the simplest single-celled organism, and we certainly can't wait around for nature to make another one for us. So, why not preserve and protect threatened *living* masterpieces as we would our own? This is exactly what some people on Mauritius and many others around the world are doing. And because of it, the future is looking brighter for the island's kestrel, pink pigeon, and echo parakeet, plus a host of the earth's other animals and plants.

MAURITIUS KESTREL

One of the great triumphs of 20th-century conservation has been the virtual resurrection of the Mauritius kestrel, a diminutive falcon found nowhere else on earth. Centuries of deforestation for sugar cane plantation and lumber had destroyed this tiny raptor's habi-tat; introduced rats, crab-eating macaque monkeys, mongoose, and feral cats preyed on eggs and young; and finally, DDT sprayed in the 1950s and 1960s to combat malarial mosquitoes poisoned its body and thinned its eggshells. A species can only take so much, so by 1974 there were only four Mauritius kestrels left, just one of them female. It was considered the rarest bird in the world.

About the size of a blue jay, this forest-dwelling brown and white mottled falcon was probably never very abundant, given the limited area of its small island home. Its diet is similar to other species of kestrels around the world, eating a variety of small prey, including geckos, insects, songbirds, and introduced mice and shrews. The female lays two to five eggs in natural cavities in volcanic rock cliffs or in tree holes, which she incubates for about a month. Since its recovery, the Mauritius kestrel has also frequently nested in artificial nesting boxes that have been provided as part of the recovery effort.

The species might not have been saved had it not been for the dedicated work of Carl Jones, a Welsh conservationist first sent to the island by the International Council for Bird Preservation (now BirdLife International) in the late 1970s to *close down* their project to save the Mauritius kestrel. Pessimism about the fate of the bird was understandable: the effort had had little success since it began less than a decade earlier; the species was no better off. But once he arrived, Jones refused to give up on the kestrel, stayed in Mauritius, and began working with the Durrell Wildlife Conservation Trust in 1985. They used a captive breeding technique new to Mauritius, known as double or multiple clutching, where the first clutch of eggs is taken from the nest to be artificially hatched and the young reared in captivity before being released into the wild. This forces the female to lay a second clutch, which she raises naturally, doubling her reproductive output. By the early 1990s, Jones and his Mauritian Wildlife Foundation had developed a successful captive breeding program.

Driven by his unflinching commitment to saving the species (even as a young boy in Wales he bred native kestrels), Jones helped increase its population from just 4 to over 200 in the early 1990s. Once again, the diminutive falcons could be seen flashing through what was left of the island's subtropical evergreen forests—especially those in the Black River Gorges area in the southwest part of the island. So successful was the recovery effort that the captive breeding program was ended when the population reached a self-sustaining 300 birds in 1994, the same year the International Union for Conservation of Nature, the official global authority on threatened species and more commonly known as the IUCN, downlisted the species to the Vulnerable category of its Red List of Threatened Species.

Since then, the Mauritius kestrel has rebounded even farther on its own, and today the population stands at around the 1,000 mark, a number that biologists feel might be about the maximum sustainable, given the amount of suitable habitat left for the kestrels on the island. Future plans include translocating a number of birds to islands around Mauritius and to the island of Réunion, whose own endemic kestrel went extinct some 300 years ago. As for Carl Jones? He remained in Mauritius and would be a key factor in the survival of the pink pigeon and the echo parakeet.

PINK PIGEON

Despite the kestrel's successful recovery, only 9 of the nearly 30 native bird species that once lived on Mauritius survived, so it was no time for Jones and the Mauritian Wildlife Foundation to rest on their laurels. The once abundant pink pigeon suffered from the same habitat destruction, introduced pests, and DDT spraying as the little raptor. In fact, the two species appeared to have declined almost in lockstep. By the mid-19th century, the pink pigeon was already rare.

Similar in size and shape to the familiar rock pigeon found on city streets around the world, the Mauritius bird is named for its distinctive pink head, neck, belly, and legs. Like other members of the dove family, the species is vegetarian, eating the seeds, fruits, and buds of the island's native plants. It is also a devoted parent, and both females and males incubate the eggs and feed the young. Although hunting was largely to blame for the extinction of its relative the dodo (also a pigeon, albeit a giant one), it appears to have played only a minor part in the pink pigeon's decline because its flesh was thought to be poisonous. Indeed, the pink pigeon may have occasionally made people sick, since the bird itself ingested toxic seeds that were a natural part of its diet. Ironically, this may have saved the species from being hunted to extinction long ago. Nevertheless, it was listed as critically endangered on the IUCN Red List. By 1990, there were only 10 pink pigeons left in the wild and time was running short. The Mauritian Wildlife Foundation did everything it could to help the species recover before it was too late.

The bird's population began to grow as the result of eradicating rats that ate its eggs, providing supplemental food to overcome a shortage of fruit and seeds in its habitat, and ramping up the reproductive output of the species by starting a captive breeding program (including multiple clutching where eggs were removed to be incubated and reared in captivity by another more common pigeon species, forcing the pink pigeon female to lay another clutch, which she reared naturally). By 2000, its situation had improved enough that the IUCN downlisted it from critically endangered to endangered. Today, there are approximately 400 of the birds living in the forests of Mauritius, and about 150 living in captivity, in aviaries on Mauritius and in dozens of zoos worldwide.

Echo Parakeet

Decimated by many of the same factors as the Mauritius kestrel and the pink pigeon, at one point the echo parakeet was the rarest parrot in the world and the last native parrot species surviving on any of the islands in the tropical Indian Ocean. By the 1980s, only about 20 remained. Its cousins on Réunion, Rodrigues, and the Seychelles had all gone extinct.

Fortunately for this medium-sized emerald green–and blue-tinged parakeet, wildlife conservationists in Mauritius had practice snatching birds from the edge of extinction. Successes with the kestrel and the pink pigeon proved it could be done. Their experience would be put to the test again.

Since they shared the same forest habitat, much of what was learned during the recovery efforts for the other two birds also applied to the parakeet. However, in addition to suffering from deforestation and predation by introduced species such as rats and monkeys, the echo parakeet was also being starved into extinction. Introduced weed species, such as the guava plant and starfruit, had a severe impact on the parakeet. These exotic plants, which quickly dominate an ecosystem once they're established, choked out the saplings of native tree species, preventing the forest from regenerating properly. Over time, the trees the echo parakeet depended on for sustenance began to disappear. It wasn't possible for the bird to simply switch to eating the weeds, since they didn't fruit during its breeding season, when an ample supply of food is critical for feeding hungry nestlings. Virtually no chicks were fledged between the 1970s and the mid-1980s, when the population had reached rock bottom.

Though there had been an earlier effort to save the species, an effective recovery program for the echo parakeet wasn't begun until 1987. With help from the Durrell Wildlife Conservation Trust, the World Parrot Trust, and Wildlife Preservation Canada, Carl Jones and the Mauritian Wildlife Foundation would again play a lead role. The list of what they've done to save the parakeet from extinction is long: control of introduced rats, pigs, monkeys, and deer; control of introduced ring-necked parakeets and Indian myna birds that competed with the echo parakeet; removal of weeds and the planting of native trees; the provision of supplemental feeding stations; the placement of artificial nesting boxes; enhancing breeding success by leaving one nestling in each of the wild nests to be brooded by its parents while removing the other to be captive fed and reared before being released back into the wild (since there was a food shortage in the wild, it was easier for the parents to find enough food for only one chick); regular inspection of nests, and rescuing any chicks that were underweight or sick; and establishing the 68-square-kilometre

Black River Gorges National Park in 1993 (which also contains the habitat of the kestrel and pigeon).

The echo parakeet's recovery has been a resounding success. In 2007, it became the third Mauritius bird (after the kestrel and the pink pigeon) to be downlisted on the IUCN Red List from critically endangered to endangered. There are now about 400 of them in the wild.

Saving endangered species and the rest of the earth's living treasures is within our grasp.

Here's some proof: if you added together the populations of the Mauritius kestrel, the pink pigeon, and the echo parakeet just a few decades ago, you would have come up a number of less than 35. Thirty-five. Total. Tally them up now and you'd be closing in on 2,000 individuals, thus proving Margaret Mead's famous dictum, "Never doubt that a small group of thoughtful, committed citizens can change the world; indeed, it's the only thing that ever has."

A NOTE ON THE IUCN (INTERNATIONAL UNION FOR CONSERVATION OF NATURE)

There is mention throughout the book of this Switzerland-based international organization and its Red List of Threatened Species. The IUCN (International Union for Conservation of Nature), according to its website, is the "the world's oldest and largest global environmental network—a democratic membership union with more than 1,000 government and NGO member organizations, and almost 11,000 volunteer scientists in more than 160 countries." Its Red List of Threatened Species is the de facto global benchmark for the evaluation and assessment of the conservation status of the planet's animals and plants.

The most relevant Red List category for this book is Critically Endangered. The IUCN says animals and plants in this category are "considered to be facing an extremely high risk of extinction in the wild." Since all species in this book currently have minuscule populations, it isn't surprising that most of them are considered critically endangered. The other important Red List category for us is Extinct in the Wild. In fact, there are species in the book that are no longer found anywhere in the wild after exhaustive searches of their traditional ranges; organisms that, according to the IUCN's criteria, are known only "to survive in cultivation, in captivity, or as a naturalized population well outside its past range." This isn't to say that some might not be returned to the wild in the future. The good news is that species can and sometimes do get downlisted to a less dangerous category, such as Endangered or Vulnerable, like the birds on Mauritius did.

A NOTE ON POPULATIONS

The population stated for each species is the best estimate or census available at the time of writing; please bear in mind that such small populations can quickly change. Unless otherwise indicated, these numbers reflect the population in the wild.

SPECIES FEATURED IN THIS BOOK

Alabama sturgeon (*Scaphirhynchus suttkusi*)
Population: 2

Alagoas curassow (*Mitu mitu*)
Population: 100 in captivity

Amsterdam albatross (*Diomedia amsterdamensis*)
Population: under 100 breeding birds

Amur leopard (*Panthera pardus orientalis*)
Population: under 40

Anjouan scops owl (*Otus capnodes*)
Population: 50 or fewer breeding pairs

Arakan forest turtle (*Heosemys depressa*)
Population: 5

Archey's frog (*Leiopelma archeyi*)
Population: possibly under 100

Armoured mistfrog (*Litoria lorica*)
Population: possibly under 100

Asiatic cheetah (*Acinonyx jubatus venaticus*)
Population: 70 to 100

Attwater's prairie chicken (*Tympanuchus cupido attwateri*)
Population: 75 to 90

Bachman's warbler (*Vermivora bachmanii*)
Population: unknown, possibly extinct

Baiji (Yangtze) dolphin (*Lipotes vexillifer*)
Population: unknown, possibly extinct

Bali myna (*Leucopsar rothschildi*)
Population: 24 or fewer

Black-footed ferret (*Mustela nigripes*)
Population: from presumed extinct to about 1,000 today

Black stilt (*Himantopus novaezelandiae*)
Population: under 100

Blue iguana (*Cyclura lewisi*)
Population: from 5 to 250 today

Burmese roofed turtle (*Batagur trivittata*)
Population: 5 to 7 breeding females

Cahow (Bermuda petrel) (*Pterodroma cahow*)
Population: from under 50 to over 200 today

California condor (*Gymongyps californius*)
Population: from 22 to about 200 today

Campbell Island teal (*Anas nesiotis*)
Population: between 48 and 100

Carrizal seedeater (*Amaurospiza carrizalensis*)
Population: under 50

Catalina mahogany (*Cercocarpus traskiae*)
Population: 7

Cat Ba langur (*Trachypithecus poliocephalus*)
Population: 65

Chatham Island black robin (*Petroica traverse*)
Population: from 5 (including just 1 breeding female) to about 250 today

Chinese crested tern (*Thalasseus bernsteini*)
Population: under 50

Chinese giant paddlefish (*Psephurus gladius*)
Population: unknown, possibly extinct

Crested ibis (*Nipponia nippon*)
Population: from 7 to 997 today

Devils Hole pupfish (*Cypronidon diabolis*)
Population: under 100

Eastern North Pacific right whale (*Eubalaena japonica*)
Population: 28

Echo parakeet (*Psittacula eques*)
Population: from 20 to about 400 today

El lobo (Mexican wolf) (*Canis lupus baileyi*)
Population: 50

Enigmatic owlet-nightjar (*Aegotheles savesi*)
Population: under 50

Eskimo curlew (*Numenius borealis*)
Population: unknown, possibly extinct

Fabulous green sphinx of Kauai (*Tinostoma smaragditis*)
Population: under 100

Floreana mockingbird (*Nesomimus trifasciatus*)
Population: possibly 100 or fewer

Franklin's bumblebee (*Bombus franklini*)
Population: under 100

Ganges river shark (*Glyphis gangeticus*)
Population: under 100

Gilbert's potoroo (*Potorous gilbertii*)
Population: under 100

Greater bamboo lemur (*Prolemur simus*)
Population: probably under 100

Guam rail ko'ko' (*Gallirallus owstoni*)
Population: approximately 200, none self-sustaining over the long term in the wild

Hainan gibbon (*Nomascus hainanus*)
Population: 20

Hawaiian crow ('alala) (*Corvus hawaiiensis*)
Population: 77 in captivity

He-cabbage tree (*Pladaroxylon leucadendon*)
Population: under 50

Iberian lynx (*Lynx pardinus*)
Population: from under 100 to about 200 today

Iranian Gorgan mountain salamander (*Paradactylodon gorganensis*)
Population: under 100

Iriomote cat (*Prionailurus iriomotensis*)
Population: under 100

Irrawaddy river shark (*Glyphis siamensis*)
Population: under 100

Javan rhinoceros (*Rhinoceros sondaicus*)
Population: 50 to 60

Kakapo (*Strigops habroptila*)
Population: from 65 to 120 today

La Gomera giant lizard (*Galliotia bravoana*)
Population: 90

Lord Howe Island giant stick insect (*Dryococelus australis*)
Population: under 20

Madagascar pochard (*Aythya innotata*)
Population: 20 to 25

Mangrove finch (*Camarhynchus heliobates*)
Population: under 100

Mariana crow (*Corvus kubaryi*)
Population: 100 or under

Maui's dolphin (*Cephalorynchus hectori maui*)
Population: possibly under 100

Mauritius kestrel (*Falco punctatus*)
Population in 1974: from 4 to about 1,000 today

Milu (Père David's deer) (*Elaphurus davidianus*)
Population: over 2,000 in captivity

Miss Waldron's red colobus monkey (*Piliocolobus badius waldrone*)
Population: unknown, possibly extinct

Molokai thrush (*Myadestes lanaiensis rutha*)
Population: unknown, possibly extinct

Mountain bongo (*Tragelaphus euryceros isaaci*)
Population: under 50

Nene (Hawaiian goose) (*Branta sandvichensis*)
Population: from 30 to over 1,500

Niceforo's wren (*Thryothorus nicefori*)
Population: 77

Norfolk Island Phreatia orchid (*Phreatia limenophylax*)
Population: 5

Northern hairy-nosed wombat (*Lasiorhinus krefftii*)
Population: from 35 to over 130 today

Northern river shark (*Glyphis garricki*)
Population: under 100

Northern sportive lemur (*Lepilemur septentrionalis*)
Population: probably under 100

Northern white rhinoceros (*Ceratothenium simum cottoni*)
Population: 7 in captivity

Oahu creeper (*Paroreomyza maculate*)
Population: unknown, possibly extinct

Philippines crocodile (*Crocodylus mindorensis*)
Population: under 100

Phillip Island wheatgrass (*Elymus multiflorus kingianus*)
Population: under 50

Pink-headed duck (*Rhondonessa caryophyllacea*)
Population: unknown, possibly extinct

Pink pigeon (*Nesoenas mayeri*)
Population: from 10 to about 400 today

Pinta Island Galapagos giant tortoise (*Geochelone abingdoni*)
Population: 1

Przewalski's horse (*Equus ferus*)
Population: from extinct in the wild to over 300 today

Puerto Rican amazon (*Amazona vittata*)
Population: approximately 50 breeding birds

Rabb's fringe-limbed tree frog (*Ecnomiohyla rabborum*)
Population: several males and a single female in captivity

São Tomé fiscal (*Lanius newtoni*)
Population: under 50

São Tomé grosbeak (*Neospiza concolor*)
Population: under 50

Scimitar-horned oryx (*Oryx dammah*)
Population: 1,500 in captivity

Seychelles magpie robin (*Copsychus sechellarum*)
Population: from 12 to about 200 today

Seychelles sheath-tailed bat (*Coleura seychellensis*)
Population: 60

She-cabbage tree (*Lachanodes arborea*)
Population: under 10

Short-tailed albatross (*Phoebastria albatrus*)
Population: from presumed extinct to nearly 3,000 today

Sicilian fir (*Abies nebrodensis*)
Population: 30

Slender-billed curlew (*Numenius tenuirostris*)
Population: unknown, possibly extinct

South China tiger (*Panthera tigris amoyensis*)
Population: 20 or under

Spix's macaw (*Cyanopsitta spixii*)
Population: between 70 and 80 in captivity

St. Helena ebony (*Trochetiopsis ebenus*)
Population: 2 mature trees

Sulu hornbill (*Anthracoceros montani*)
Population: under 40

Tahiti monarch (*Pomarea nigra*)
Population: 40 to 45

Thermal water lily (*Nymphaea thermarum*)
Population: over 50 in cultivation

Vancouver Island marmot (*Marmota vancouverensis*)
Population: from 30 to about 300 today

Virginia round-leaf birch (*Betula uber*)
Population: 8

White-collared kite (*Leptodon forbesi*)
Population: 50 or fewer breeding pairs

Whooping crane (*Grus americanus*)
Population: from 21 to about 400 today

Wisent (European bison) (*Bison bonasus*)
Population: from 9 to over 800 today

Wollemi pine (*Wollemia nobilis*)
Population: under 100

Wyoming toad (*Bufo baxteri*)
Population: thousands in captivity

Yangtze giant softshell turtle (*Rafetus swinhoei*)
Population: 1 in the wild, 3 in captivity

Yunnan box turtle (*Cuora yunnanensis*)
Population: unknown, but thought to be under 50

PART ONE

TROUBLE WITH THE NUMBERS: UNDER 100

We usually think of populations of species as being in the billions (humans), millions (white-tailed deer), or thousands (American black bears). But under a hundred? This is the realm of the rarest living things. They are all critically endangered. With such small numbers, from 1 to 99, it wouldn't take much—a disease, a bad storm, a little poaching, or habitat destruction, say—for any of them to disappear completely. In fact, a few of these species may be already gone, having not been seen in years, sometimes decades. But the odd one might still hang on, so they haven't been declared extinct under the IUCN's criteria that "there is no reasonable doubt that its last individual has died."

Besides their vanishingly small populations, almost all of these animals and plants have another thing in common: their survival is being championed by people (sometimes many, sometimes a few) who want to see them flourish once again.

OUR CLOSEST KIN: MAMMALS

As a rule, most mammal species are small, shy, nocturnal, and rarely seen. But not all. Some, like the big cats, the great whales, rhinos, and antelopes are among the most spectacular living things inhabiting the planet with us, while our primate cousins share virtually our entire genetic code. As a mammal species barely 100,000 years old, we are still wet-behind-the-ears newcomers, junior players to practically all others on the evolutionary stage.

Unfortunately, we happen to be, by far, the most abundant species of mammal ever to exist on the face of the earth. And it's precisely owing to this success that many of our fellow warm-blooded, live-bearing, young-suckling mammalian relatives are hurting so badly. Twenty percent, or 1,134, of all wild mammal species are in danger of extinction worldwide according to the IUCN Red List of Threatened Species. Essentially, we are crowding them off the planet as we make room for an additional 80 million people, every year.

Hainan Gibbon

The primates have flourished since the first shrew-like ancestor climbed into a tree eons ago and never left. There are now more than 600 species. The bad news is that over 300, or more than half them, are at risk of extinction.

Gorillas, chimpanzees, bonobos, orangutans, gibbons, and humans are all members of the Hominoid super-family, commonly referred to as the apes. How closely related are we? Humans' and chimpanzees' DNA—the blueprint of life—is more than 98 percent identical. Everything that sets us apart from our chimp cousins—hairlessness, upright walking on two legs, complex language, abstract thought, and so on—can be accounted for by a mere 2 percent difference in our genes. To put this into perspective, that's less than the genetic difference between the white-eyed and Philadelphia vireos, two very closely related songbirds of eastern North American forests.

Even the DNA of the gibbons, our most distant cousins among the apes, is about 95 percent identical to ours. In fact, the ancient Chinese (whose country was the stronghold of gibbons before most were wiped out due to habitat loss) referred to gibbons as the "gentlemen" of the forest, and Taoists believed they lived for 1,000 years and could turn into humans.

Today, gibbons have the distinction of being the most endangered family of primates in the world. Of the 16 surviving species, 15 are either endangered or critically endangered. It's not as if these are creepy insects or obscure plants that might be hard to empathize with; after all, gibbons are highly intelligent, warm-blooded animals. Because gibbons are smaller at about 60 centimetres in length and weigh just seven kilograms or so, they are referred to as the "lesser" apes. Perhaps this is why they get little media attention compared with the "great" apes and receive just a fraction of the conservation funding of gorillas, chimpanzees, and orangutans.

The most critically endangered of all gibbon species lives on the 13,000-square-kilometre island of Hainan in the South China

Sea. Only about 20 Hainan gibbons survive. Their last refuge is the Bawangling National Nature Reserve, the site of some of the last virgin tropical forest in China, where they live in two matriarchal family groups in undisturbed forest on the northeastern side of the reserve. Here, the seven-kilogram apes swing through the trees on their long arms, a way of getting around known as brachiation. Spanning gaps of 15 metres at speeds of up to 50 kilometres an hour, the agile apes travel gracefully through the canopy, stopping often to eat fruit. No animal surpasses them in their mastery of arboreal travel. Yet, as spectacular as their tree-top peregrinations must appear, a Hainan gibbon is much more likely to be heard than seen.

Songs are socially important to gibbons. The all-black males and the yellow-coated females form long-term pair bonds and sing duets that echo through the jungle for up to a kilometre. But no matter how strongly they profess their love for one another, their reproductive output is inevitably low. Hainan gibbons have just one young every two years; therein lies one of the biggest hurdles to rebuilding the population.

In the 1950s, about 2,000 gibbons survived throughout the island. Then the state converted 8,000 square kilometres of Hainan's lowland rainforest to rubber plantations, wiping out about half of the little apes' habitat. What's more, they had to endure relentless hunting for traditional Chinese medicine by the local Miao people of Hainan. Entire subpopulations of the animal were exterminated by the hunt.

Because the entire remaining population lives within a protected area, the apes should be safe, but illegal poaching in the reserve is reportedly still an issue. With only 20 gibbons left, even the death of one animal is devastating to the species. Because all of their typical lowland forest habitat has already been destroyed, the reserve is at a less fertile, higher elevation than gibbons naturally prefer, and they must work harder to get enough food. The human population continues to grow, and the collection of firewood and clearing for farming is fraying the edges of even this last sanctuary. With so few individuals left, a severe typhoon, disease, an imbalance in the ratio of males to females, inbreeding, or any number of non-human related causes could wipe out the species. If there's anything here to hang some hope on, it's that the Hainan gibbon's population, though still tiny at 20, was even smaller in the 1970s, when there were only 7 left.

CAT BA LANGUR

Across the Gulf of Tonkin, just 200 kilometres west of Hainan Island, Cat Ba Island is the home of the Cat Ba langur monkey, also known as the golden-headed langur for the gorgeous, brightly coloured mane of fur surrounding its black and expressive heart-shaped face. Although it displays the usual outward characteristics of other monkeys, such as long limbs and a very long tail, its exclusive taste for vegetation has resulted in an unusual adaptation that is more reminiscent of a cow. In order to digest the tough cellulose of their strictly herbivorous diet, langurs have a multi-part, complex stomach similar to hoofed grazing animals. This adaptation allows these "leaf-eating monkeys" to consume just about any tough vegetation, such as fibrous leaves, bark, shoots, flowers, and fruits, some of which are even poisonous to other animals.

As bulletproof as the Cat Ba langur's digestive system is, it is bullets themselves that have made it one of the world's most endangered primates. Poaching for the traditional Asian medicine trade has decimated its numbers. A population of nearly 3,000 in the 1960s had collapsed to a low of just 53 in 2000. Today, fewer than 100 individuals remain. They live only on Cat Ba Island in the archipelago of the same name in northern Vietnam. The archipelago has been a UNESCO Biosphere Reserve since 2004.

Nearly 2,000 islands, islets, and rocks make up the archipelago, which was formed when the sea level began to rise about 10,000 years ago, creating Halong Bay. This left the tops of cave-ridden limestone hills and small jagged peaks stranded as islands. Many of these karst formations rise vertically from the shallow marine waters, creating a distinctive landscape that draws thousands of international tourists each year. Verdant evergreen tropical monsoon forests cover most of the larger islands, including Cat Ba Island itself, the largest in the archipelago at 130 square kilometres. Over half the island is a national park, protected for its phenomenal biodiversity, which includes more than 20 endangered species. However, with 13,000 people living on such a small island and hundreds of thousands of tourists visiting each year, there's little room left for wildlife (or humans, for that matter).

Cat Ba's limestone forest, the langur's preferred habitat, has been highly fragmented by the cutting of trees by local people for firewood and building materials. The result is that no single block is large enough to sustain its whole population at once, so the monkeys have been forced to split into seven tiny subpopulations scattered throughout the island. Only four of the seven groups include both males and females, so animals in the remaining ones can't reproduce. As a result, the species is falling short of its reproductive potential, as the number of baby langurs born each year is lower than it should be given the overall population.

In 2000, when the Cat Ba Langur Conservation Project was begun by conservation organizations from Germany, the population was just over 50 animals. They've had success against poaching, and in the last decade, numbers of the Cat Ba langur have grown somewhat, to 65 animals—still critically endangered, but a move in the right direction. To boost the population further, future plans include relocating some monkeys into other groups to balance the sex ratio and establishing protected natural corridors so non-breeding individuals and groups have access to breed with other subpopulations.

NORTHERN SPORTIVE LEMUR

While lemurs are primates as surely as gibbons and langurs, eons of evolution in geographical isolation have taken them in a different physiological direction, so there's no mistaking these iconic Madagascar species for apes or monkeys.

Ever since it separated from India 80 to 90 million years ago (and from Africa and Antarctica before that), Madagascar has been host to a giant evolutionary experiment. Isolated from mainland populations, the animals on the world's fourth-largest island have evolved in unique ways, free from the influence of species living in the rest of the world. One of the most fruitful experiments has been the lemurs, today with over 90 species. Lemurs, named after the Latin word for "ghost"—in homage to their eerie vocalizations, often nocturnal habits, and strange facial expressions that make them looked eternally spooked—first appeared 50 to 65 million years ago in Africa. They arrived on Madagascar soon after, possibly floating across from the mainland on rafts of vegetation. In fact, recent evidence suggests that ocean currents at the time would have been just about right to deliver early lemurs from the mainland of Africa.

It is lucky for lemurs that monkeys never made it to Madagascar, though, because everywhere else on earth where the two coexisted in the distant past, monkeys out-competed their "ghostly" cousins, driving them to extinction. Although lemurs had thrived for millions of years on their island sanctuary, these days Madagascar is not a good place to be a wild animal. With a burgeoning population of 21 million people and crushing poverty, out of necessity the island's forests are being rapidly stripped with little heed for the future of either humans or wildlife.

In a nation known for the desperate straits of its fauna, the status of the northern sportive lemur ranks among the most dire. Named for the "sportive" upright, boxer-like stance it takes when threatened, the northern sportive lemur is a small primate about 30 centimetres tall, not including its long tail. Large, round, forward-facing reddish-brown eyes, small erect ears, and a coat of rich grey-brown fur give it the look of a forever-surprised plush toy. It uses its powerful hind legs to jump from branch to branch through its home in dry forest. By day it sleeps the hours away in hollow trees, where it might occasionally be seen poking its head curiously out of a hole. As a nocturnal animal, its life history is still very much a mystery. A few things are known, however. Northern sportive lemurs tend to be solitary and eat mostly leaves and other kinds of difficult-to-digest vegetation. In a curious twist on the theme of "waste not, want not," they will eat their own droppings—a behaviour also practised by rabbits—to glean every last bit of goodness from nutritionally poor food by digesting it a second time. They reproduce slowly, giving birth to just one young at a time, so increasing the population is a slow process.

A few scattered scraps of dry forest in the far north of Madagascar are the last refuges for the northern sportive lemur. Hunting and the harvest of trees for charcoal production put the small primate at an especially high risk of extinction. A small group of 20 individuals lives in the Andrahona mountain forest. This tiny forest is sacred to local people, though not legally protected. That the sportive lemurs continue to inhabit Andrahona suggests they may be able to sustain themselves on very little land, providing some hope that small protected patches of habitat (which is pretty much all that's left in

Madagascar) might be enough to save the species in the long run. Scientists believe there could be fewer than 100 left on earth, tying it with the greater bamboo lemur as Madagascar's most endangered primate.

GREATER BAMBOO LEMUR

Why is it that some wildlife species, like racoons, crows, and gulls, to name a few of the more familiar ones, thrive, while many others can barely hang on to existence? What do they have going for them that so many others don't? Generally, they are generalists. If one type of food becomes rare or unavailable, they can survive on another. And they can more readily adapt to new habitats if old ones are destroyed. Adaptability to a wide variety of food types equals adaptability to a wide variety of habitat types equals healthy, widespread populations. To see this played out to the nth degree, look no farther than our own species, the ultimate generalist. We eat practically everything and live practically everywhere—and are followed into every nook and cranny and to the ends of the earth by generalist parasites, such as rats and cockroaches.

Madagascar's greater bamboo lemur is the antithesis of a generalist. It fits the definition of a specialist perfectly, depending on pretty much one kind of food and one habitat type. Its name says it all: this cute, woolly, bushy-tailed, wide-eyed, and gregarious primate survives on an abridged menu featuring the parts of one bamboo species and the occasional flower, leaves, or fruit. This exclusive taste limits greater bamboo lemurs to living only in forests of the outsized grass, which are rapidly disappearing.

Today, the greater bamboo lemur's range may be as small as 1 percent of what it used to be. Slash-and-burn agriculture, bamboo harvesting, mining, and hunting have nearly wiped out the species and its habitat. Global warming is likely also playing a part as the climate becomes drier and water scarcer. Although there are other bamboo-dependent lemurs in Madagascar, none is as endangered as this one. The greater bamboo lemur is also distinct for being the only species of lemur where family units (some with as many as 28 individuals have been seen) are dominated by males. Keeping these large social groups together may be the reason for the species' varied vocal repertoire.

On the upside, a hitherto unknown population of greater bamboo lemurs was recently confirmed in the Torotorofotsy region of the country, about 400 kilometres north of the animal's previously known range. Several family groups totalling up to 60 animals inhabit this area, which borders an important protected wetland and a national park. One family unit appears to live within the wetland itself. As encouraging as this new find is, the other populations to the south are declining. Most greater bamboo lemurs live outside protected areas, so establishing formal reserves for them is a priority. It is estimated there could be 100 or fewer greater bamboo lemurs left in the wild. Yet even this population dwarfs that of the next primate discussed, possibly the rarest on the planet.

MISS WALDRON'S RED COLOBUS MONKEY

Willoughby Lowe, an employee of the Natural History Museum in London, did what good collectors do: he shot animals for a living. Before the mid-20th century, when museums finally became enlightened to the havoc they were wreaking on the natural world, all shapes and sizes of animals were shot or trapped to be taken back to London, Berlin, New York, or wherever, to be added to museum collections. It isn't known exactly how many have been killed to fill the drawers of such institutions. However, if you combine the collections of three of the largest natural history museums in the English-speaking world, the American Museum of Natural History in New

York, the National Museum of Natural History (Smithsonian) in Washington, and London's Natural History Museum, you're closing in on 100 million, including insects. Among these are thousands of specimens of African colobus monkeys.

In 1933, Lowe was in what is now Ghana, West Africa, where he collected eight curious specimens of a type of red and black colobus monkey never before recorded. He was assisted on the expedition by one Miss F. Waldron, a fellow employee of the same museum. It wasn't until three years later that the monkeys were examined and described scientifically as a new subspecies by British Natural History Museum mammalogist R.W. Hayman. He named it *Procolobus badius waldroni* in honour of Miss Waldron because, in his words, she "contributed much to the success of the expedition." Apparently, in the old days you could have a species named after you for just helping somebody shoot it!

Western red colobus monkeys were once found in their millions across much of Africa. Overall, they are now considered the most threatened group of primates on the continent. In addition to Miss Waldron's, the Pennant's red colobus, Preuss's red colobus, and the Niger Delta red colobus are all threatened with extinction. The Bouvier's red colobus hasn't been seen in 30 years and may already be history.

Standing about a metre tall, sporting a silky black body and tail and a bright auburn forehead and thighs, Miss Waldron's red colobus is a noisy species, in constant communication with others of its kind using loud calls and shrieks. Family troops of 20 or more individuals (if they still exist) live in the high canopy of rainforests, where they feed on up to 100 kinds of leaves. As a group they're all eyes and ears, as each one acts as a sentry against danger and warns the entire group if something threatening lurks.

Possessing a multi-chambered stomach like a cow, the monkeys can digest the tough cellulose found in coarse vegetation that few other species can. This specialized diet allows them to live high above the ground among the luxurious greenery of tall old-growth forest trees. And therein lies the trouble for the Miss Waldron's monkey: 90 percent of the rainforest in Ghana and Ivory Coast where they live is already gone. What's left are fragmented islands of forest surrounded by a sea of farms and villages. To make matters worse, as the human population grew, so did the appetite for bush meat, so everything that moved in the forest was fair game for the gun, including monkeys. But more than just monkeys are dodging bullets to survive in these dwindling scraps of original woodland; other iconic species, such as forest elephants, leopards, and chimpanzees, are also feeling the crush of habitat destruction and the bush meat trade here.

Miss Waldron's monkeys were already becoming rare less than two decades after they were discovered. Logging and poaching had taken its toll on yet another of the planet's treasures. By 1978, one hadn't been seen in decades. After six years of searching the forests of Ivory Coast and Ghana, the authors of an article in the October 2000 issue of the journal *Conservation Biology* concluded that the Miss Waldron's red colobus monkey was probably extinct. If true, it would be the first primate wiped off the face of the earth in 200 years. So was Miss Waldron's red colobus monkey gone only a matter of decades after it was first described? Maybe not. Soon after the *Conservation Biology* article, a series of small but intriguing discoveries had cast some doubt that the monkey was extinct.

Between 2001 and 2003, three bits of evidence surfaced: a tail, a skin, and a photo of a dead red colobus monkey. All three pointed to the continued existence of the Miss Waldron's monkey in Ivory Coast. It appeared the species was still hanging on, if only by the slimmest of threads. Even though later searches between 2004 and

2006 failed to turn up anything other than one claim of a single vocalization, the IUCN listed the Miss Waldron's monkey as critically endangered and *possibly* extinct. The species simply did not yet meet the criteria for extinction.

If Miss Waldron's monkey still survives somewhere, it may be in Ehy Forest of eastern Ivory Coast. It was near here, on the edge of a large lagoon surrounded by villages, that scientist Scott McGraw—who had been searching for years in vain for the elusive animal—found that aforementioned skin of a Miss Waldron's monkey. Whether this individual monkey was the last of its kind isn't known. So, as scant as the evidence is, Ehy Forest may nevertheless contain the last vestiges of the Miss Waldron's red colobus monkey. It might be a long shot, but an awareness and education campaign has been ongoing in the villages around Ehy Lagoon in the hope that more information about the existence of this curiously named monkey will come to light.

South China Tiger

While primates such as the red colobus and other monkeys and apes might be charismatic because of their close evolutionary relationship to us, the big cats are known in scientific circles as charismatic megafauna for their size alone. They are spectacular animals. In fact, it's because of their universal appeal that they are often chosen as flagship or umbrella species representing the broader biodiversity around them. The theory goes that if you protect the large habitat of, say, a tiger, you'll also save all the smaller, more obscure species that live in the same ecosystem. Therefore, if these big cats can be saved, so might countless organisms they share the land with.

The South China tiger is thought to be the mother of all tigers—known as the stem tiger—from which all other *Panthera tigris* subspecies have descended. In other words, it appears the world's biggest cat has been living in this part of China longer than tigers have lived anywhere else on earth. As recently as the 1950s, 4,000 of them roamed the humid, mountainous forests of south-central China, where they hunted anything from mice to wild cattle (and the occasional local farmer, reportedly).

In 1959, as part of China's Great Leap Forward plan to transform the country from an agrarian society into an industrial state, leader Mao Zedong inexplicably ordered the eradication of all tigers and other big predators. The ensuing slaughter, coupled with habitat loss, shrank the South China tiger population to a few hundred by the 1970s, when it was finally given protection. Although unseen in the wild by biologists since then, it is not yet officially extinct, as occasional unconfirmed sightings by local people and the report of tiger tracks in the early 1990s sustain a flicker of hope that tigers persist in southern China. No hard evidence has been found since, but experts believe there are still a few left, estimating the population in the wild at fewer than 20. As insurance against extinction, there are still several dozen South China tigers in captivity, and the Chinese government intends to reintroduce some of these animals into their former haunts one day. However, nobody knows exactly where the wild tigers currently live, so if they survive at all, there's little at present that can be done to protect them. Fortunately, things look brighter for the better-studied Amur leopard, another big cat whose range includes China.

Amur Leopard

A few hundred thousand years ago, African leopards reached Asia. They got as far east as the Sea of Japan, to an area where today southeastern Russia, northeastern China, and North Korea meet. As a geographical nexus of three head-strong nations, the area is politically sensitive. What's more, this place of great biodiversity and beautiful forests is also heavily populated. It's hard enough for spectacular cats like leopards to survive anywhere; in a place like this it's almost impossible.

Living farther north than any other member of *Panthera pardus,* the Amur leopard subspecies has evolved a thick, cream-coloured coat for bitterly cold winters (it turns a more familiar reddish-brown in summer), and longer legs for stalking deer and other prey in deep snow. Distinctive rosette markings and pale blue-green eyes make for a striking creature, even for a leopard.

Only 25 to 40 animals are thought to survive in a slender band of habitat within the Primorye region of Russia near Vladivostok, along with a few across the border in the adjoining forests of China. This handful of leopards shares the forest with about 10 Amur tigers (not to be confused with the South China tiger), the largest cat species on earth. Once as rare as the leopard, the recovery of this tiger subspecies is an example of successful conservation: its population has grown from fewer than 50 animals a few decades ago to about 500 today. It's lucky for the leopards that so few of the bigger cats live this far south, since they compete with them for prey such as sika and roe deer. What's worse, tigers have been known to eliminate their competition by eating them. But, so far, there's little evidence of conflict between the two species here. The leopards have bigger problems.

There's only so much food to go around any ecosystem, and in the Primorye region the cupboard is getting bare as poachers compete directly with the leopards by overhunting deer to the point of scarcity. This lack of prey is thought to be one of the greatest barriers to the population recovery of the Amur leopard. It's hard to rear young when you can't feed them.

It is even more difficult when local villagers set fire to the forest to create better growing conditions for a type of edible fern that is popular in the regional cuisine and sold at market. Leopards and their prey don't survive well in burned-over forests. Moreover, Primorye is a border region and economic corridor with a large, growing population, and illegal poaching of the cats for their coats is a problem. There is also constant pressure to develop new gas and oil pipelines, and expand road and rail networks, logging, and mining. Despite this, the leopard's population has remained relatively stable over the past 30 years.

Thankfully, the Amur leopard and its tiger cousin have allies in their struggle to survive. A coalition of a dozen or so conservation groups known as ALTA (Amur Leopard and Tiger Alliance) has the big cats' best interest in mind. In 2006, ALTA helped stop plans to build an oil pipeline terminal within the range of the leopard. And the recent creation of a tiger-leopard reserve in China that borders other wildlife refuges in Russia is a sign of hope for the species. While ALTA and others educate the public and push for measures to protect habitat, captive breeding programs for the Amur leopard in zoos in Europe and Russia are also ensuring a pool of animals for possible future reintroduction programs. Although the leopard is still perilously rare, recent footage from hidden camera traps in 2011 suggests that there may be a few more animals in the population than originally thought. So it appears this distinctive, great cat still has a fighting chance.

Asiatic Cheetah

The antithesis of a forest dweller such as the Amur leopard, the sleek, athletic cheetah—the world's fastest mammal with a top speed of 110 kilometres per hour—inhabited the open savannahs and grasslands of India, Pakistan, Afghanistan, Arabia, and Iran until the 1940s.

In the late 16th century, this Asiatic subspecies of the cheetah was so plentiful that the great Mogul emperor Akbar had a stable of at least

1,000 of them that he used for hunting gazelle and deer (the cheetah's natural prey species). This spectacle was often depicted in Indian and Persian art of the time. Keeping cheetahs as pets or hunting animals wasn't limited to royalty, however, and their widespread use by the wealthy continued into the 1800s. But the exploitation didn't end there. The predator became the prey as the relentless killing of chee-tahs, coupled with the elimination of the deer they needed to survive, reduced the cats' numbers drastically by 1910. Add the destruction of native grassland habitat for agriculture, and the Asiatic cheetah was all but history. By the mid-20th century, the species was wiped out in India and southwestern Asia—the last three shot in 1947 by the Maharaja of Surguja, who also slaughtered 1,157 tigers during his life, thus playing an important role in ushering another Asian cat to near non-existence. And, lest you think he was some kind of anom-aly, another of his ilk nearly equalled these exploits with 1,000 tiger kills. Still another killed 300. And none other than King George V of England, who, with his princely son in tow, bagged himself no fewer than 39 tigers (plus four bears and 11 rhinos) on a hunt in Nepal in 1911. Such cruelty for "sport" defies the imagination.

Now, all that is left of the once-abundant cheetah in Asia is a relic population of between 70 and 100 widely dispersed animals scratching for existence on the arid central plateau of Iran, a dan-gerous crossroads of drug smugglers and armed outlaws. Here, on top of the destruction of their habitat by agriculture and develop-ment, the desertification of grassland by the overgrazing of cattle, and the decline of their prey species, cheetahs are illegally hunted by poachers coming into the desert on newly created mining roads. However, in a sweetly ironic twist, it appears that illegal hunting might be on the wane, as the poachers are afraid they might be killed by drug-running thugs in the area.

Iran's cheetah strongholds consist of five widely dispersed protected areas. Although these national parks and wildlife refuges cover millions of hectares, much of the habitat is fragmented into smaller bits by roads and development. Moreover, some cheetahs live in unprotected areas, making them difficult to safeguard and accurately count.

As if all that weren't enough, the world's cheetahs have always been cursed with a very limited gene pool stemming from a "genetic bottleneck" they passed through about 12,000 years ago. At that time, some kind of environmental catastrophe such as climate change or overhunting by paleolithic humans left only a handful of cheetah survivors to act as the breeding stock from which all of today's cheetahs have descended. With little genetic variability, the species is particularly vulnerable to disease, and its cubs experience high mortality. Findings from a recent DNA study published early in 2011, however, suggest that the various subspecies of cheetahs (which range from Iran to southern Africa) possess more genetic variability than originally thought.

The homegrown Iranian Cheetah Society was established in 2001 to save the subspecies. That same year, the Conservation of the Asiatic Cheetah and Its Associated Biota program was begun by the Iranian government in cooperation with the United Nations Development Fund. Several international conservation organizations are also involved, including the Wildlife Conservation Society and the IUCN. Unfortunately, strict Iranian laws barring Western conservation scientists from the country limit access to the wealth of field experience they've had in the recovery of other large cat species around the world, making it all the harder to save this remarkable animal.

Despite scant evidence it still exists there, Iran's neighbour Afghanistan added the Asiatic cheetah to its own endangered species list in 2010, thus outlawing its killing. And India, 60 years without cheetahs, has begun efforts to reintroduce them, although that country will be using an African subspecies as breeding stock.

IRIOMOTE CAT

In contrast to the three cats discussed above, which are regional races of species that range across nearly an entire hemisphere, the diminutive Iriomote cat has lived exclusively in the mist-shrouded, primeval jungle and mangrove swamps of its namesake island in the East China Sea since tectonic forces separated it from mainland Asia 200,000 years ago. What's more, fossil evidence suggests the Iriomote may have existed as a species even earlier than that, nearly two million years before Iriomote was an island. Some paleontologists see it as a living fossil, possibly one of the original species of cat. But with its population at fewer than 100 and shrinking fast, its long tenure is threatened.

The animal was apparently unknown until 1967, even though Iriomote-jima (nearby is the famous World War II battle island of Iwo Jima) is a relatively compact 280-square-kilometre island that has been occupied by humans for centuries. How the presence of a wildcat—even a small one like the Iriomote—could have gone unnoticed for so long is a testament to its secretive nature. Even today, most of the scientists who study the cat have seen it only through the lenses of the remote cameras they've set up throughout the island to monitor the species—rarely are they seen in the flesh. Maybe this feline's painfully shy, skulking nature or its craggy, wet, vegetation-entangled habitat has something to do with it. Whatever the reason, this ghost cat has been seen by few human eyes, and as its population slides toward zero, it's likely few ever will.

The Iriomote cat is about the size of a big tabby. Its dark brown fur is adorned with even darker lateral stripes. Short legs, short rounded ears, and a short tail have evolved as an adaptation for hunting in extremely dense vegetation. Its diet includes small mammals, birds, fruit bats, insects, and frogs. Like the closely related fishing cat on the Asian mainland, the Iriomote has partially webbed feet and is unable to fully retract its claws, similarities that suggest it too may obtain some of its prey from the water. Given its preference for the wet lowlands and mangrove forests of the island, fishing or at least hunting for crabs and other such aquatic animals might not be a far-fetched idea.

Because of the limited available habitat on the island, its number was probably never large, likely peaking at several hundred individuals. Despite its success at avoiding contact with humans, it has been completely unsuccessful at avoiding their accelerating impacts on its habitat over the past few decades. Even though the island has a permanent population of just over 2,000 people, it attracts every year some 400,000 visitors, who come to visit its tropical coral reefs and beaches. A few even come for an unlikely glimpse of the Iriomote cat itself. And, although practically never seen in the flesh, its presence looms large on the island, as its stylized cartoon image is splashed on buses, road signs, businesses, and in advertising. There are even sculptures of it. In short, the Iriomote cat is somewhat of a celebrity, if a spectral one. Ironically, the popularity of this mysterious species is in a small way responsible for the rapid expansion of the tourism industry, with its new hotels and resorts and widened roads, all of which have eaten into the island's natural habitat that is so necessary for the cat's survival.

Its threats are diverse. Primary among them is habitat destruction on an already small, 289-square-kilometre island whose main highway runs directly through the heart of the cat's natural home. Add to that the exponential increase in the number of vehicles to serve the tourist trade and you've got several cats being road-killed every year. Three or four per annum may not seem like a lot, but consider how small the population is already. And there's more. Scientists are concerned that a large population of feral house cats could transmit harmful diseases such as feline leukemia to the Iriomote. It is also feared that a fungus now spreading through the world's frog populations might reach the island and wipe out the native frogs that are one of the cat's important staple foods.

As rare as the Iriomote cat is, "never say never" must surely be the motto of those who are trying to save it. The island's Iriomote Wildlife Conservation Center has been working for more than a dozen years to protect the cat. Besides educating islanders and visitors about its plight, it has installed signs along roads warning drivers to be on the watch for them and has built more than 80 underpass crossings for them along the main road. The centre also takes in and rehabilitates injured or sick animals and has taken steps to protect the island's frogs from the deadly chytrid fungus by laying out antifungal mats at Iriomote-jima's ports so that it doesn't enter the island on visitors' shoes.

It's easy to be pessimistic about the fate of the feline, but the effort and the faith shown by those trying to save it inspire a glimmer of hope for the Iriomote cat. After all, it has survived *without* our help on this little island in the Pacific for eons. Can it now survive *with* it?

El Lobo (Mexican Wolf)

It is ironic that we've allowed the Iriomote cat and the little Mexican wolf to be pushed to the brink of extinction. You'd think we'd care a little more than this about such close cousins to our beloved domestic cat and dog companions.

Known as el lobo, the Mexican subspecies of *Canis lupus* is the rarest wolf in North America. Weighing in at just 23 to 39 kilograms, it is the smallest wolf on the continent. It used to range over vast areas of Arizona, New Mexico, Texas, and Mexico and appears to have lived as far north as Colorado.

El lobo's troubles began in the late 19th and early 20th centuries as ever more people settled the southwest. As populations of wild elk and deer dwindled because of overhunting by the growing hordes of settlers, without an adequate supply of wild food the Mexican wolf had no choice but to turn to livestock to survive. Who could blame it? Apparently, just about everyone. The scorn of the US government and western ranchers soon festered into an all-out, one-sided war. Mexican wolves were poisoned, shot, and trapped, and their dens were even dug up with mom and pups inside—anything to rid the region of "varmints," as they were called. By the 1950s, el lobo was all but gone from the deserts of the southwest. The last confirmed Mexican wolf in the United States was killed in west Texas in 1970. Only a tiny remnant population survived in the roadless wilds of northern Mexico.

Almost too late, in 1976 the United States listed the Mexican wolf under the Endangered Species Act (a law that didn't exist before 1973), and collaborated with its neighbour to the south on its recovery. After scouring the Mexican desert during the three years between 1977 and 1980, biologists were able to find only four males and one pregnant female. The entire known population of the Mexican wolf could be counted on one hand.

With so few left, it was as good as a death sentence to just leave them in the wild. Legal protection from hunting would do little to protect the animals against the vicissitudes of the desert: poachers, trapping, poison bait, starvation, disease, and so on. So, the five wolves were captured in a last-ditch effort to save them. The goal was to eventually grow this population enough so that el lobo could be reintroduced into the wild with a fighting chance to survive and maybe even thrive someday on its own.

In 1998, after nearly 20 years of captive breeding, the US Fish and Wildlife Service (USFWS) finally reintroduced a small pack of 11 carefully reared Mexican wolves into the 18,000-square-kilometre Blue Range Wolf Recovery Area of the Gila and Apache National Forests of western New Mexico and eastern Arizona. In the years since, they have begun to readapt to a landscape their ancestors had roamed for millennia. Like wild wolves everywhere, they are forming family packs, hunting deer and elk, and having pups. They should be thriving, but they aren't.

Although the USFWS program's target was a population of at least 100 by 2008, by 2011 it stood at half that. The poor result might have something to do with the official designation the wolf was originally given when it was listed under the Endangered Species Act. Rather than declaring it endangered under the law, which would have given it the fullest protection possible, the government listed the Mexican wolf as "an experimental, non-essential population." That the last few animals of an entire subspecies could be seen as non-essential may seem counterintuitive, but in the face of strong opposition from the anti-wolf lobby, it was apparently the best the little wolf was going to get. As a consequence, any wild Mexican wolf that attacked livestock three times in one year could be legally culled or captured. Ranchers graze livestock on the same public lands in Gila and Apache National Forests where the reintroduced wolves live, and natural prey species such as deer are less common than in the past, so it's not surprising that a rare encounter between a hungry wolf and livestock might occur. It was only a matter of time before ranchers would be demanding wolves' heads. And so, history had come full circle: the animals were hunted as vermin once again. According to some wildlife conservationists, such culling is the main reason the population hasn't reached the targeted 100 animals. In defence of the USFWS, this culling and capture option was used only after 2003, when the federal agency turned over management of el lobo to a committee headed by the Arizona Game and Fish Department. The US government has recently taken over the management of the Mexican wolf again and has stated it would no longer exercise the option to kill them.

Cole Porter's cowboy song "Don't Fence Me In" would seem to be the perfect anthem for a species that freely roams the vast deserts of the America southwest, as el lobo does. Thousands of kilometres away, however, in East Africa, it may in fact be a fence that ultimately saves another mammal species, the mountain bongo.

MOUNTAIN BONGO

What is possibly the world's longest wildlife fence was completed in Kenya in 2009. The 400-kilometre-long, 2.5-metre-high electric barrier, under construction for 20 years, encircles the Aberdare mountain range north of the capital city Nairobi. The Aberdare watershed supplies 90 percent of Nairobi's drinking water and almost half its hydroelectricity, so protecting it is as important to people as it is to wildlife.

The enclosed 2,000-square-kilometre upland forms the eastern rim of the Great Rift Valley and is East Africa's most important mountain forest. It's home to some of the continent's most spectacular wildlife, including black rhinos, elephants, and lions. Living amid this who's who of wildlife is one of the world's rarest large mammals and Africa's most endangered antelope, the mountain bongo.

Although we typically think of antelopes running gracefully across the open savannah, the extremely shy mountain bongo is strictly a forest species that relies on its dense wooded habitat for food and protection. (There is also a less threatened lowland bongo subspecies in western Africa.) It thrives on steep wooded mountainsides where landslides and tree falls have left openings in the canopy, allowing sunlight to penetrate to the forest floor and support the densely growing plants and bamboo the bongo eats.

The largest of the forest antelopes, bongos can weigh over 400 kilograms and stand 1.3 metres high at the shoulder. Add large spiral horns, vertical white stripes on a chestnut background, and a brushy mane running from shoulder to rump and it's not surprising this striking animal was once a popular zoo acquisition. Ironically, with the completion of the megafence around the Aberdare range, most of the wild mountain bongos still in existence are in essence captive—though it's an internment that might ultimately save them.

The concept and construction of the fence was spearheaded by the group Rhino Ark, whose original intent was to protect the shrinking black rhinoceros population and its ecosystem by keeping illegal loggers and poachers out. But it also keeps much of the wildlife in, especially elephants and rhinos, which used to destroy local crops and gardens. Fewer such confrontations have reduced animosity toward the area's large wild animals.

The mountain bongo has also benefited from the fence. By the late 1980s, when its construction began, mountain bongos hadn't been seen for years and were feared extinct. Before it was built, poachers and illegal loggers from the region's crushing throng of humanity had decimated the bongo's numbers and habitat, in spite of its preference for living in nearly impenetrable high-altitude forest.[1]

In time, the fence reduced logging and poaching, resulting in ideal habitat for bongos. In addition, a cull of the large lion population in the Aberdares (many were actually introduced to the area, resulting

---

1. A burgeoning human population is an acute problem in East Africa. Growing faster than any other country in the world, it took only eight decades for Kenya's population to swell from about 3 million to nearly 40 million today. For an idea of how rapid that growth is, if the population of the United States had expanded at the same rate over that time, it would now be home to almost 1.6 billion people.

in overpopulation), reduced predatory pressures on any of the animals that may have survived. Yet, despite such favourable conditions for the antelope, it would be years before one would be seen.

A single carcass found in the Mount Kenya forest (a separate, unfenced habitat west of the Aberdares) in 1994, however, was a sign that the species still existed in East Africa.

Hope for the animal's survival was ephemeral, though, and that carcass would be the last anyone would see of a mountain bongo until 2004, when after a decade of searching, a population of some 30 animals was finally located in the Aberdare Mountains. The fence likely played a crucial role in their survival. Since then, more animals have been found in the Aberdares region, as well as a few in the nearby Eburu Forest and in the Mount Kenya forest.

To determine the genetic health of the remaining population, conservationists have been recently collecting dung samples, which are preserved, then sent to the Cardiff University in Wales for DNA analysis. The results are worrying: it appears the entire population is descended from the lineages of just two females. This means the bongo has very low genetic diversity, likely the result of years of inbreeding among the small group. The upshot is that the recovery of the mountain bongo could be stymied by an increased susceptibility to disease. Such is often the reality of tiny, remnant populations.

Yet there is another "pool" of the antelopes. Descendants of Kenyan mountain bongos sent to zoos in the United States in the 1960s and 1970s have returned home to Kenya. Eighteen of them arrived at the Mount Kenya Wildlife Conservancy in 2004. The original plan was to reintroduce some of the first-generation offspring of these animals into native habitat to strengthen the wild population. Unfortunately, since their return to Kenya, it's been discovered that the captive animals have no immunity to some common African bovine diseases. Experts are now suggesting that any introduction to the wild be delayed until a second generation of bongos has been produced by these captive animals. By then a natural resistance to the diseases should have developed. Though it may be some time well into the future, an injection into the wild of the captive-bred bongos could result in a much-needed boost to the wild mountain bongo's genetic diversity, thereby increasing its prospects for long-term survival.

Unlike the bongo, some wild living things can't rely on the practice of captive breeding to help with population recovery. The Javan rhinoceros, for one, fares quite poorly when pent up.

Javan Rhinoceros

Imagine Manhattan practically disappearing from the face of the earth one day. That's what happened to the similar-sized island of Krakatau off Java, Indonesia, on August 27, 1883. Among the largest volcanic eruptions in recorded history, the explosion that let loose with a force of 13,000 atomic bombs hurled millions of tonnes of rock and ash into the air. It was heard thousands of kilometres away. A tsunami 40 metres high slammed into the shores of eastern Sumatra and western Java, killing 36,000 people. On Java's Ujung Kulon Peninsula, just a few kilometres away, all traces of humanity disappeared. It was never repopulated.

Free from human settlement, Ujung Kulon Peninsula rebounded to become one of the richest repositories of flora and fauna in Indonesia and the most important remaining refuge for the Javan rhinoceros. Protected since the early 20th century (comparatively easy to do because nobody lived there), Ujung Kulon would eventually be designated as a national park and a UNESCO world heritage site in the early 1990s. Ironically and fortuitously, the volcano helped keep the Javan rhino from going extinct. For without the eruption of Krakatau, people would still live on the peninsula, the national park may have never been created, and the already rare rhino would have long since been hunted to extinction.

Once the most widespread of the rhinos, living throughout much of Asia, the Javan today is the rarest of the five members of its family. All told, between 50 and 60 of the extremely shy, forest-dwelling animals survive, 40 to 50 of them in Ujung Kulon National Park. Here, they're safe because they are actively guarded against poaching within the 1,200-square-kilometre park. But with so few left, the status quo of merely a stable population is not enough. It might be only a matter of time before a disease or a natural disaster wipes out the rhino here. Its numbers need to grow, so scientists are hoping that another self-sustaining population can be established on Java using translocated animals from Ujung Kulon, thus improving the odds of the species' survival.

While the detonation of Krakatau may have been an unlikely saviour of the Javan rhinos on the island of Java, explosions of a more sinister kind had the opposite effect on the only other population of Javan rhinos, in Vietnam.

The havoc wreaked on wildlife by the bombs and gunfire of the Vietnam War is unimaginable. Moreover, Agent Orange defoliator and napalm were dropped from American aircraft, destroying huge swaths of the country's forests and grasslands, along with the animals that lived there. Many areas have never recovered. When the war was over, thousands of guns were left behind to be used by poachers, so it's no surprise that by the early 1970s most experts thought the Javan rhino was already extinct in Vietnam.

However, as fate would have it, one was killed by a hunter in 1988, nearly two decades after it was presumed extirpated from the country. A few years after that, a survey of lowland forest in Cat Tien National Park, north of Ho Chi Minh City, found evidence of a small population of rhinos. Vietnam's most important national park, home to sun bears, Asian elephants, gibbons, and langur monkeys, was later expanded to include the rhino's habitat. But the story may not end well. The recent approval of a hydroelectric megaproject just a few kilometres from the rhinos may have sealed the species' fate, as its last habitat will be flooded. An estimated 1,000 tonnes of explosives will be used during construction. This is bitter irony for a species whose original decline here was the result of the explosion of bombs during the Vietnam War and the din of poachers' gunfire. The Javan rhinoceros in Vietnam faces a tenuous future, at best. (Sadly, the story of the rhinoceros in Vietnam has ended, the result of illegal hunting. The Vietnam subspecies of the Javan rhino was declared extinct in October 2011.)

The Javan isn't the only member of its family facing extinction. The Sumatran, black, and Indian species, as well as the northern subspecies of the white rhino, are also endangered.

There's nothing new about the plight of the rhinoceros. They've been on this one-way road of decline for as long as any animal on the planet, largely because of the millennia-old belief in traditional Asian medicine that rhino horns cure fever, rheumatism, headaches, typhoid, and a host of other maladies. That it is illegal to trade in rhino horn anywhere in the world—rhinos are protected under the Convention on International Trade in Endangered Species—hasn't dampened demand. And, despite being totally disproved by modern medical studies as an effective treatment for *anything*, doctors and pharmacists throughout Asia continue to prescribe rhino horn to patients. Even if it *were* shown to be effective (which it is not), since rhino horn is nothing but keratin—the same protein found in birds' bills, horses' hooves, and yes, human fingernails—patients might just as well save themselves the time and expense of a trip to the doctor and stay home and nibble their nails.

Records of trade in rhino horn go back as early as 2600 BC.

During the Tang Dynasty (around AD 600–900), the animals had already become so scarce in China that they began importing horns from Africa and Arabia, as well as Java, Vietnam, Borneo, Sumatra, and Malaysia in Southeast Asia. Populations were being decimated very early on. Thus, China's insatiable demand for horns from Southeast Asia thousands of years ago bears some responsibility for the sorry state of Asian rhinos today.

As a booming Chinese economy puts more money into more people's hands, the demand for rhino horn grows. As the beleaguered animals become rarer and harder to find and kill, basic supply-demand economics kicks in: a very low supply and a high demand have pushed the price of rhino horn to US$60,000 per kilogram (in 2010), making it worth roughly its weight in gold. Such prices have drawn organized crime into the illegal trade in rhino horn. In the first half of 2011, criminals using automatic assault rifles from helicopters killed nearly 200 southern white rhinos in South Africa alone. Sadly, it is in the criminals' interest that rhinoceros are pushed toward extinction, for each kill that makes the animals rarer drives the market price even higher, increasing profits in the short term (poachers and thieves aren't noted for looking at the future with an eye on sustainability!). Despite ever-shrinking populations and stronger conservation efforts, more rhinos were killed in 2009 than in any of the previous 15 years, and 2011 looks poised to surpass it.

Excessive killing for whale oil, another animal "commodity" that was as valuable in its day as rhino horn is today, is responsible for the dire straits of the eastern North Pacific right whale, whose population is only half that of the Javan rhino.

EASTERN NORTH PACIFIC RIGHT WHALE
Why did whalers call them right whales? They were abundant. They were slow. They didn't sink when dead. And most importantly of

all, a single animal could yield 100 barrels of oil. They were the "right" whales to kill.

Eighteen metres long and weighing in at 100 tonnes, the right is a chunky, grey-coloured whale with no dorsal fin and a tail that measures four metres across. Its enormous head is about a third of its body length. Its mouth, big enough to fit a small car, is full of long slats of cartilage, known as baleen, that hang like vertical window blinds on either side of its gaping maw. Several tonnes of food in the form of shrimp-like zooplankton are filtered out by the baleen every day.

There are three species of right whales: the southern, found off Argentina, Australia, and South Africa; the North Atlantic species along the US Eastern Seaboard and eastern Canada; and the North Pacific right whale. There may be up to 10,000 rights living in the southern hemisphere, but the northern species are faring poorly. Both the western North Atlantic and western North Pacific Oceans are home to small populations of just a few hundred animals each. Even worse, the eastern North Pacific right whale of the Bering Sea and the Aleutian Islands has barely one-tenth that number, making it the rarest whale in the world. (Right whales off Peru and Chile, and in the eastern North Atlantic, have already disappeared, the victim of the whaler's harpoon. And so have the bowhead whales of Svalbard in the Scandinavian Arctic, a closely related species.)

Eastern North Pacific right whales were rediscovered in 1996 after an absence of decades. Based on genetic analysis published in 2010, the current population is just 28 animals, only 8 of them females. Most are lone individuals dispersed over a vast area of the Bering Sea. Just a few calves have been seen since 2002.

The story of the right whale's decline in North American waters began nearly 500 years ago on the Labrador coast. Centuries of slaughter along the European coast, and around Iceland and

Greenland, had already made the species scarce, so to make a profit in the 1500s, there was little choice but for European whalers to sail great distances across the Atlantic to the coast of North America.

In 1550, Basque whalers from the Bay of Biscay set off looking for whales to kill. They found lots of them in Labrador and subsequently built seasonal butchering and oil-rendering stations on its southern coast. The largest facility, at Red Bay (named not for water turned red by whales' blood but for the colour of shoreline rocks), was the first industrial complex in the New World, hosting as many as 15 ships and 600 men every summer for half a century.

Thousands upon thousands of right whales were slaughtered here so that tens of thousands of barrels of oil could be shipped back to the Old World for use in lamps and as candle wax. By the beginning of the 17th century, the animals were no longer plentiful enough to make the whalers' yearly 8,000-kilometre round trip from Europe worthwhile. The "right" whale would have to be found elsewhere. Eventually, it was.

In the 19th century, primarily American whalers but also Japanese and Russian began pushing into the remote North Pacific to find their quarry. They discovered right whales in abundance in the 1830s in the Gulf of Alaska and the Bering Sea. It is estimated that up to 37,000 of the animals were taken in these waters, nearly 30,000 of them between 1840 and 1849 alone.

No population of such slowly reproducing animals—a female gives birth to only one young every three to five years—can withstand this kind of pressure without collapsing. And collapse it did. North Pacific rights were scarce by the late 1800s and early 1900s. Just a few hundred were legally taken between 1911 and 1946, the year right whales finally became fully protected around the world.

That they were protected meant nothing to the Soviet Union whaling industry. It illegally killed nearly 400 of them during an intensive hunt in the Bering Sea in the 1960s. This war against the gentle animals was especially brutal in 1965. That year, the giant factory-whaling ships *Dal'nii Vostok* and *Vladivostok* steamed into the Gulf of Alaska and secretly slaughtered 300 eastern North Pacific right whales. This wiped out most of the remaining population at a time when the species was finally beginning to rebound from the American-led hunt of the previous century. The Soviet Union and Japan also "legally" killed 10 and 13 of the endangered whales respectively during the 1950s and 1960s for "scientific research."[2]

Almost nothing is known about the biology of eastern North Pacific right whales. Is the tiny population increasing or decreasing? Where do they migrate during the winter? How large is their range? Where are their calving grounds? How long do they live? What are their specific habitat requirements? How do you protect a species you don't really understand? These questions remain unanswered. Nevertheless, early steps are being taken to try to safeguard the population.

---

2. The exploitation of the "scientific research" loophole in the International Whaling Commission's ban on commercial whaling continues to this day. Japan "legally" hunts whales using massive factory ships, satellite tracking, and grenade-tipped harpoons. There is little, if any, scientific value in it. It is condemned by whale biologists around the world, who see it for what it really is: a scientifically worthless and cynical justification for the mass killing of whales. Between 1988 and 2009, Japan has thus taken over 12,000 whales in the North Pacific and around Antarctica. None of them (at least that we know of) was a northern hemisphere right whale, since those are just too rare to be hunted profitably. Despite Japan's insistence that the hunt is done strictly for research, the meat ends up being sold in its restaurants and markets. Mercifully, the Japanese public appears to be losing its taste for eating cetacean flesh. In fact, demand has dropped so much that by 2011, some 6,000 tonnes of whale meat were stockpiled in warehouses throughout Japan. Yet, despite this glut, Japan will resume its "scientific research" whaling in the western North Pacific in the summer of 2011. Although it isn't targeting the eastern North Pacific right whale, since it is endangered, Japan hopes to kill some 200 smaller minke whales in the name of science. The question must once again be asked, what exactly will be accomplished by such slaughter?

A huge right whale "critical habitat" area of about 95,000 square kilometres in the southeastern Bering Sea was established in 2007 by the federal government under the US Endangered Species Act and the Marine Mammal Protection Act. A smaller area was later designated in the Gulf of Alaska. But even in these areas the whales face potential conflict with humans. Commercial fisheries and shipping both occur within the designated habitats. And in a world of shrinking oil supplies, it may only be a matter of time before offshore petroleum and gas exploration begins here. The hard reality is that it's difficult to imagine a few whales standing in the way of an energy-hungry nation expanding its domestic oil supply. How much of a difference these designated habitats will ultimately make in the fate of the last eastern North Pacific right whales is anybody's guess.

A little less guesswork—and a little more success—is involved in the conservation of the world's smallest cetacean (it would take a thousand of them to make up the weight on one right whale), a well-studied species found a quarter of a world away, off the coast of New Zealand.

MAUI'S DOLPHIN

Few would argue that dolphins are exquisitely built for the sea, from the blowhole for breathing to the torpedo-shaped body to the powerful tail to the streamlined flippers and dorsal fin. But look closely at any dolphin embryo and you'll see something unexpected and telling: the beginnings of hind legs. Although they stop developing early in the embryonic stage, tiny limb bones remain part of every dolphin's skeleton. This vestige of terrestrial locomotion is evidence of a land-based ancestor for the ancient Delphinidae family: an otter-like land animal that first took to the sea some 50 million years ago. What drove this incipient dolphin into the ocean?

Perhaps there was more food there. Maybe the sea was safer. It is safe no longer. We need look no farther for evidence of this than the world's rarest dolphin, the Maui's dolphin of New Zealand.

It's easy to understand why it might be harder to get a good population estimate of a marine species compared with a land-dwelling one. The sea is very large and its creatures are usually hidden beneath it in three-dimensional space. The Maui's dolphin is an exception whose numbers *can* be estimated well because it lives within a small, defined area along the shallow waters of the west coast of New Zealand's North Island. Possibly fewer than 100 to 150 animals survive.

At a metre and a half long and weighing just 50 kilograms, the Maui's dolphin is the smallest of the 40 species of dolphins worldwide. Named for *Te Ika a Maui,* a Maori term for North Island, it is physically and genetically distinct from the more numerous Hector's dolphin of the South Island. The two have been isolated from one another for thousands of years and are considered separate subspecies.

This chunky-bodied, grey and white dolphin, with its black dorsal fin shaped like Mickey Mouse's ear and its black tail, flippers, and eye patches, is usually found in water no deeper than 20 metres. Here, small pods of up to five to eight individuals are seen engaging in mock chases, leaping and lobtailing; the young dolphins often blow bubbles and frolic with seaweed. Such antics may be more than simply play, perhaps filling an important role in learning, communication, and social bonding. Females don't reproduce until they are seven to nine years old, and even then have only one baby every two to four years. The young stay with their mothers and other females in small nursery pods for protection. Such a slow reproductive rate means population recovery won't be swift. It's been estimated that even one human-caused death of a Maui's dolphin every seven years would be enough to stymie any growth in their numbers.

The single biggest threat to this intelligent marine mammal is entanglement in fishing gear. Like other dolphin species, Maui's dolphins have evolved sophisticated sonar for hunting fish and navigating. But they seem to have trouble detecting the thin nylon filaments used in commercial and recreational gillnets, often becoming ensnared in them while on their way to the surface to breathe. Many drown. To prevent this, the New Zealand government has imposed a ban on setting nets in dolphin habitat along the North Island's west coast. Other protective measures include a very slow "no wake" speed for boaters when in the vicinity of the animals, a ban on swimming with or feeding them, and a strict no-trash policy. These are positive steps. However, the dolphins' near-shore habitat exposes them to a more insidious threat much harder to control: runoff of land-based farming pesticides and industrial pollution. Many of these nasty chemicals bioaccumulate, which means they get more toxic each step up the ocean food chain, a problem for species at the top, like dolphins. Young animals get a dose of these toxins through their mother's milk, which may lead to reproductive problems and weak immune systems in adulthood. To complicate matters, very small populations of organisms often have reduced genetic diversity. The Maui's dolphin is no exception. Today, only one of its three known genetic lineages of the past survives, possibly the result of inbreeding. This raises questions about its future ability to adapt to diseases or a changing environment.

But the good news for the Maui's dolphin is that critical steps to save it are being taken. Continued research and a public dolphin-reporting program are giving scientists better data that are so vital for conservation. Besides the all-important fishing net bans (which continue to be expanded and adjusted as new information is collected), public and school awareness programs are teaching New Zealanders that they are custodians of the one of the world's rarest dolphins, a distinction I'm sure they'd be happy to relinquish.

BAIJI (YANGTZE) DOLPHIN

As rare as the Maui's dolphin is, there are doubts whether the Baiji dolphin of China's Yangtze River exists at all.

This small cetacean was venerated in Chinese mythology as the reincarnation of a princess who was drowned in the Yangtze River because she wouldn't consent to marry someone she didn't love. Known as the Goddess of the Yangtze, the Baiji was once seen as a symbol of peace and prosperity.

Found only in the Yangtze, where it grows up to two and a half metres long, the light-coloured dolphin is a sleek, hydrodynamic animal with a long rostrum (snout). Because it typically lives in murky waters, its eyesight is quite poor, so it uses highly developed sonar for navigating and finding fish. It is one of four species of river dolphins worldwide; the others are found in the Ganges and Indus Rivers in India and the Amazon and Rio de la Plata in South America. Baijis are known to reach speeds of 60 kilometres per hour when fleeing danger, something that they've likely had to do a lot while dodging the juggernaut of modern China's economic, industrial, and population expansion along the Yangtze.

Much of the respect shown this animal for centuries came to an abrupt end during the Great Leap Forward of the late 1950s and early 1960s, when China's cruel Communist leadership outlawed the veneration of animals and mandated an ethos of brutal exploitation of nature. People living along the Yangtze complied and began hunting the defenceless animal. This marked the beginning of the end for the intelligent mammal with a perpetual smile, which according to fossil evidence had lived in the river for 20 million years. The Yangtze had been the Baiji's home for 100 times as long as *Homo sapiens* have walked the earth.

Just before the Great Leap Forward, the Baiji's population was estimated at a healthy 6,000 animals within its historic range along 1,700 kilometres of the Yangtze's middle reaches, almost as far south as Shanghai. Although it became illegal to kill the dolphins in the 1970s and several protected areas were established by the early 1990s, it was too little too late. In 1997, an organized search for the Baiji was able to come up with only 13 dolphins. Fast-forward less than a decade to 2006, when the last organized search for the Baiji took place. Not a single dolphin was found. Five decades of losing habitat to megadams, being drowned in fishing nets, struck and killed by ships, deafened by underwater shipping noise, poisoned by pollution, electrocuted by electro-fishing (whereby a powerful electrical charge is passed through water to kill fish), and being butchered for their meat may have been too much.

Nevertheless, some are not ready to give up on the Baiji just yet. Still categorized as critically endangered, it has yet to be declared officially extinct. A few conservationists feel that the search conducted in 2006 may have not lasted long enough to cover the vast stretch of potential Baiji habitat in the Yangtze. Maybe they were right, because in August 2007 a large white animal was filmed swimming in the river. It was later tentatively identified as a Baiji. Perhaps there are a few left, but if they are isolated from potential mates by dams, or too old and too sick to reproduce, it might still be too late. If so, the Goddess of the Yangtze will have become the ghost of the Yangtze.

GILBERT'S POTOROO

Kangaroos with little joeys and baby koalas riding around in their mothers' backs are icons of Australian fauna. In one of the great quirks of evolution, all the mammals Down Under are marsupials, the young famously carried in a parent's pouch while they develop. The marsupials encompass an impressive diversity of species that parallel that of placental mammals living on other continents. The most endangered one of all is the Gilbert's potoroo.

Weighing in at about a kilogram or less and reaching 30 centimetres in length, the potoroo is categorized as a rat kangaroo. Cute in a quirky way, it has a chubby body and long rat-like tail. Like a kangaroo, its powerful rear legs and long hind feet work like springs to bounce it along the ground. When sitting or standing still, it looks hunched over, a bit like a giant squirrel. It uses its short front legs only when manoeuvring very slowly and when foraging. The front feet are tipped by long, sharp claws for digging and are dextrous enough to manipulate objects it brings to its mouth.

The potoroo lives almost entirely on fungi, a unique trait among mammals. In fact, over 90 percent of its food is made up of truffles. It snuffles through the undergrowth, nose to the ground, until it smells the tasty morsels buried just beneath the surface. After digging them up, it eats the cherry-sized truffles, which are fungi's fruiting bodies. This is exactly what the fungi "wants" the potoroo to do, so it produces an odour that is irresistible to the little marsupial. In exchange for a meal, the potoroo helps spread the fungi's spores to new sites when it later defecates. It is a simple yet elegant example of the mutualism that occurs in nature.

At one time, the little Gilbert's potoroo was abundant in southwestern Western Australia, prompting the namesake of the species, naturalist John Gilbert, to write in the 1800s that "immense numbers could be captured by aborigines in a single afternoon." Alas, much has changed. By the late 1870s, it was thought to be extinct, but like so many species currently surviving on the edge of oblivion, it was rediscovered. In 1994, a small colony was found living on a single promontory in the Two Peoples Bay Nature Reserve near Albany, Western Australia. Between 30 and 40 Gilbert's potoroos currently survive there. Despite searches, the species hasn't been found outside this small area, where it is limited to a few dense patches of vegetation that hasn't been burnt in over 50 years, a rare commodity in this part of Australia. However, 10 of the original potoroos were translocated to two additional conservation colonies between 2005 and 2007. They have reproduced very well since their move. Today, these colonies hold between 40 and 50 of the cute marsupials, in addition to the originally discovered colony.

SEYCHELLES SHEATH-TAILED BAT

Pity the bats. They don't have the benefit of being cute like potoroos, a trait of real utility when it comes to garnering support for conservation. Of all the mammals, none is more misunderstood or unjustly maligned than the bat. Ignorance of bats runs deep, and nowhere is this more evident than when one gets loose inside a house or flies around the backyard during a barbecue. Fear is struck into the hearts of helpless humans, and a code-red state of panic ensues. Everybody makes for whichever door puts them on the side of the wall not occupied by the bat. There's usually one brave soul who stays behind to deal with the beast, courageously stalking the intimidating canary-sized menace with a broom. Flailing in futility with the makeshift weapon, the intrepid would-be bat wrangler ducks like a hitter dodging a fastball every time the tiny animal swoops near. Faces pressed against the window watching the struggle blanch at the sight of the beast flitting, butterfly-like, around the room.

The truth about bats is far less dramatic. Bats don't get in the hair, they don't carry disease (except rarely, like any animal), they don't suck blood (well, some that live in faraway places do, but not humans' blood), and they don't turn into vampires. What bats *are* is the largest order of mammals on the planet with 1,150 species; warm-blooded creatures that give birth to live young, suckle them, and mother them; the owners of a sonar system so sophisticated they can see with sound as well as we can see with light; highly social animals with tight-knit communities and complex communications; the planet's most effective and withal cheapest method of mosquito control; barometers of the state of the environment thanks to their sensitivity to chemicals and changes in their insect food supply; and one of the most important pollinators of plants on earth, including more than a few human-grown crops. The most tragic fact about bats is that nearly one-tenth of them are endangered or critically endangered.

One of the rarest bats on earth lives on the remote Seychelles Islands in the Indian Ocean, off Africa. Named for a membrane that stretches between its hind legs, which is used for flight manoeuvring, the reddish-brown, 10-gram Seychelles sheath-tailed bat lives on two small islands: Silhouette and Mahe. Here, it roosts among boulder fields in woodland along the coast, where it also breeds, giving birth to a single pup late in the year. It feeds using echolocation to locate insects in mature woodland near the coast.

Already extirpated from several other islands in the Seychelles, where it was once quite common, the bat now numbers about 60. The causes for its decline haven't been pinpointed, but the best guess is a combination of human disturbance of the roost sites, hunting by introduced barn owls and feral cats, invasive kudzu vine, loss of habitat, and a decline of important food items such as beetles and moths due to pesticides. And so goes the common refrain in the realm of endangered species: there isn't one but many reasons for decline.

The removal of introduced kudzu and introduced cinnamon plants to allow native flora to flourish again on Silhouette Island has helped restore the insect population there. This appears to have helped the bats. After hitting a low of as few as 14 animals in the 1990s, the population had bounced back to 40 by 2010. Meanwhile on Mahe, where 90 percent of the people in the Seychelles live, three small roosts are home to just a handful of bats. Unfortunately, living as they do in woodlands along the coasts on both islands, there's the inevitable and ever-present threat of housing and tourism development. To complicate matters further for the little bat, they have no legal protection in the Seychelles. Gaining full protection for the species is a conservation priority. Control of feral cats and barn owls, public education, and continued management of the bat's habitat are also critical if the Seychelles sheath-tailed bat is to be rescued from extinction.

FRAYING FEATHERS: BIRDS

B irds are a paradox of conservation. On one hand, as brightly coloured, often musical creatures that are generally active during daylight hours, they are an ever-present visual and audible part of our everyday world, the single most popular group of wild animals on earth. Hundreds of millions of bird aficionados around the world are only too ready to support the protection of their feathered friends. On the other hand, the enormous diversity of birds (there are about 10,000 species) means they are spread across the globe, on every continent and island, in every nook and cranny, often remote and therefore difficult to help. The majority of the threatened ones are located on small oceanic islands and in the tropical forests of continents and large islands such as New Guinea and Borneo. Currently, there are 1,253 bird species on the IUCN Red List of Threatened Species.

SÃO TOMÉ FISCAL

What pops into your head when you think of a songbird? A canary, a warbler, a robin, a sparrow? Whichever it is, probably the last thing that comes to mind is a ruthless predator. But that's exactly what the São Tomé fiscal is. Like other members of the family of birds known as shrikes, the São Tomé fiscal has a reputation as an efficient, albeit diminutive, hunter. As if it were a tiny hawk, it swoops down on a potential meal and plucks it from the ground with its bill. That's the predatory part. The ruthless part comes next: even when it's no longer hungry, this bird keeps hunting for more. So, when it can't stuff anything else into its full belly, it takes its prey—which might be anything from a small insect to a nestling bird to a small lizard—and impales it on a big thorn or a spike on a barbed-wire fence to save it for later. And sometimes, larger quarry, like a writhing lizard, might be too much for the shrike to handle, so the thorn also comes in handy as a vice to hold the animal while the bird pecks and tears at it until it's dead. Not surprisingly, the nickname "butcherbird" has stuck for members of the shrike family. So have other unflattering names, such as the "hangman" or "the murderer." The name "shrike" comes from "shriek," for the shrill call made by these unusual songbirds. Naturally, one member of the family has to be the rarest, and that distinction falls to the São Tomé fiscal.

The species is found on the small equatorial island of São Tomé, which lies in the Atlantic Ocean about 300 kilometres off the coast of Gabon, in West Africa. With an area of only about 1,000 square kilometres, the country of São Tomé and Principe, Africa's smallest, was formed by now extinct volcanoes. Despite its limited size, the nation is home to 28 species of birds found nowhere else in the world. São Tomé is a crucible of evolution, much like its Pacific counterparts the Galapagos and the Hawaiian Archipelagos.

The São Tomé fiscal, with a population estimated to be under 50, not only is among the rarest birds on the islands, it's one of the most endangered songbirds on earth. In fact, for six decades it was thought to be extinct, until rediscovered in 1991, when a single bird was observed during an extensive survey.

Slightly smaller than an American robin, the fiscal has a striking appearance with its black back and mask, a creamy belly, a long tail, and a typically heavy shrike bill with a hawk-like hooked tip. It is found only in a small remnant of primary or old-growth lowland and mid-altitude forest. Very little of this original habitat is left on the island after centuries of clearing for sugar cane (São Tomé was the world's largest producer of sugar in the 16th century), cacao, and coffee plantations. Although little is known of its habits, the fiscal appears to prefer a habitat with a closed canopy of trees above a bare, rocky forest floor; this would presumably suit its style of swoop-down hunting. It also feeds on seeds and fruit in the understorey. Nest predation by introduced black rats, civet cats, and weasels may have also had an impact on the species' ability to successfully reproduce.

Although direct development of the birds' remaining habitat has largely stopped (some of which is protected in a small, newly established national park), newly built roads in the area are nevertheless improving access for local people to illegally cut wood, harvest plants, and hunt in the forest. It's also making it easier for the introduced species that prey on nests to penetrate deep into the fiscal's habitat. With such a tiny population, the species can ill afford the loss of even one individual or to suffer greater disturbance of its forest habitat. Several other threatened endemic birds of São Tomé, including the São Tomé grosbeak and the dwarf olive ibis, also depend on this primary forest. With an extremely dense human population of 170 people per square kilometre (about 140,000 people live on the island) and scant natural habitat remaining, the future of the fiscal shrike and many of the island's species, such as the São Tomé grosbeak, are up in the air.

São Tomé Grosbeak

With a total population of fewer than 50, the critically endangered, endemic São Tomé grosbeak is one of the least-known birds in the world. Until it was rediscovered in 1991 (the same year as the island's fiscal) in southwestern São Tomé, a single specimen collected in the 19th century was all anyone knew of the grosbeak. This large, 18-centimetre-long, rusty brown finch inhabits lowland rainforest, where it uses its massive conical bill to crush seeds. With its tiny population and a preference for spending time in the forest canopy, the bird is rarely seen. Despite the reputation finch species around the world have for their ebullient singing, the São Tomé grosbeak evidently rarely vocalizes, though it does occasionally whistle like a canary. This generally quiet nature might be one of the reasons the species is seldom noticed.

Centuries of widespread destruction of the island's lowland rain-forest for the development of sugar cane and cocoa plantations has left this and other species of native São Tomé birds with little viable habitat, and newly built roads are making it easier to exploit what little forest remains. Much of the species' habitat is located within the small Obo National Park. Apparently a park in name only, very little conservation enforcement takes place there. Introduced black rats, feral pigs, stoats, and civets also live in the area. The grosbeak remains poorly studied, so it isn't known what, if any, effects these invasive species may be having on its population. A paucity of ecological knowledge about the grosbeak also makes it difficult to assess which human-caused factors are most impacting the species.

With such a small population and so little known about it, the São Tomé grosbeak is in a precarious position. Unfortunately, the species isn't even protected under São Tomé law; without such legal status, its future is completely a matter of chance. Legal protection is the number one goal of conservationists, but they must first learn more about the species so that recommendations on a recovery plan can be made to government. Research into its population size, its distribution on the island, and its ecology is underway. A program to train local residents in population monitoring and conservation has recently been completed. It is hoped that the community's knowledge of rare species such as the São Tomé grosbeak and the São Tomé fiscal will engender an appreciation of them, thereby helping to secure their future. But, with just a few dozen grosbeaks left, there is little time to waste in protecting them and their habitat.

As much as habitat loss threatens the world's island birds, it may not be the most important problem facing wildlife living on another tiny island, nearly halfway around the world, where the Mariana crow and other native species of Guam in the South Pacific are struggling with a more insidious threat.

MARIANA CROW

Crows are one of the most successful groups of large birds on earth. About 40 species are found around the world, and some, like the American crow, are so cagey and have such a huge population that they've become pests. It's no fluke that many crow species have been able to adapt so well to the modern world. They are highly intelligent, claimed by some researchers to be the smartest non-human species. Maybe being called a birdbrain isn't such an insult after all.

But sometimes no matter how intelligent you are, circumstances get the better of you. That's exactly what's happened to the Mariana crow, a species exclusive to Guam and Rota Island of the Northern Marianas Islands, in the Pacific Ocean, about halfway between Japan and Australia.

Looking all the world like an everyday, typical crow, the Mariana species is dubiously distinguished as the current record holder for rarest of its kind on earth. This isn't surprising when you consider the three-metre-long menace it has had to contend with: the brown tree snake, an accidentally introduced species normally native to Australia and New Guinea. This nocturnal, tree-climbing snake has devastated the island's ecosystem since arriving on Guam after World War II. With concentrations of up to 5,000 per square kilometre, legions of them slithered their way over the island, eating practically every small wild animal in sight, killing thousands of domestic pets, and causing frequent power outages as they weighed down and shorted-out electrical lines.

Because the native birds of Guam evolved in the absence of predatory snakes, they were unable to adapt to this efficient predator, which caused the extinction of several small endemic species by the 1980s. The Mariana crow, perhaps owing to its larger size or to an intelligence that allowed it to adapt somewhat to a novel threat, managed to survive the serpent's onslaught a little longer. But not much: in 1981, only 250 crows were left on Guam.

The crow was listed as endangered on the heels of the extinction in the wild of the Guam rail, Guam flycatcher, and rufous fantail in the 1990s. Soon after, biologists captured and placed 10 of them in US zoos (Guam and the Northern Marianas are territories of the United States) to stock a captive breeding program. Although six captive-bred birds were later released on the island, in 1997, and more than 20 since, only two (both males) survive on Guam today, neither of which are native-born, making the species functionally extinct there. Even the use of electrical tree barriers has failed to protect the crow's eggs and chicks from tree snakes. There's little hope of re-establishing the Mariana crow on Guam until the snake has been eradicated from the island. So far that hasn't been possible.

Fortunately, Mariana crows are also found on the tiny island of Rota, 60 kilometres north of Guam. Until recently, the population was thought to be relatively safe there, with a tally of over 1,300 birds in 1982. Since then, however, that number has crashed to only about 100, a decline of over 90 percent in less than three decades. Although the brown tree snake hasn't been found on the small island yet (its potential arrival is a serious worry that keeps conservationists up at night), many other factors have been involved in the crow's decline there. Typhoons have destroyed much of the bird's forest habitat, some of which has also been cleared to make way for golf courses and resorts, housing developments, and farming. On top of all that, rats and monitor lizards kill crow nestlings, and locals shoot the adults. A final insult is the black drongo, an introduced bird, which now competes with the crows for nesting sites.

Although the Mariana crow has been listed as a critically endangered species for decades now, its present predicament is not for a lack of effort. Some of its habitat has been protected on both Rota and Guam, birds have been translocated from the former to boost numbers in the latter (unsuccessfully), attempts have been made to protect it against the brown tree snake, and even a small captive breeding program was started. Although the dual forces of invasive species and habitat destruction aligned against it seem almost overwhelming, hope holds that the Mariana crow will survive.

Tahiti Monarch

Perfect weather, swaying palms, turquoise lagoons, pristine black sand beaches, mist-shrouded mountains, and sunsets, don't forget the sunsets. What could be better than living in Tahiti, one of the most beautiful places in the South Pacific? Who wouldn't jump at the chance? As we just learned about Guam, however, life on a tropical Pacific island isn't always what it seems to be. Tahiti is no different. Eighty percent of the 29 terrestrial bird species here are endangered, and nearly one-fifth are classified as critically endangered. The king of scarcity is the Tahiti monarch, a 15-centimetre-long, sparrow-sized flycatcher. Despite its grandiose name, this little songbird looks anything but regal in its plain, shiny black plumage and pale blue bill and legs. It is rare like any monarch: only 40 to 45 birds are left.

The Tahiti monarch is the rarest member of the *Pomarea* genus, a highly threatened group of birds found throughout Polynesia. Two of the species are critically endangered, two are endangered, and one is considered vulnerable. Moreover, another four species of *Pomarea* flycatchers have already gone extinct.

Occupying a total range of just 28 square kilometres of the island, the monarch lives in forest habitats of giant ferns, mara trees, and flowering hibiscus that are located in four of the island's deep valleys at elevations between 80 and 400 metres. Highly territorial birds, they announce their presence with a rich and complex flute-like song. Like many flycatcher species around the world, monarchs feed on insects in both the forest canopy and its undergrowth.

Black rats, introduced to Polynesia centuries ago, have long been a menace for the beleaguered members of the *Pomarea* genus. Though nobody knows with certainty, they were probably instrumental in the decline of the Tahiti monarch. Rats are known to climb to the nests of the endangered bird and eat its egg or young, thus wiping out the entire breeding season for the parent birds. And because Tahiti monarchs lay only a single egg—very unusual for a songbird—they are slow to rebound from losses. Happily, an ongoing rat eradication program in the four valleys where the monarch is found has had a real positive effect on the endangered bird's prospects for survival.

But there's more than rats to worry about. Red-vented bulbuls and common mynas, both introduced birds, have also made recovery difficult for the monarch. The myna is thought to prey on eggs and nestlings, and the bulbul may compete for nesting sites. So far they appear to be less of a threat than the rats, and no eradication programs have been carried out on them. Even invasive plants such as the African tulip tree are at odds with the little songbird, dominating its forest habitat by threatening to squeeze out the mara tree in which the monarch builds its nest. Removal of tulip trees from its habitat is thus an important part of the recovery plan. As a contingency in case of a disastrous nesting season, a hurricane, or some other factor decimating the population, plans are in place to take some birds into captivity for a breeding program if it becomes absolutely essential or to translocate some to other islands. Still, this is only a contingency.

Barely 40 of these little musical songbirds hang on. This may be a small, small number, but it's better than it was. Less than a decade ago, there were only 20 Tahiti monarchs struggling against invasive organisms, the scourge of many a threatened ecosystem, including the famed Galapagos Archipelago, 5,000 kilometres across the South Pacific.

FLOREANA MOCKINGBIRD

One of the biggest myths in all of science is the role that the so-called Darwin's finches of the Galapagos played in the great naturalist's formulation of the theory of evolution. Truth be told, he didn't even specifically mention finches in *The Origin of Species,* his masterwork published in 1859. But what he did mention, both in *The Origin* and in journals he wrote while on the HMS *Beagle* soon after leaving the Galapagos in 1836, were mockingbirds. Mockingbirds, not finches, were instrumental in his idea that species evolve through adaptation to their surrounding environments and come from common ancestors—as opposed to the long-held view that species never change.[3]

One bird in particular, the Floreana mockingbird, got him thinking when he noticed how different it was from the other three

---

3. Darwin wasn't the first person to propose evolution. His grandfather Erasmus Darwin, among others, did earlier, but Charles, along with Alfred Russel Wallace, who came to the same conclusions independently, was the first to show how it worked through natural selection.

mockingbirds of the archipelago. Darwin asked, did one of those other three species somehow end up on Floreana Island, only to evolve novel traits after generations as it adapted to the peculiarities of its new environment? The answer, of course, was yes.

Floreana mockingbirds are large songbirds of about 25 centimetres in length that spend much of their lives on or near the ground among cactus and other desert shrubbery. They are also noisy birds. In fact, it's hard to miss the boisterous vocalizations of any one of the 35 members of the mockingbird family found throughout the Americas. All of them, including the four on the Galapagos, are intelligent, musical birds, with complex songs and raucous calls.

With a dark back, light belly, a long tail, and a curved bill, the Floreana bird resembles the northern mockingbird of the United States and southern Canada. The Galapagos bird's diet is broad and includes such delicacies as insects, little crabs, lizard and bird eggs, fruit, nectar, seeds, centipedes, and ticks plucked from the skin of living iguanas (an unintentional favour for which the reptiles must be grateful). Living in small groups, the rearing of the young mockingbirds is a cooperative affair, with non-breeding adult members of the family helping to feed nestlings.

This famous mockingbird is at risk of disappearing forever. It no longer lives on its namesake island, where it was wiped out by introduced black rats, cats, goats, and human occupation in the late 1800s. Who knows, maybe rodents that escaped from Darwin's HMS *Beagle* decades earlier even contributed to the bird's disappearance from Floreana. Fortunately, a few still survive on two nearby satellite islets, Champion and Gardner-by-Floreana—mere rocks in the sea with a combined area of about one square kilometre. Although the population fluctuates, as few as 100 or even fewer adult birds cling to existence there.

Steeped as Floreana mockingbird is in the history of science, it's not surprising that a lot of effort is being made to ensure its survival. The major goal is to eventually reintroduce birds from the two satellite populations back onto Floreana. Oddly enough, after nearly two centuries, the hand of Darwin may have a small part to play in the survival of the species. Two of the mockingbirds he collected there in 1835, currently housed in the Natural History Museum in London, are being used in the effort to conserve the bird. In 2009, scientists extracted DNA from these old specimens to use as a benchmark to learn how much the current birds' DNA had changed (i.e., evolved). The analysis revealed that the living Champion and Gardner-by-Floreana populations have only recently begun to evolve apart from one another, though they are not yet separate species. This suggests that the now extinct population on Floreana Island acted as a bridge between them, enabling the mixing of genes across all three islands in the past. So today, now too far apart physically to interbreed, the mockingbirds have begun to "go their own way" in an evolutionary sense.

The upside is that the slight evolution that has occurred in these two populations means the overall genetic variation within the species is greater. This should improve the chances of success for any introduction of the Champion and Gardner-by-Floreana birds to Floreana: the more diverse a population, the more resilient it is and the better its chance of survival. On top of all this, the rapid genetic change in the two populations confirms what we have known ever since Darwin: new species are evolved from older ones by adapting over generations to their specific environments—exactly what is happening to the birds on Champion and Gardner-by-Floreana.

Once the rats, cats, goats, and other introduced animals that wiped out the mockingbird on Floreana in the first place have all been removed, the reintroduction of the species will proceed, helping the Floreana mockingbird's chances at surviving well into the future.

Mangrove Finch

Though we now understand that the mockingbirds of the Galapagos were the more important inspiration for the theory of natural selection, "Darwin's finches" did nevertheless play a role in the refinement of his ideas. They've also inspired scientists after Darwin, such as biologist David Lack, who used his studies of the finches in the mid-20th century to fill in some of the technical details of evolution that Darwin missed.

Splitting into new species as they adapted to new ecological niches throughout the archipelago over generations, 13 finches would ultimately evolve from one common ancestor.

All quite similar in that they are "LBJs" or little brown jobs, the Galapagos finches are pretty plain birds. Plain, that is, except for the beak, which needs to be well adapted to the surrounding environment for a bird to efficiently feed itself. Some of the finches' beaks are short and thick for cracking hard seeds, some are long and thin for reaching into flowers to sip nectar, others are pointed and of medium girth for grasping cactus spines as tools to dig beetle larvae out of rotten wood. None of the finches is abundant, living as they do in specialized habitats on relatively small islands, but by and large they've fared quite well. Except for one. The mangrove finch, one of the two tool-using birds on the islands (the other is the very similar woodpecker finch), has become very rare.

Found nowhere else in the world, this 14-centimetre-long brown and beige songbird once lived throughout the coastal areas of Isabela Island and neighbouring Fernandina Island. Inhabiting dense, drier stands of mangrove trees, the mangrove finch feeds on insects, worms, spiders, and grubs it gleans from shoreline leaf litter that has yet to be washed out to sea by the tide. By the 1970s, the bird was gone from Fernandina. Now teetering on the brink of extinction with fewer than 100 left, it is found only in three small patches of mangroves on Isabela, its known habitat totalling just one square kilometre.

While loss of habitat isn't a pressing issue, since all of it is protected as part of Galapagos National Park, rising sea levels caused by climate change could affect the suitability of the dense groves of mangrove currently inhabited by the finch. As the sea creeps inexorably higher up the shore, there's a risk that the leaf-litter environment favoured by the birds will become too wet for feeding (no longer drying out at low tide). Of more immediate concern, however, is the black rat, the enemy of island birds everywhere. These rodents—and to a lesser extent introduced feral cats and introduced smooth-billed anis, a blackbird-like species with a grotesque beak—have decimated the finch's population by preying on eggs and nestlings.

What's more, a tiny invader from the South American mainland has emerged as a major new threat to the mangrove finch. The larvae of a species of fruit fly known as *Philornis downsi*—which probably got to the Galapagos in a shipment of fruit—now infests all of the mangrove finch nests (as well as many nests of the other finch species on the archipelago). These unsavoury parasites, which suck the blood of nestlings, killed their first mangrove finch in 2007. Finding out how to stop them is a conservation priority. One idea is to breed a genetically altered sterile version of the fly that would then be released to mate with and sterilize the rest of the population. Whether this will work is anybody's guess. And as if all that weren't enough, the first case of avian pox, a disease that could potentially cause big problems for the vulnerable species, was recently recorded.

Despite all of this, the recovery of the species has enjoyed modest success. A program to control rats has worked quite well: fledgling survival went from just 6 in 2006, when the rat program started, to 17 a year later. It's hoped that as more young are successfully fledged they will naturally begin to move to new habitat. This might already be occurring, as yearling finches have been observed moving about in mangrove trees outside their traditional home range. Moreover, as the population of young birds continues to expand, it is hoped some of them can be captured and relocated to suitable habitats that have been identified on the other side of Isabela. In 2010, nine birds were part of a trial relocation to new habitat on Isabela.

Remember that closely related tool-using species the woodpecker finch? Not wanting to risk experimenting with the highly endangered mangrove finch, scientists are using some of these other birds in captive breeding trials in order to develop techniques and experience that could be applied to a future mangrove finch breeding program. The ultimate goal is to increase the population enough to one day reintroduce the mangrove finch throughout most of its former range. Fortunately, DNA tests show the species still has enough genetic variation to grow and survive, so a captive breeding program should have a fair chance of succeeding.

NICEFORO'S WREN

As fascinating as the avian life is on oceanic islands like those of the Galapagos or Tahiti, these generally aren't the best places to see a big variety of birds. If you want that, go to Colombia. With nearly 1,900 species, it has more of them than anywhere else, about one-fifth of all the birds on earth (by contrast, Canada, with a geographical area about 10 times the size, hosts only about 500 species). There's just something special about the combination of diverse forest habitats found in the deep Andes mountain valleys and the equatorial climate that drives avian variety. What's more, Colombia boasts 74 bird species found nowhere else in the world, the rarest of which is the Niceforo's wren.

This small, rufous and white songbird with a thin, slightly down-curved bill and nearly vertical, skyward-pointing tail lives in an

Blue iguana » The fact that the Cayman Island blue iguana has a light-sensitive spot on the top of its head (a third eye, if you will), did little to defend it against centuries of predation by introduced rats, cats, and dogs. By 2003, the colourful lizard was almost extinct, with as few as five of them surviving. Happily, since then, the determined efforts of the Blue Iguana Recovery Program have resulted in a stunning comeback for the long-lived lizard, and today there are 250 thriving on the island.

Black-footed ferret » The slender and elegant black-footed ferret spends much of its time underground, either sleeping, raising its kits, or hunting the burrowing black-tailed prairie dog, its primary source of food. This plains-dwelling member of the weasel family has been the focus of one of the most intensive wildlife recovery efforts in North America, which has brought the species back from the brink of extinction to a total population of about 1,000 today, living both in captivity and in the wild.

Pink pigeon » The pink pigeon was never heavily hunted, and it may have avoided the fate of the extinct dodo (also a species of pigeon) because its meat was thought to make people sick, possibly owing to its diet, which includes toxic seeds. Even without the threat of hunting, by 1990 there were only 10 pink pigeons left in the wild. Today, through the efforts of the Mauritian Wildlife Foundation, there are about 400 living in the wilds of Mauritius.

Vancouver Island marmot » A mascot of the 2010 Winter Olympics, the Vancouver Island marmot had the dubious distinction of being Canada's rarest mammal. Less than a decade ago, there were 30 marmots left in the wild, the only survivors of clear-cut logging and predation by wolves, cougars, and eagles. Conservationists have been working tirelessly to ensure their survival, and by 2010 the population had increased dramatically, to 300.

Northern sportive lemur » Named for the upright, boxer-like stance it takes when threatened, this nocturnal animal is largely a mystery. The northern sportive lemur is one of the rarest of the planet's primates; possibly fewer than 100 survive in small, scattered bits of forest in northern Madagascar, where they spend their days sleeping in hollowed-out tree trunks. Conservationists are working to save its last forest habitats.

Rabb's fringe-limbed tree frog » In a most unfroglike way, the newly discovered Rabb's fringe-limbed tree frog will launch itself from high atop the trees, spreading its toes and using its four very large webbed feet like parachutes to drift softly to the ground. The species is no longer found in the wild, and just a handful of frogs exists in captivity. Conservationists are attempting to breed them, so that this remarkable amphibian might someday restock former wild habitats in its native Panama.

Burmese roofed turtle » If it weren't for the sanctuary provided by a Buddhist temple pond in the middle of the city of Mandalay, we might still think the brilliant green Burmese roofed turtle was extinct. That's where three of them were discovered alive and well in 2002, prompting further searches for the species. In 2004 a few more were found in the wild, along a river in northern Burma, and the following year a recovery program was initiated. There's still a long way to go, but some progress is being made toward a time when this rare turtle might thrive in the wild again.

Mountain bongo » Africa's most endangered antelope, the mountain bongo, was thought to be extinct due to poaching and tree-cutting in the mountain forests of East Africa. Then a herd of 30 of them was discovered in 2004. Now, with its habitat protected by the world's longest wildlife fence (which also protects a host of other animals), and with a captive breeding program in place, this striking species, with its reddish-brown fur and vertical white stripes, may yet make a comeback.

Andean valley of dry tropical forest in north-central Colombia. It was discovered by Brother Niceforo Maria, a Frenchman formerly called Antoine Rouhaire, who travelled to the country as a Catholic missionary in 1908. He went on to become one of the leading naturalists in his adopted homeland, founding the natural history museum in Medellin in 1911 and helping to discover many animals new to science. Based on specimens he collected and provided to museums around the world, scientists were able to describe over 150 new species, including 13 mammals, 14 amphibians, and 8 birds. In recognition of his contribution to science, 4 of these species have been named in his honour: Niceforo's big-eared bat, Niceforo's marsupial frog, Niceforo's pintail duck, and the wren.

In the 1940s, Niceforo discovered his wren in dry tropical forest in a valley on the west slope of the Andes, not far from the Venezuela border. It then disappeared for a half century before turning up again in 1989. That it took so long for another to be recorded isn't surprising, considering just how tiny its range and population was. It lived in just one valley, the Chichamocha. Niceforo's wren had become legendary as South America's rarest, most endangered bird. Today, around 20 birds are found at the original site, along with very small populations at two other nearby sites. Only about 77 birds are thought to exist.

Niceforo's wren was probably never common. This is not particularly unusual for organisms living in tropical regions with high biodiversity where the cost of great variety is a relatively small population for any given species. That's the polar opposite (pardon the pun) of high-latitude ecosystems that host only a few species but at very large abundances—think caribou in the Arctic or penguins in Antarctica. However small the wren's population might have naturally been, its current numbers are far below that which are sustainable over the long term.

Once again, it appears habitat loss is playing the major role in propelling a species toward non-existence. Niceforo's wren depends on a dense undergrowth of perennial vegetation on the forest floor. This rich understorey has been largely destroyed by centuries of grazing by goats and cattle. Much of the forest has also been cut down to make way for coffee, plantain, and sugar cane plantations.

There was very good news for the endangered bird in 2009, though. With support from the American Bird Conservancy, the World Land Trust-US, and the local government, Fundación ProAves, a Colombian bird conservation group, purchased 1,400 hectares of the prime wren habitat and established the Niceforo's Wren Natural Bird Reserve. Not only did this create a safe, protected home for one of the world's rarest birds, it preserves a slice of dry tropical forest, one of the world's rarest ecosystems. Two other highly endangered birds, the chestnut-bellied hummingbird and the Apical flycatcher, also found in the reserve, will benefit as well. No doubt, Brother Niceforo Maria would have been pleased.

As rare as Brother Niceforo's lovely wren is, it has nevertheless been well studied in recent years, something that can't be said for the rather mysterious Carrizal seedeater, one of the world's least-known birds, living just across the border in neighbouring Venezuela.

CARRIZAL SEEDEATER
Can a species go extinct before it even becomes a species? This is precisely what nearly happened to one South American bird. In 2001, Edelca, the state-owned electric company in northeastern Venezuela, commissioned a survey of wildlife in areas that would be affected by the construction of a new hydroelectric dam on the Caroni River. While surveying Isla Carrizal, an uninhabited, spiny bamboo–covered island located in the middle of the massive river,

biologists discovered a songbird that had never been seen in this part of South America before. They didn't know if it was new to science or one of several seedeater species that also lived in other parts of Latin America.

By the time it was announced in 2003 that the bird was, in fact, a unique species never seen before, it looked like it was already too late: Isla Carrizal, the only known home of the newly named Carrizal seedeater, had been destroyed, its vegetation completely razed during the development of the hydro dam. The little bird had apparently become extinct even before it officially existed; it was a birth announcement and obituary all rolled into one. Alas, and happily, reports of its demise were premature.

Small even for a songbird, the Carrizal seedeater reaches a length of only 12 centimetres, about the size of an American goldfinch. The males are a glossy blue-black with bright blue shoulders and black wings, and sport a relatively large, cone-shaped bill, typical of a seedeater. Females are light brown.

Even though the ecosystems along the Caroni River had been fairly well explored over the years, the Carrizal seedeater might have remained unknown as long as it had because it spent most of its time in groves of spiny bamboo. Growing in dense stands and wielding long, razor-sharp thorns, spiny bamboo can be a nasty weapon against large, soft-skinned mammals like humans. Living in such a fortress of inaccessibility, it isn't surprising nobody had become acquainted with the Carrizal seedeater earlier. Because of this, of course, very little is known about its ecology, although we do know that its bill is adapted to feeding in a bamboo habitat and it may eat weevils that are associated with the giant grass.

Surveys of the Caroni River Basin in the vicinity of Isla Carrizal in 2007 and 2008 found the birds in several locations. This is obviously good news; however, it appears the surviving population is still very, very small, estimated at fewer than 50 in total. To make matters worse, none of the species' known range is protected, a crucial step that's needed to ensure its survival. Although it will be a challenge to save the Carrizal seedeater, searches for more of its potential habitat along the Caroni and nearby Orinoco River are planned. But even this won't be easy, since the bird's preferred habitat of spiny bamboo grows beneath the dense forest canopy, so it can't be seen during aerial surveys. The challenge to save the Carrizal seedeater is made much more difficult because it's so hard to find. Bali mynas, on the other hand, another of the rarest songbirds on earth, are threatened with extinction in part for the opposite reason: they are simply too *easy* for the wrong people to find.

BALI MYNA

There are few birds on earth more distinctive than the Bali myna (also known as the Bali starling). It is snow white—a rare colour for a songbird. Black wing tips and tail contrast with the pure brilliance of its body. A bright blue mask, the shape of a falcon's wing, wraps around the eyes, and its head is topped by a drooping crest of long, delicate feathers. About the size of a northern cardinal, its natural habitat is the lowland rainforest along the northwest coast of the island of Bali, in Indonesia. In fact, the Bali myna is the only endemic species that still survives on the island (unique to Bali and found nowhere else). The only other species known to be endemic to the island was the Bali tiger, which went extinct in 1937. Destruction of the forest for agriculture and wood decreased the myna's total habitat from about 30,000 hectares in the 1920s to about one-tenth that today, all of it inside Bali Barat National Park. But habitat destruction is only a part of the troubles faced by this species.

Like so many desired objects, the Bali myna has a beauty that is uniquely its own—a beauty that unfortunately also excites the greed of collectors of rare wild birds. As the official bird of Bali, for some Indonesians it is an "object" of status, a symbol of power and wealth. The demand for it has boosted the amount it fetches on the black market for caged wild birds, contributing greatly to its decline. Although trade in the species became illegal when it was listed under the Convention on International Trade in Endangered Species in 1970 (an international agreement regulating trade in threatened animals and plants), collectors in Bali and Java still pay poachers thousands of dollars to own one. Extreme rarity (that is, proximity to extinction) only adds to the cache of owning one. The illegal bird trade, and to a lesser extent the destruction of the bird's natural habitat, has made the Bali myna one of most endangered songbirds. Nobody knows for sure how many there are, but it is thought anywhere between zero and about 24 birds survive in original, natural habitat.

Like other members of the starling family, the Bali myna has a rich and varied vocal repertoire and can mimic human speech.[4] The myna's best-known call is a chatter song, but it also whistles, squawks, chortles, and warbles its way though life, either in small flocks in the non-breeding season or with its mate while nesting.

To attract a mate, a male Bali myna will approach a female with his crest raised as he bobs his head up and down and makes clucking sounds. If all goes to plan, the female will requite his love by perching beside him while they perform a duet of bobbing and singing. Like other members of the starling family, abandoned tree holes that have been excavated by other birds are used for nests. The female will lay two or three eggs twice a year. Although two sets of chicks are produced annually, the species was probably never abundant.

---

4. In fact, Mozart had a pet European starling (closely related to the Bali bird) that he taught to speak and to mimic his music. He eulogized it in a short poem when it died.

With so few birds remaining in the wild, captive breeding and release has become the only alternative for the self-sustaining survival of the species in natural conditions (hundreds of birds live in captivity throughout Indonesia and the rest of the world, many of them poached wild birds). Although the Bali myna has proved to be relatively easy to rear in captivity, it has been much more difficult to control the dark side of human greed.

Because the bird is worth so much money on the black market, theft by poachers is a huge problem that has largely stymied efforts to ensure its survival. Case in point: in 1999, 39 birds were stolen from the breeding facility in Bali Barat National Park just before they were to be released into the wild. A well-organized armed gang tied up the guards who were supposed to be protecting the birds and stole their guns. The poachers apparently had inside information, since they knew the specific cages of the birds that were awaiting release. The bandits escaped in a boat across the narrow Strait of Bali to the neighbouring island of Java. In a suspicious twist (another hint of an inside job), the stolen guns of the guards were mysteriously returned to the breeding facility in a cardboard box a month later.

Poachers also routinely enter Bali Barat National Park at night and capture birds that have already been released. Over the years, several separate attempts at preventing the disappearance of the Bali myna have been foiled by such criminal activities.

Clearly, a different approach to saving the bird was needed. So, in 2004, the Begawan Giri Foundation (now the Begawan Foundation) for the conservation of the Bali myna and the Friends of the National Parks Foundation began to release captive-reared birds into the wild on the small island of Nusa Penida, located off Bali's coast. Nusa Penida was chosen because many of its communities still followed traditional laws against killing birds, and these are taken very seriously on the island. If the mynas could successfully breed in the wild on the island, then perhaps there would be a chance that the local inhabitants would protect them against poaching. The program was spearheaded by Bayu Wirayudha, a Bali native, avian veterinarian, and myna breeder. His experience told him that the species was relatively easy to breed and adaptable in the wild.

Although the release of birds into the wild on Nusa Penida was criticized by some because it is not the traditional habitat of the Bali myna, the proponents of the program argue that it may be the last hope for the bird to survive *anywhere* in the wild. So far it appears to be working. At last report, of the 65 birds released onto Nusa Penida by Wirayudha and his collaborators, 45 have bred and hatched offspring, helping pull the wild population of the species back from the brink of extinction.

Perhaps the Bali myna will survive somewhere in the wild after all. Unfortunately, for a delightful yellow songbird half a world away in the United States, such hope is very slim.

BACHMAN'S WARBLER

Warblers are most aptly named. In wooded habitat across North America, from great forests to small thickets, untold millions of them tirelessly warble, whistle, lisp, and chirp their way through spring and summer. And if their melodious songs weren't enough, their brilliant, often beautifully patterned plumage offer a palette's worth of colour: reds, yellows, oranges, greens, blues, black, and everything in between, there for the enjoyment of anyone willing to look. As Thoreau put it: "They are of every hue. Nature made them to show her colors with. There are as many as there are colors and shades."

Over 50 species of warblers—all belonging to the family Parulidae—inhabit the continent's woodlands, most of them in the east. Some, like the yellow-rumped and the magnolia, are widespread and abundant; others—the endangered golden-cheeked and Kirtland's warblers come to mind—are found only in very specialized habitats and are quite rare. Even these, however, can't hold a candle to the Bachman's warbler in the scarcity department.

Last seen in Louisiana in 1988, Bachman's warbler is possibly extinct but still listed as endangered under the US Endangered Species Act and critically endangered on the IUCN Red List. According to the US Fish and Wildlife Service, its current population number is unknown. That number, if it is anything other than zero, must be vanishingly small, possibly in the double or even single digits.

The bird was first described in 1833 by John Bachman, a Lutheran pastor and naturalist from South Carolina. He sent skins of the bird to his close friend, John James Audubon. Although Audubon never saw the bird in the wild, he included a painting of it in his famous work *Birds of America*. Interestingly, the artist simply painted the pair of warblers into an original illustration of a franklinia bush by Maria Martin, Bachman's second wife and one of the first female natural history illustrators in the United States. That Audubon never observed a living Bachman's warbler is evident in the stiff poses of his painted birds, which contrasts with Martin's exquisite rendering of the franklinia.

Bachman's warblers inhabit cypress swamps with an understorey of saw palmettos in the southeastern United States. Here they build their little cup-shaped nests of grass and Spanish moss in the canebrakes (stands of bamboo), brambles, and other undergrowth. Three or four nestlings are fed a diet of insects for a couple of weeks before they can fly on their own. At the end of the breeding season they migrate south to Cuba for the winter.

The little yellow-faced bird with its black throat and cap, delicate down-curving bill, and a buzzing trill of a song has been somewhat of a mystery in the southeastern United States for the last two centuries. Early reports of its abundance were often contradictory: some said there were many, others said few. Perhaps it depended on whether birds were counted during migration, when their numbers tend to be concentrated, or during nesting season when they are spread out. In any event, the species apparently went missing for several decades during the 1800s, until a few dozen of them were shot by one Charles Galbraith in 1888, a hunter for the ignominious hat trade. (Back then, women's hats were decorated not only with the exotic plumes of egrets but with stuffed whole songbirds. In fact, one of the specimens of the Bachman's warbler in the American Museum of Natural History was literally plucked from a hat.)

It wasn't until 1897 that the first Bachman's warbler nest was discovered, more than 60 years after being scientifically described by its namesake. Around the same time, the species stronghold appeared to be in the swampy woods bordering the lower Suwannee River in Florida. Since then, however, the population has plummeted. As early as the 1940s, Bachman's warbler was the rarest songbird on the continent. In spite of its near absence for many decades, the species wasn't listed as officially endangered until 1967.

The cause of its decline is far from clear. Loss of cypress swamp forest seems to be only a contributing factor because there appears to be enough presumably good habitat left to support at least a few breeding pairs. The extensive destruction of the vast canebrakes of the southeast, in which the species is thought to nest, is also likely an important agent in the decline. Perhaps the clearing of forest to make way for sugar cane plantations where the species wintered in Cuba ushered it down the path of extreme rarity. Or maybe severe hurricanes killed off so many Bachman's warblers during migrations that it became hard for survivors to find mates to breed with. On the other hand, if the bird has always been rare, its decline may have been inevitable in the face of human progress in the south-eastern United States. The most likely cause for its precarious state is *all of the above*. The official nail of extinction has yet to be driven into the species' coffin, however, since much of its nearly inaccessible potential habitat, such as the vast Congaree Swamp of South Carolina, hasn't been fully surveyed. So there's a very slim chance the bird may still exist.

But is this just wishful thinking? Probably. Yet, in January 2002, a bird closely resembling a female Bachman's warbler was videotaped in Guardalavaca, Cuba. Experts from the Cornell Lab of Ornithology later examined the video and pronounced it inconclusive—but found it intriguing enough to post on the lab's website, with an invitation for further opinion on the evidence. The identity of the mystery bird in Cuba has never been confirmed.

On an island in the Pacific, ornithologists are equally anxious to catch sight of another species whose continued existence is also questioned.

MOLOKAI THRUSH

Hawaii may be a Pacific paradise and the most isolated archipelago in the world, but it is struggling with the loss of its amazing biodiversity, especially birds. Dubbed the "extinction capital of the world" by conservation biologists, half of the state's 140 known endemic bird species have already disappeared. Trouble in paradise began when the first Polynesians arrived about 1,600 years ago, long before the first Europeans set foot on the islands. The Polynesians killed the islands' birds for food, and for their colourful feathers to be used as currency. What's more, feathers decorated their ceremonial dress, most notably the raiment of kings, whose elaborate capes were festooned with tens of thousands of colourful songbird feathers. The robe of King Kamehameha the Great is said to have required nearly a half *million* brilliant yellow feathers from the O'o bird, now extinct.

In 1779, Europeans brought invasive species such as goats, pigs, feral cats, rats, and even introduced bird species like cardinals and bulbuls. All have wreaked havoc on the native birds, which were not equipped to deal with aggressive mainland organisms. A third of all of the endangered birds in the United States are exclusive to Hawaii. Though native Polynesians may have exploited the birds pretty heavily, all bets were off for the future of the archipelago's avifauna once Europeans colonized the islands.

Their most insidious import was the mosquito. Hawaii was free of the pest until about 1820, when it arrived as an accidental stowaway on ships from the mainland. Unfortunately, the earlier release of domestic pigs into the islands' forests produced perfect conditions for mosquitoes to really take hold. With an abundance of food, the pigs multiplied and became feral. Soon they were tearing apart the trunks of native tree ferns and creating cavities for standing water— perfect breeding places for mosquitoes, which would soon thrive. As vectors of deadly avian malaria, the pesky insects threatened the very survival of many native birds. Some escaped the insects by moving up the mountains to where it was cooler. But warming temperatures owing to climate change may soon render this strategy useless. And, as the islands' human population has grown, ever more of the unique forest habitats so crucial for Hawaii's birds have been destroyed for urban and agricultural development. This has pushed native species, already reeling from hunting by humans, introduced animals, plants, and disease, into an ecological corner.

The ubiquitous American robin, a member of the thrush family, may be one of the most abundant birds in the world, but another member of the same family, also a resident of the United States, is among the rarest. The endemic brown and grey Molokai thrush

(*Oloma'o* in the native Hawaiian language) is unusually drab for Hawaii, where most birds are brilliantly plumaged, like the state's famous scarlet honeycreepers. What this thrush lacks in bright feathers, however, is made up for by its brilliant voice. Its song is remembered as a chorus of liquid, ventriloquial, flute-like notes, often sung all the day long and even through the night. Today, the gist of the Molakai thrush's colourful music is preserved only in written records, since its song has never been recorded.

The species was first listed as endangered in 1970, and the last confirmation of the bird's existence was in 1980. Despite its long absence, it has not been declared extinct, since there is still a small chance it survives—though habitat destruction and avian malaria have so devastated its population that if it does exist, the population would be tiny indeed. The only thing that can be done at this stage is to continue surveying for evidence of the species, restore its historically known habitats, and remove harmful invasive species. Realistically, though, there isn't a whole lot of hope that the Molokai thrush will be found. And the status of a bird next door on the island of Oahu is every bit as tenuous.

OAHU CREEPER

Members of Hawaii's creeper guild (a group of various bird species in a natural community using similar techniques to gather similar food types) are found only in the archipelago. Today, five separate species of Hawaiian creepers survive: one each on Hawaii and Kauai, both relatively common; one on Maui, endangered but with a population in the thousands; the extinct Molokai creeper; and the hairbreadth-from-extinction Oahu creeper.

The theory of evolution tells us that every species does its own thing to survive. Sparrows hop along the ground picking up seeds and bugs, swallows swoop through the air scooping flying insects into their gaping beaks, and warblers flit about the forest canopy, picking insects off leaves. So it goes, each using its own proven method of getting a meal. The Oahu creeper's name is a dead give-away for how *it* gets a living: by inching up and down the trunks of trees, with its ear to the bark listening for unsuspecting beetle larvae underneath. Little is known about the 10-centimetre-long warbler-like bird, with its brilliant yellow belly and face and bright olive-green back. It remains largely a mystery. In addition to its distinctive foraging techniques, it's thought to lay two eggs in a nest made of soft mosses and tiny rootlets. Its song has never been described.

First discovered by science in 1850, biologists today are uncertain whether the Oahu creeper survives. Although its last confirmed record was on Christmas Day in 1985, there have been several more recent sightings in lowland native wet forest along the Poamoho Trail, in the island's Ko'olau Mountains. These haven't been confirmed, however, since the creeper is easily confused with the very similar amakihi, a more common Oahu species. But the understandable reluctance to declare the species officially extinct has delayed any such move until every last scrap of its potential habitat has been thoroughly explored.

Some suitable creeper habitat still survives on Oahu—the largest piece a 1,500-hectare tract of native forest administered by the Nature Conservancy of Hawaii—so habitat loss doesn't appear to be the sole reason for the species' decline. It's likely that the main culprit in the whole matter is avian malaria, the mosquito-borne disease that is responsible for the decimation of much of Hawaii's bird life. On the US endangered species list since 1970, the bird also remains listed as critically endangered on the IUCN Red List.

Like Hawaii, Amsterdam Island, home to the world's rarest albatross, is one of the remotest islands in the world, with an ecosystem that is also being destroyed by invasive species.

AMSTERDAM ALBATROSS

The greatest travellers among earth's creatures, albatrosses have been the embodiment of freedom for as long as humans have known them. Among seafarers they were synonymous with the wind, as immortalized in Coleridge's "The Rime of the Ancient Mariner": "For all averred, I had killed the bird / That made the breeze to blow." Throughout history, sailors also believed that albatrosses carried the souls of their lost seafaring brethren.

Few living things are as well adapted to live in the vast wilderness of the earth's high seas, especially those in the southern hemisphere. On long slender wings evolved for gliding just above the water, albatrosses use air currents and updrafts formed when wind blows across the waves to carry them over vast distances with minimal flapping and maximum efficiency. During a lifetime—they can live up to 50 years—some species travel more than 16 million kilometres, or the equivalent of 50 round trips to the moon. One of these great wanderers may soon disappear.

Found only on Amsterdam Island in the Indian Ocean, the Amsterdam albatross, with a wingspan of nearly four metres, is one of the largest birds on earth. It is also one of the rarest. Initially thought to be a subspecies of the wandering albatross, it was first described by science only in 1983. With its brown breeding plumage, the Amsterdam Island albatross is unusual among a family of typically white birds. The puffiness of the feathers covering the head, the large pink bill, and the jet-black eyes residing beneath a prominent brow give the bird an endearing puppet-like appearance.

Nowhere in the animal world is there a more dedicated parent. Mating for life and bearing a single chick every two years, the Amsterdam albatross invests a great deal of effort into ensuring its offspring survives. Both parents participate in all aspects of its upbringing. While one adult stays with the young (the parents will alternate), the other embarks on a journey across 4,400,000 square kilometres of the southern Indian Ocean in search of food to feed the hungry, rapidly growing chick. This continues for seven months until the nestling takes its first flight. Once its feathers are fully formed, the young bird makes several awkward attempts to get airborne. To be fair to the neophyte bird, all albatrosses, seasoned adults included, are less than graceful whenever they're leaving or landing on solid ground. They become airborne by running down a slope into a headwind to generate enough lift. Once in the air, young albatrosses fly out to sea, embarking on a journey of hundreds of thousands of kilometres around the southern hemisphere's oceans. They won't touch land again until they return to Amsterdam Island five years later, when they are sexually mature.

Amsterdam Island is very remote. Only 55 square kilometres in area, it lies in the middle of the southern Indian Ocean, exactly midway between Africa and Australia. It is a testament to our planetary reach that a group of creatures so wide ranging in its oceanic peregrinations, so far flung from our own centres of population, is affected by human activities. In fact, although it is the most imperilled member of its family, the Amsterdam albatross isn't alone in its struggle to survive: two-thirds of the two dozen species of albatross are today threatened with extinction. The major culprit for many of them is longline fishing, where high-seas boats tow long hooked lines heavily weighted with bait. For surface-feeding seabirds, such gear, loaded with tasty, attractive food, is irresistible—and deadly. The birds get snagged while trying to get the bait and subsequently drown as the line sinks. Some 100,000 albatrosses are killed this way every year. Although scientists think longline fishing has contributed to the dire situation the Amsterdam albatross finds itself in, other factors may be even more important.

Except for a small research and military station (the island belongs to France), Amsterdam Island has never been permanently settled. That's not to say it hasn't been tried. One attempt, made long ago, marked the beginning of real trouble for the albatross. In the spring of 1870, a peasant family from the distant island of Réunion was left on Amsterdam with a few cows to establish an outlier cattle station. The family didn't last long in the harsh environment and eight months later abandoned the island, leaving behind their livestock. Left to run amok across the uninhabited landscape with no predators and lots of grass to eat, the original population of a few cows grew to many thousands. The feral cattle stomped and ate their way through Amsterdam albatross habitat over the past century and a half, reducing its breeding range—and hence its population—on the island. Now the few birds left are relegated to a tiny area in a bog on the island's central plateau that the cows can't reach. What's more, feral cats—the scourge of island birds everywhere—left behind by visiting ships over the decades have taken a toll on vulnerable albatross chicks.

The number of cattle has been reduced to about 1,000 by an eradication program over the past two decades, and fences have been erected to keep the remaining ones out of the nesting area. As well, plans are in place to cull the feral cat population and to manage vegetation to enhance nesting habitat. However, this may not be enough. The Amsterdam albatross faces a new, serious challenge in the form of deadly avian diseases that have been found infecting another seabird species on the island.

When the Amsterdam albatross was described as a new species just over a quarter of a century ago, its entire known breeding population consisted of just five pairs. Today, its numbers have increased to about 80 mature birds (of which only 10 to 20 pairs will breed in any given year). Yet there is evidence that the newly discovered avian diseases may have already caused a decrease in chick survival rates. So, despite some success in restoring its numbers, scientists now fear the population may begin declining again. If true, and the disease has already taken hold, the future of this magnificent species just got a bit less certain.

CHINESE CRESTED TERN

Even a soaring albatross can't surpass the grace and elegance of a tern in flight. As light as butterflies on the wing, 44 species of these slender, delicate creatures inhabit the earth. Found on every continent and sometimes mistaken for gulls, terns are generally white with black accents (a few, like the noddies, have all dark plumage) and are among the most abundant larger birds. Most migrate, a few incredibly so. One of them, the Arctic tern, migrates over a million kilometres in a lifetime—nearly enough to make it to the moon and back *twice*. By following the summer season to the alternating poles of the planet, it sees more daylight than any species. Thankfully, this champion traveller is still abundant. One migratory tern, however, may soon cease to see daylight at all, ever again. The Chinese crested tern, restricted to just two breeding sites along the east coast of China, is the rarest of its family and one of the most endangered birds on earth. White with light grey wings, a large head with a shaggy black crest, and a black-tipped yellow bill, the Chinese crested tern is also among the larger members of its family, growing to a length of 43 centimetres.

First discovered in the early 1860s, the crested tern was once widely distributed along China's coast, as far north as Shandong Province. Until just recently, its last reliable confirmed record anywhere was from 1937, and it was presumed extinct by the late 20th century. Then, in 2000, four chicks and four adults were found amid a colony of greater crested terns, a more numerous but similar species, on an island in the Matsu Archipelago off the coast of mainland China's Fujian Province—an area administered by Taiwan. In 2004, a few more birds turned up farther south in the Jiushan Islands of Zhejiang Province. Today, these two areas account for the sum total of Chinese crested terns in existence.

According to the IUCN Red List, the count is fewer than 50 surviving birds, though in fact, no more than about 20 birds, including chicks, have actually been counted at any one time since their rediscovery. In winter, Chinese crested terns migrate to warmer climes, where they used to be seen feeding at tidal mudflats in several Southeast Asian countries such as Thailand and the Philippines. In late 2010 on a wetland in Indonesia, a single Chinese crested tern was observed during the non-breeding season, the first record of a wintering bird in more than 70 years.

The main threat to the species now and in the past is the collection of eggs for food by fishers. This, along with hunting, is thought to have all but wiped out a once relatively common species. Ironically, the bird owes its survival at least in part to international political tensions between China and Taiwan. Fishers may have been discouraged from stealing eggs from the Matsu Archipelago tern colony because of the constant military presence in the waters between the two quarrelling jurisdictions.[5] This is one case where human discord could end up helping to save a very rare living thing from extinction.

By 2000, the nesting islets in the Matsu Islands became a fully protected national nature reserve, where the Taiwan coast guard seizes the nets of any fishers caught raiding seabird colonies for eggs. The other colony in the Jiushan Islands wasn't so lucky, how-

---

5. A similar situation exists in the depopulated demilitarized zone between North and South Korea, where scores of otherwise endangered species thrive in the half-century-long absence of human activities.

ever. Four of the imperilled terns bred there in 2007 and success-fully laid eggs in their nests, but fishers took them all before any hatched. The Jiushan terns soon abandoned the islands (who could blame them?) and moved to a nearby nature reserve to breed, where they triumphantly fledged two young in 2009.

Egg collecting remains the most immediate threat to the Chinese crested tern's survival—it still happens occasionally, despite the bird's protected status. But at least it's a problem that can be con-trolled through the enforcement of laws coupled with increasing local people's awareness of the bird's plight. What is impossible to control, however, is the widespread destruction of wetland habitat along China's coast due to rapid economic development and the effect widespread industrial and domestic pollution has on the fish eaten by the terns.

Nevertheless, China has had some success saving endangered bird species. In 1981, only seven Asian crested ibis—a large stork-like bird—were known to exist in the wild. Today, after decades of captive breeding, reintroductions, and strict government protection of habi-tat, the once critically endangered bird's population in the wild has climbed well into the hundreds. The crested tern might also someday find itself receding from the brink of extinction, the beneficiary of the same committed involvement of the Chinese government that helped the ibis. In contrast, another species in desperate need of help half a world away on politically unstable, poverty-stricken Anjouan Island is getting little support from government.

ANJOUAN SCOPS OWL

On Anjouan Island in the Indian Ocean and on neighbouring Madagascar there live two populations of identical-looking little owls—really just bundles of feathers not much bigger than a fist. One, the Anjouan scops owl, was only rediscovered by science in

1992 after an absence of over 100 years (apparently nobody had consulted the locals, who claim to have known about the bird all along). Although it had been considered one and the same as the Madagascar scops owl, the Anjouan birds are separated from the larger island by hundreds of kilometres of ocean, so biologists have suspected for some time that they might be a separate species.

So, since it is exceedingly rare, with as few as 50 pairs clinging to survival, it was important to establish the specieshood of the Anjouan bird. If it is simply a separate population of the more numerous Madagascar scops owl, its disappearance—as terrible as it would be—would result in the loss of a population rather than an entire species. If, on the other hand, it is a distinct species, it goes extinct. A big difference.

Fortunately, taxonomists are able to use DNA analysis to distinguish separate species among similar organisms. In a nutshell it works like this: A DNA molecule is shaped like a twisted ladder, a shape known as a double helix. The "rungs" of the ladder are made of paired combinations of four different chemical compounds called bases. The sequence of these base pairs along the length of the double helix will determine all the characteristics of an animal (or plant). If the base pairs of the DNA in two similar organisms don't match closely enough, they are considered separate species. Recent DNA tests confirm that the Anjouan scops owl is indeed a separate species from the Madagascar scops owl. This puts the little bird in the unenviable position as the rarest, most endangered owl on earth.

Known to local people as the *badanga*, the tiny owl occurs in two colour schemes, one greyish brown, the other rufous, both of which have prominent yellow eyes surrounded by a corona of cream-coloured feathers and topped by the two small ear tufts typical of scops owls and their close relatives, the screech owls. The species' only habitat is in fragments of undisturbed old-growth forest on steep slopes in the island's mountainous interior. But there isn't much of it left—only about 10 to 20 square kilometres' worth.

Knowledge of the bird's natural history is scant. Before its rediscovery in 1992, biologists probably missed it because of its nocturnal habits, densely forested habitat, extreme rarity, and decidedly un-owl-like repetitive *pee-oo, pee-oo* call, which sounds more like a shorebird's plaintive cry. What *is* known is that it apparently hunts insects at night, nests in tree cavities, and roosts in dense vegetation during the day. That's just about all that's known of the Anjouan scops owl's biology. It isn't much, and with its precarious grasp on existence, there might not be much of an opportunity to learn more.

An extremely high population density of nearly 700 people per square kilometre live on the small island. The result is abject poverty and an enormous pressure on limited natural resources. The biggest threat to the owl's survival is the ongoing loss of its remaining forest habitat for lumber, charcoal production, and agriculture. Moreover, despite its critically endangered status, it appears the species is still hunted for food. Introduced common myna birds may also be having a negative effect on the owl's breeding success by competing for limited nesting cavity sites. Besides all that, the political stability of Anjouan is tenuous at best. After eight years of rule, a regime claiming independence for the island was ousted with bloodshed in 2008 by troops of the Comoros government and the African Union. Although elections for a new president were held in June of 2008, the political tension still runs high—not a conducive atmosphere for conservation.

There were plans to try to capture, then move, the owls to the nearby island of Moheli, but the subsequent discovery on that island of a separate, previously unknown scops owl species, itself critically endangered, scuttled the idea. The United Nations Development

Programme and the Comoros government have plans to establish a protective reserve on the mountain in the centre of Anjouan, where the bird survives. Although this is a tall order when the human population itself appears to be rapidly running out of room, it at least provides a flicker of hope. Other steps such as captive breeding, the placement of nest boxes in the remaining habitat to improve the success of breeding, and working with locals on sustainable forestry plans are also being considered. But, realistically and tragically, the long-term survival of the species is a long shot.

SULU HORNBILL

Like the Anjouan scops owl, the Sulu hornbill has the odds stacked high against it, not only because of the destruction of its habitat but also because of similar political, social, and economic conditions on its home island, thousands of kilometres distant, in the Celebes Sea.

There are 54 species of hornbills. Found exclusively in Africa and Asia, these large birds all possess one feature that sets them apart from other birds: a truly enormous bill shaped, not surprisingly, like a cow's horn.[6] As if an oversized beak weren't enough, hornbills sport long eyelashes—actually made from modified feathers—which only adds to their whimsical appearance. From just 30 centimetres in length for the smallest forest species to over a metre for the giant ground-dwelling birds of the African savannas, hornbills span one of the broadest size ranges for any family of birds.

Most hornbills live in tropical forests, spending much of their time in the canopy exploring for fruits, large insects, small lizards,

---

6. The toucans of South America also have large bills but aren't closely related. They do live in similar habitats and eat the same kinds of food, however, illustrating how nature arrives at similar solutions for adapting to similar ecological niches thousands of kilometres apart—a concept known as convergent evolution.

and other small animals. Despite their large, apparently awkward bills, eating small berries and insects is a breeze: grabbing an item gingerly by the tip of their huge bills, they deftly flick the morsel into the back of their throats with an upward toss of the head.

Hornbills mate for life, prompting several local cultures to consider them symbols of fidelity. Their nesting strategy is one of the strangest in the avian world. Once a pair chooses a nest site, typically a cavity in a large tree, the female enters. Using mud, fruit pulp, and their own droppings, the mated pair builds a wall over the entrance to the nest, imprisoning the female inside, where she is separated her from her mate and the outside world save for a small slit just big enough for the male to pass food through. She lays her clutch of eggs in the darkness and incubates them, all the while being fed by her mate. He also brings food to the young once they've hatched. When they're ready to leave the nest, the female chisels an opening in the plaster wall, freeing herself and her offspring. Depending on the species, she may have been sequestered in the nest cavity for up to four months. Exactly why the hornbills employ such a bizarre nesting strategy is unknown, although protection from predators may be one reason.

The Sulu hornbill, the rarest of its family, lives in the Sulu Archipelago off the southern Philippines. This critically endangered bird is found nowhere else. Because it's so scarce, little is known about its ecology, and much of its life history must be deduced from the lives of more abundant relatives. What *is* known is that it is a 70-centimetre-long, overall blackish bird with a dark green sheen on its upperparts and a long white tail. Sitting atop its enormous black bill is a heavy ridge known as a casque. A raucous bird whose cackling and shrieks penetrate its equatorial moist tropical forest habitat, the Sulu hornbill, like other hornbills, eats fruits, lizards and other small animals, and insects.

Fewer than 40 Sulu hornbills survive. Although it was common in the 19th century, today the species lives only on the island of Tawitawi, having already been driven to extinction in most of its former range by rampant habitat destruction on Jolo and Sanga Sanga Islands—both of which have been cleared of natural forest. And things aren't much better on Tawitawi. Only a few hundred square kilometres of natural forest remain on the island, all of it in rugged, mountainous areas. Because such places are so hard to reach, they are usually the last to be destroyed by humans. These remnant forests are the final refuge for the Sulu hornbill. The bird needs old, large trees to survive, both for the fruit they produce and the nesting holes they provide. Unfortunately, big trees are also valuable to humans, and therein lies the crux of the problem: such value does not go unexploited for long. To make matters worse, these scraps of remaining old-growth forest are completely unprotected, and it's only a matter of time before they are chopped down—putting the Sulu hornbill out of business for good. But that's not all the beleaguered bird must contend with.

Armed militias on Tawitawi, warring for the island's independence from the Philippines, thoughtlessly use wildlife, including hornbills, for target practice. If that weren't enough, local people also invade the sanctity of the nesting birds and take the baby hornbills to eat as a delicacy; adults are actively hunted. Furthermore, Tawitawi is a very dangerous place for people. Eight villagers, including women and children, were gunned down in a local village in 2008, so it's not surprising that conservation takes a back seat. Little has been done to save the species. The island also has a very high human population density, especially after the Philippines government forcibly resettled a quarter of a million illegal immigrants there in 2001.

What's left of the forests must first be protected, then surveyed to establish the population and distribution of the remaining hornbills. The local public needs to be made aware that one of the world's rarest living things lives in their midst. It's a real uphill battle for this species, and although a difficult pill to swallow, the Sulu hornbill may be extinct very soon.

WHITE-COLLARED KITE

Every ecosystem that is under threat should have its own flagship species, a charismatic animal that can be used in the public relations battle to save it—think of the giant pandas in Chinese bamboo forests, grizzlies in the American Rockies, or the tigers in the jungles of India. It's a way to put a "face" to a place, an important step to garnering the support needed to save habitat from destruction. The white-collared kite could play such a role for the Murici forest reserve in Brazil. One of the five critically endangered birds found there, the kite is a spectacular 50-centimetre-long forest-dwelling raptor, black and white with a white band around its neck. It is the most endangered bird of prey in South America. Possibly fewer than 50 breeding pairs survive on earth.

Given distinct species status only in 2005—before that it was considered a subspecies of the more populous grey-headed kite—the white-collared kite has been recorded just a few times at a handful of sites in the Brazilian states of Pernambuco and Alagoas, and recently in the adjoining state of Sergipe. It's estimated that less than 1 percent of the kite's original forest habitat remains, supporting probably no more than 1 percent of its original population.

Very little is known about this rarely seen bird. Typical of many hawk species, the white-collared kite's call is a rapid series of harsh notes. They are also known to perform courtship flights where one bird will hold its wings above horizontal and rapidly flutter them to impress its mate. Based on the natural history of the very similar, better-known grey-headed kite, it's also likely that the white-collared kite feeds on a wide variety of prey, including lizards, and smaller birds and their eggs. It may rear two or three young in a nest located high in the forest canopy.

The epicentre of the white-collared kite's existence is the Murici forest reserve, which lies in Alagoas near the easternmost reach of South America, a point just below the equator where the continent bulges toward Africa. (If you look closely, you can see where this coastline would have fit jigsaw-like with the coast of Cameroon before the two continents were split apart by continental drift over 200 million years ago.)

Murici, a small patch of Atlantic coastal forest no larger than Manhattan, could well be the most important piece of real estate for its size on the planet for birds. It is the last, biggest, and withal best fragment of highly endangered, virgin northeastern Atlantic coastal forest ecosystem anywhere in South America. Though today it's only a 6,000-hectare sliver of an ecosystem that once stretched for 1,000 kilometres, this "island" of biodiversity in a sea of sugar cane and cow pastures is nevertheless home to nearly 300 species of birds. Five of them are critically endangered, two of which, the Alagoas foliage-gleaner and the Alagoas antwren, are found nowhere else on earth. What's more, countless plant species, including rare orchids and palms, as well as rare reptiles, amphibians, and insects, make Murici their home.

Whittled down to a nub by centuries of human activity, Murici is a calm eye of nature amid a cyclone of agriculture, logging, and development that has decimated virtually all of Brazil's Atlantic forest ecoregion. Only 2 percent of this original ecosystem type remains. But although Murici was designated in 2001 an Ecological Station, Brazil's highest official level of land protection, it is effectively a "paper park," a euphemism for a place that is a park in name only; a place, owing to a lack of money or political will, no real effort is made to protect.

The case of the Alagoas curassow is a lesson of what could happen to other species if more isn't done to protect this endangered ecosystem. The last vestige of this large ground-dwelling bird's habitat near Murici was decimated, causing the curassow to become extinct in the wild. So, for the white-collared kite and the other critically endangered Murici birds, the only hope for survival is to stop further destruction of the forest. However, even if it was left alone and fully protected, it is so small that it might not be able to support the full spectrum of biological diversity for long. The process of exponential decay may have already begun. This occurs when small "islands" of habitat are left in the midst of a human-altered landscape. Every species has a definite minimum habitat size, beyond which it will eventually go extinct, no matter if the land is protected or not. The frequency of extinctions accelerates as the habitat patch shrinks. What the future ultimately holds for the white-collared kite will depend on how it fares in such patchy habitats, and whether more members of the species will be discovered in Atlantic coastal forest areas outside Alagoas and Pernambuco, such as those birds observed in Sergipe.

BLACK STILT

Shorebirds, in contrast to typically solitary raptors such as the white-collared kite, are usually observed in massive flocks, turning this way and that through the air as they move like a single organism just above the beach. But imagine a shorebird so rare that just a decade ago you could count the number of breeding pairs on your two hands with enough fingers left to call a strikeout. Seven pairs, that is how close the black stilt of New Zealand came to extinction.

Typically elegant like other species of stilts and avocets around the world, this all-black species, 40 centimetres in length, is an ebony plumaged, lanky, fragile-looking shorebird with long skinny red legs, a long neck, and a delicately pointed, slightly up-turned bill. Like others in its family, it feeds by probing under rocks and in muddy water for insects and the occasional tiny fish. Atypical for its family, the black stilt generally doesn't migrate.

It was widespread across New Zealand's North and the South Islands in the late 18th century. By the early 20th century, however, it had disappeared from the North Island and had dwindled to dangerously low numbers on the South Island. Decades of predation by introduced species such as ferrets, minks, and brown rats had decimated the species. A successful government program that killed off a plague of introduced rabbits in the 1940s eliminated a major food source for the South Island's large feral cat population, which in turn switched to eating the native birds to survive. The black stilt, a ground nester, was one of the species most affected. Not all of the stilt's problems can be blamed on introduced species, however. Large-scale hydroelectric development in its last nesting stronghold, the MacKenzie Basin of South Canterbury, destroyed much of the braided river bottom habitat where it nested. The projects resulted in flooding in some areas and draining of wetlands in others, neither of which are good conditions for a bird that lays its four eggs in a scraped-out hollow on a braided gravel bar in the middle of a riverbed.

By the time the New Zealand government began a recovery program for the black stilt in the early 1980s, only 32 were left. Had it not been for a captive breeding program begun then, plus predator-control programs to get rid of the introduced species that kill the shorebird and eat its eggs, the black stilt would likely be extinct now. Fortunately, although the growth in its population has been slow, today, thanks to the recovery program, there are almost 100 birds living in the wild.

Not every rare shorebird is so fortunate to have its population increased because of a sustained recovery effort. In fact, two of the northern hemisphere's curlews have become so rare in recent decades that their very existence is questioned.

Eskimo Curlew

On October 7, 1492, after a month out of the sight of land, Christopher Columbus's crew spotted a flock of what are thought to be Eskimo curlew shorebirds flying westward over the sea. Taking their cue from the birds, the sailors of the *Niña,* the *Pinta,* and the *Santa Maria* changed direction in the hope of making landfall. It turned out to be a good idea. A few days later, on October 12, Juan Rodrigo Bermejo, on the *Pinta,* spotted land. Columbus named it San Salvador Island (now a district of the Bahamas). The first contact with the New World had been made.

It seems only fitting that it was a flock of Eskimo curlews (possibly along with some lesser golden plovers, a species with which they often migrated) that led Columbus to land. October was the peak of their southward migration. As one of the most abundant bird species in the western hemisphere, millions of them would have been on their way south along the Atlantic coast of North America, having recently left behind autumn feeding areas in Nova Scotia and Newfoundland. So enormous was the fall migration of curlews that vast single flocks of hundreds of thousands of them would cast shadows on the earth, living clouds blotting out the sun.

A stilt-legged shorebird with a long, thin, downward-curving bill; a 70-centimetre wingspan; and mottled brown plumage, the Eskimo curlew is easily confused in the field with the closely related, more numerous whimbrel; only by their calls can the two be reliably told apart. This similarity is one of the reasons it's hard to conclusively say the curlew is gone or is still with us—there may be a few still mixed in with groups of whimbrels and lesser golden plovers, species with which it was known to flock. On the other hand, the odds are that any Eskimo curlews reported—and reports are few and far between—may in fact be whimbrels. Declaring a species extinct is a serious step, so *any* report of their continued survival, however unlikely that might be, could cast some doubt on the decision.

Little is known of the Eskimo curlew's life history. They spend (spent?) their summers nesting on the arctic tundra west of Canada's Mackenzie River and into Alaska. The female lays four olive-brown eggs in a depression on a carefully chosen hammock of soft moss. The downy chicks emerge from the shells after about four weeks of incubation by both the male and female. In the fall, young and adults begin an epic migration that is surpassed by few birds. After flying east across the top of the continent to Labrador, they turn down into Atlantic Canada before heading due south to the Lesser Antilles of the Caribbean (Columbus would have seen them on this leg of their migration). Finally, there's a long flight deep into South America, where they winter on the great grasslands of the pampas. The following spring they take a much more direct route straight through the centre of North America to their breeding grounds in the western Arctic. Throughout their migratory peregrinations, the birds continuously communicate by twittering soft, melodious whistles to each other, said by some to resemble bluebird songs.

Known as doughbirds for the thick layer of fat carried during fall migration, they weigh over 400 grams, making them popular with hunters. Running a deadly migratory gauntlet every year that covered 30,000 kilometres, Eskimo curlews were shot in the fall along the US Eastern Seaboard, blasted on grassland wintering grounds in Argentina, and ambushed by gunners in Texas and the Great Plains while returning north to breed in the spring. Slaughtered both for the market and for the sport, like the ill-fated passenger pigeon, they were treated as though their numbers were infinite.

Like most shorebirds, Eskimo curlews are gregarious. The loyalty they show to their own kind is extreme, and the way hunters exploited this is heartbreaking. Flocks had a habit of circling back time after time to the scene of a shooting, drawn by the sight of their recently downed flock mates on the ground. And an almost complete lack of fear of humans—even when being fired upon—plus a propensity to clump together en masse in huge flocks, rendered them easy pickings, even for short-range shotguns. Little thought was given to the fate of the species as dozens at a time were taken down by single shotgun blasts. They were scooped up dead from the ground by the wagonload.

Big congregations of Eskimo curlews were a thing of the past by the late 19th century. The last large flock anywhere was observed in 1890 on the Magdalen Islands in the Gulf of St. Lawrence. Since then, there have been sporadic reports of mostly single or a few birds at a time throughout the 20th century. Some were confirmed sightings, most weren't. Given the aforementioned difficulty in telling this species apart from the whimbrel, we'll never know exactly how many sightings were actually of Eskimo curlews.

By the time Canadian author Fred Bodsworth's classic *Last of the Curlews* was published in 1954, nearly five centuries after Columbus's landfall, the Eskimo curlew had been extremely rare for decades. No flock of more than 25 birds had been seen since 1916, and when the curlews were by chance observed, it was only one or two birds at a time.

Bodsworth wrote about how close they had come to extinction in his day (the 1950s): "The odd survivor still flies the long and peril-ous migration from the wintering grounds of Argentine's Patagonia, to seek a mate of its kind on the sodden tundra plains which slope to the Arctic sea. But the Arctic is vast. Usually they seek in vain. The last of a dying race, they now fly alone."[7]

An American birding magazine reported the sighting of a sin-gle bird on a rocky headland near Peggys Cove in Nova Scotia in 2007. The purported Eskimo curlew was observed by a very expe-rienced birder and professional biologist, who took great pains to arrive at an accurate identification of the bird before reporting it. Unfortunately, he wasn't able to take a photograph or record its call, so the sighting remains unconfirmed. The IUCN Red List still lists the Eskimo curlew as critically endangered and *possibly* extinct. So even today, over 500 years after they helped an explorer from the Old World discover the New, there might be a few Eskimo curlews out there somewhere, following age-old tracks across the sky from the tundra to the pampas and back again in search of a future.

SLENDER-BILLED CURLEW

The plight of the slender-billed curlew echoes that of its closely related New World cousin. A hundred years ago, tens of thousands of slender-billed curlews migrated from Siberia in a southwesterly direction across eastern and central Europe. These large (40 centi-metres in length), grey-brown, mottled shorebirds, sporting long necks, long legs, and long, slender down-curving bills, made their way to wintering grounds in coastal and inland wetlands around the Mediterranean and in North Africa. Despite their abundance, only a few nests of this species were ever discovered. These were found between 1900 and 1925 in subarctic scrub forest in the vicinity of

---

7. Fred Bodsworth, *Last of the Curlews* (London: Longmans, Green, 1955), 9.

Novosibirsk in southwest Siberia. Typically shorebird like, the nests were simple cups on the ground made of grasses and moss and holding four eggs. Very little else is known about the ecology of this enigmatic shorebird. And that's too bad, because today we need every bit of knowledge we can garner on the slender-billed curlew to save it from extinction; but it just might be too late.

Listed as critically endangered on the IUCN Red List, the population of this shorebird is estimated to be fewer than 50. And even that might be optimistic. There hasn't been a confirmed observation of a group of more than 100 slender-billed curlews since a flock was seen in Morocco in 1974. In 1995, a handful of curlews were videotaped in Morocco, the last time more than one bird was seen at the same time. And there is no irony in the fact that this particular little group of birds was apparently later shot, since it was unrestrained hunting of the species during its migration and on its wintering grounds that has put it on the edge of extinction, if not over it.

The last time an individual was confirmed was during migration in 2001 in Hungary. With the exception of this single bird, several search expeditions across the slender-billed curlew's range over the past two decades have come up empty-handed.

Despite many human eyes watching for it over the massive span of the slender-billed curlew's range, it's conceivable the bird might be missed. It is a difficult species to positively identify. Because it is similar in size to the relatively abundant whimbrel and similar in appearance to the still common Eurasian curlew, both of which it historically mingled with, a single or even a few slender-billeds travelling among a throng of these birds might easily go unnoticed. To this end, in 2008, the Slender-billed Curlew Working Group, established under the Convention on Migratory Species, created what's being called "the greatest Western Palearctic birding challenge" ("Palearctic" is the biogeographical term applied to species nesting in northern Eurasia).

The idea was to rally teams of volunteers living in the 35 countries for which records of the species exist to scour every last potential habitat of the slender-billed curlew. It's the biggest effort ever to confirm the existence of a species feared extinct. So far (as of 2011), no luck. However, those who truly love nature are a stubborn lot and refuse to admit defeat; there's just too much at stake.

There is still reason to hope that somewhere out there a few remaining slender-billed curlews continue to pair up, build their nests, breed, rear downy chicks, and utter their soft *cour-lee, cour-lee* call as they migrate in autumn across Europe to warmer climes in the Mediterranean, then return home in spring to the taiga of Siberia to do it all over again.

PINK-HEADED DUCK

Compared with the two hapless curlews, both of which are well known in birding and conservation circles, the pink-headed duck is rather a mystery. Formerly found in India, Bangladesh, Nepal, and possibly Myanmar, it is a poorly known waterfowl, last conclusively observed in the wild in 1949.

First discovered in 1790, this striking chocolate brown–bodied diving duck, with its bright pink head, long pink neck, and pink bill is extremely shy of humans and lives in lowland forest swamps and secluded pools in tall grass jungles. It may also be nocturnal, further enhancing its mystique.

Living in pairs during the breeding season, they would congregate in small flocks of 30 to 40 birds through the rest of the year. About the size of a domestic duck, the species was hunted throughout its range. How big a factor hunting was in their demise isn't clear, especially since, like other diving ducks, they may not have made a particularly tasty meal. On the other hand, their spectacular colour made them a popular ornamental bird and relatively large, almost perfectly round eggs were attractive to collectors as well. Of course, with nowhere to live, a species' population is going to plummet, so the lion's share of the blame for the precarious status of the pink-headed duck goes to the cutting of lowland forests within its range and the draining of wetlands for farming.

Though rare by the late 1800s in India, a few would nevertheless turn up for sale in the markets of Calcutta into the early 20th century. In 1956, it became illegal to hunt the bird in India, but as usual, it was too little, too late—the pink-headed species was already a dead duck on the subcontinent.

Over the years its continued existence has been speculated and even occasionally reported by birders, biologists, and writers. There was even a travel-adventure book dedicated to the search for the duck along India's Brahmaputra River published in 1988. Although the author claims to have spotted the duck during his search, this, along with several other earlier sightings, are unconfirmed, though intriguing. Cryptozoologists—enthusiasts who often rely on anecdotes to prove the existence of mythical creatures like the sasquatch, the yeti, and the Loch Ness monster—have entered the fray to promote the existence of the duck. A cryptozoology website featured birder Richard Thorns's photograph of what might be a pink-headed duck. It was apparently taken in northern Myanmar, near an area thought by scientists to be the last potential stronghold of the species if it still survives. Although the bird in the photo looks similar to illustrations of the duck, the resolution is low so it's inconclusive. Adding to the difficulty of confirming the species' existence is the fact that the spot-billed duck and the red-crested pochard, similar species living in the same region, could be easily mistaken for the pink-headed duck.

Yet there's still a glimmer of hope for the species' survival in the vast, remote swamps of northern Myanmar. Between 2003 and

2006, five official scientific searches there resulted in a possible sighting by a scientist and two credible reports by local fishers in 2004, as well as a convincing description by a fisher in 2006. Still, nobody has yet to come up with actual proof—a good photo, a clear video, a pink feather, an actual duck. But there is also some doubt that it *doesn't* still exist. Given the ambiguity of it all, even unconfirmed reports such these can't be dismissed out of hand, no matter how sketchy they are, so it remains listed as critically endangered on the IUCN Red List. And even as we look for it, there's much about the bird to keep it hidden from our curious, probing eyes: extreme shyness, a tiny population, nocturnal habits, inaccessible habitat. In fact, there's little you could add to this list that would make it harder to find—except, of course, extinction.

As mysterious as a pink-headed duck might be, even stranger is a flightless one.

CAMPBELL ISLAND TEAL

Rats. Rats. And more rats. That is what nearly wiped the Campbell Island teal off the face of the earth. When sealing and whaling ships landed in 1810 on the remote subantarctic island located 700 kilometres south of New Zealand, they unleashed a rodential plague, which exponentially multiplied to become the worst on earth. More on this later.

The Campbell Island teal is a flightless duck found nowhere else in the world. Like many species of birds that inhabit isolated, oceanic islands, these small, 48-centimetre-long, dark brown waterfowl (the males sport a dark green iridescence on their head and necks) lost over countless generations the ability to fly, since a lack of natural predators meant they didn't need to get airborne for escape. The opportunity to occupy an ecological niche that would be normally filled by a mammal—none of which ever naturally inhabited the remote island—may have also contributed to the loss of flight. This doesn't mean Campbell Island teals are slow on their feet. Just ask any biologist who has tried to capture one. They move with speed and agility and apparently have a knack of deliberately disappearing into the surrounding vegetation. It helps that they frequent the chest-tall, dense tussock grass that grows so abundantly on subantarctic islands like Campbell. Oddly enough for a duck, the teals are also thought to take refuge in nesting burrows made by the island's storm petrels. They are nocturnal, too, perhaps because the aquatic invertebrates they feed on offshore are more abundant at night. During the day, the ducks forage on the shore, picking insects and other delicacies from the rotting seaweed.

Little is known of their ecology in the wild. However, captive Campbell Island teals lay a small clutch—for a duck—of an average of three to four eggs during the Austral spring, beginning in October. Brown skuas and northern giant petrels (both predatory seabirds, the latter of which must rank among the ugliest of birds) are their natural predators. Kelp gulls also occasionally prey on teal chicks. But the species likely evolved to deal with these avian threats by using its speed on the ground and the ability to find cover, so a population balance between predator and prey was maintained over the centuries. Dealing with the rats was a different story.

The pristine subantarctic outlier wasn't prepared for the rodents that jumped ship and tucked into the virtually limitless supply of food offered by Campbell Island's virgin ecosystem. Rats may have poor eyesight, but their keen sense of smell was all they needed to sniff out the nests and consume the eggs and young of the thousands of birds that inhabited the island. With no predators of their own and abundant food, the rapidly reproducing rats multiplied into the hundreds of thousands. Known as the albatross capital of the world, Campbell Island is home to six species of the giant oceanic wanderers, including the bulk of the planet's breeding southern royal albatrosses. They, along with storm petrels, became fair game for the marauding army of rodents. Fortunately, though severely affected by rats, these seabird species were also found on other islands, so none of them were threatened with extinction.

It was a different story for the Campbell Island teal, a bird which was much less abundant and, most importantly, found nowhere else—if they were wiped out here, they were gone everywhere. The rats wreaked havoc on the eggs and young of the endemic duck, which over time became rare, almost unto oblivion. The last teal on Campbell Island was observed in 1944. By everyone's lights it became extinct. Then, in 1975, a tiny population of just 20 ducks was discovered on Dent Island, a small islet sitting three kilometres off Campbell's coast. The rat-free 23-hectare chunk of rock was the final refuge for the flightless duck. Despite there being only a handful of them, the Dent Island birds represented an opportunity to eventually restore the species to its former stronghold on nearby Campbell Island.

It was crucial to ensure that those birds left on Dent Island survived as a reservoir to seed a future comeback of the species. So seven males and four females caught there in 1984 and 1990 by the New Zealand Department of Conservation were taken to begin a captive breeding program at the Pukaha Mount Bruce National Wildlife Centre on the mainland. In 1994, the first Campbell Island teal ducklings were born in captivity. Eventually, the program was successful enough that 24 birds were released on Codfish Island in 1999 and 2000. Much closer to the New Zealand mainland, Codfish Island was initially meant as a temporary home for the teal while its population grew, since the island's rats, cattle, sheep, and feral cats had already been removed to protect the kakapo, a critically endangered flightless parrot. The ducks quickly became established on the island, enjoying a high survival rate. As the new millennium dawned, with a healthy population of Codfish Island birds, plus the captive ones at the national wildlife centre, it was decided that the reintroduction of the Campbell Island teal to its namesake island would be feasible. It would have to wait a little while longer, however; before even a thought could be given to reintroducing the birds back to Campbell Island, the problem of the rat hordes would have to be fixed.

So the final crucial step was to get rid of the thousands of rats on Campbell Island. In the largest rodent-eradication campaign ever undertaken anywhere, the winter of 2001 saw over 120 tonnes of rat-specific poison bait dropped on the island from helicopters. It was risky work, given the brutal winds that blow in the subantarctic at that time of year, but the job was successfully completed. By 2003, Campbell Island was declared rat-free. Since then, over 100 teals have been reintroduced to the island. Although not all of the ducks survived, they have re-established themselves and are beginning to breed. Estimates put the current wild Campbell Island teal population at between 48 and 100 birds, including the Dent Island and Codfish Island populations, not to mention additional captive birds that are still part of the breeding program. Population growth has been slow but steady. In 1975, only 20 Campbell Island teals remained on earth, isolated on tiny Dent Island. Today, though still endangered, they live and breed on three islands: a huge step in the right direction. The future beckons for the little flightless duck.

MADAGASCAR POCHARD

Unlike its flightless New Zealand cousin, the more typical Madagascar pochard duck possesses the power of flight, though this has been of little help in fleeing the effects of a burgeoning population on the world's fourth largest island.

With most of its 21 million people being poor and rural, much of the country's natural riches have simply been cut down or plowed under. Nowhere has been more affected by this rising tide of humanity than Lake Alaotra and its environs, located on the island's Central Plateau, north of the capital Antananarivo.

The largest body of water in Madagascar at 900 square kilometres, the lake and its surroundings are the breadbasket of a country struggling to feed itself. More rice and freshwater fish is produced here than anywhere else on the island. Ever more of Alaotra's watershed is converted from natural habitat into agricultural use to feed the burgeoning populace. And the lake itself is literally disappearing as decades of deforestation on the surrounding hills have laid bare their soils, countless tonnes of which has been simply washed into the water by erosion. Despite covering an area about six times the size of Washington, DC, Lake Alaotra is literally being filled in by soil. Nowadays, it is a mere 60 centimetres deep during the dry season. Of course, a shrinking body of water is big trouble for the ecosystems and animals that depend on it, and many of the species that live here are threatened with extinction. Even non-aquatic animals such as the Alaotra gentle lemur, which inhabits what is left of the surrounding forests and is found nowhere else, is endangered.

But habitat destruction is only the beginning of Lake Alaotra's problems. Of the more than 20 species of introduced, exotic fish that have become established in Madagascar's fresh waters over the years, none is more menacing than the Asian snakehead. This large, aggressive, eel-like fish has a huge mouth and sharp teeth for snatching and swallowing its prey whole. It was deliberately and foolishly introduced to the island in 1976 as a potential food fish, a personal initiative of Madagascar's then president, Didier Ratsiraka. Once released into the environment, the fish spread like a plague across the island, invading lakes, streams, ponds, and wetlands, all of whose native species hadn't evolved to deal with such an aggressive predator. Its spread was virtually impossible to control as it used its ability to breathe air directly and leave the water to slither like a snake through the mud during the rainy season to reach new lakes and ponds.

The snakehead's nasty disposition has already resulted in the extinction of three native Madagascar fish species and one of its birds, the Alaotra or rusty grebe. This little wetland bird, found exclusively on its namesake lake and nowhere else, was already declining rapidly due to rampant habitat destruction by the time the snakehead arrived. The hungry fish simply finished the job by sneaking up from below to snatch the grebe's tiny chicks, stealing an entire generation in a few gulps. This was the last straw for the hapless endangered bird. It had finally succumbed, declared officially extinct by the IUCN in 2010. The Alaotra grebe will never be seen again.

A similar fate almost befell the Madagascar pochards that lived in Lake Alaotra. Still quite common on the lake in the early part of the 20th century, their number had plummeted by 1991, when a single male bird was captured and taken to the Antananarivo botanical garden. It died a year later. That was the last pochard ever to be seen on Lake Alaotra. Extensive searching of the lake— the only place it was known to exist at the time—throughout the 1990s right up until 2001 failed to locate even a single bird. Given the lack of evidence for its existence, the inescapable conclusion was that it was gone for good. In 2006, the IUCN listed the duck as possibly extinct. Fortunately, that wasn't the end of the Madagascar pochard's story.

A medium-sized, brown duck, the Madagascar pochard is closely related to familiar northern hemisphere species such as the ring-necked duck and the canvasback of North America and the common pochard of Europe. Like these other members of the genus *Aythya,* it is a diving species, gathering small invertebrate animals, vegetation, and seeds from the bottom of its shallow freshwater habitat. Non-migratory, it breeds from October to January, laying six to eight eggs in a nest built among the grass and reeds that grow in the shallow waters around lakes. Little else is known about its life cycle or natural history.

In late 2006, while searching for the endangered Madagascar harrier in a remote area 300 kilometres north of Lake Alaotra, Lily-Arison Rene de Roland of the Peregrine Fund and biologist Thé Seing Sam discovered a group of nine adult Madagascar pochards and four recently hatched chicks on a small lake. By a quirk of geology, the steep shores of the volcanically formed body of water weren't suitable for rice production, so there was little human disturbance to the ecosystem. And just as importantly, it didn't contain Asian snakeheads or other fish that preyed upon young ducklings.

The rediscovery of the "extinct" pochard made headlines around the world. Subsequent investigations have revealed a population of 20 to 25 birds. The pochards also visit other lakes in the area but do not breed there. Of course, such a small population is hardly sustainable, and a single event, such as poaching, a disease outbreak, or a pollution spill, could easily wipe out the species.

Today, several conservation organizations are working along with the government of Madagascar to save the pochard. The priority is to protect the few remaining birds from hunting and other direct human disturbance, so the site is now permanently guarded. But that's not enough. Conservation groups are garnering support from local people in an effort to have the pochard's habitat legally protected as a sanctuary. Low hatchling success has been observed since rediscovery in 2006. Not a single young survived in 2008, despite nesting attempts by six pairs of adults. So the following year, a few eggs were strategically removed from nests to be carefully hatched under controlled conditions. This was successful and led to the first captive-reared Madagascar pochard ducklings. The species needs such help if it is to grow in numbers. As a crucial step toward its restoration, plans for a lakeside breeding facility are in the works. Of course, there's always the possibility the Madagascar pochard could be found inhabiting as yet unsearched lakes and wetlands. And, as much as the odds are stacked against it, if enough suitable habitat can be restored at Lake Alaotra, the Madagascar pochard might one day return to the epicentre of its former range—something that seems unlikely for a grassland bird living on the other side of the world. The centre of its former range is now occupied by the city of Houston, Texas.

Attwater's Prairie Chicken

Long ago, before centuries of habitat destruction and intensive overhunting, there may have been a million Attwater's prairie chickens spread across almost two and half million hectares of bluestem Indiangrass and switchgrass prairie along the west coast of the Gulf of Mexico. This subspecies of the greater prairie chicken once had a range that stretched all the way from Corpus Christi, Texas, north to Louisiana. Today, all but less than 1 percent of its habitat has been lost to agriculture and urban development (the sprawling city of Houston is located smack in the middle of what was once prime prairie chicken habitat). Many of the habitat scraps that remain are too small to be of much use to wildlife, and even on the larger patches, fire suppression has changed the natural vegetation cycles, resulting in the growth of scrubland unsuitable for the bird to thrive in. Add to this overhunting and you wind up with one of the most endangered birds in the United States.

Prairie chickens belong to the same order of gallinaceous birds as the wild predecessors of the domestic chicken. They also look like them. Today, two species, the greater and the lesser prairie chickens, are found from North Dakota to the Gulf Coast of Texas. Both have experienced serious population declines over the last several decades. The greater prairie chicken had disappeared altogether from the northern edge of its range by 1987 and is now extinct in Canada. The Attwater's, the most southerly of all the prairie chickens, hangs on by the thinnest of threads.

Facing extinction is nothing new for prairie chickens. The heath hen, a separate subspecies of the greater prairie chicken, once lived along the Eastern Seaboard of the United States. It is thought that the Thanksgiving "turkeys" eaten by the Pilgrims were, in fact, heath hens. The subspecies used to be so abundant on blueberry barrens and coastal grasslands from Virginia to New England that it was part of the daily diet in many places—so much so that apparently people were sick of eating them: 18th-century live-in house servants in Boston demanded they not be fed heath hens more than three times a week. But this close cousin of the Attwater's prairie chicken was ultimately doomed. There may have been millions of them flourishing on coastal grasslands when the Pilgrims arrived. Moreover, they had been legally protected since 1791, when the first law against killing them during the breeding season was enacted in New York State (in fact, it was the first wildlife protection law to be enacted anywhere in the United States). But it wasn't enough. Habitat destruction and hunting did them in. The last heath hen, a male nicknamed "Booming Ben," survived alone for three years in a sanctuary on Martha's Vineyard, Massachusetts, until finally succumbing in the winter of 1932. He was one Chicken Little whose sky *did* fall. The question is, will we do a better job of saving another threatened prairie chicken?

About the size of a domestic bantam chicken, with a length of about 45 centimetres and weighing up to almost a kilogram,

Attwater's prairie chicken is distinguished by fine vertical banding of dark brown and buff feathers covering its lower body. Males have long tufts of feathers on the back of their necks that can be raised vertically like horns during courtship and possess two orange-yellow, inflatable throat sacs. In winter, the birds gather on leks or booming grounds located on rocky outcroppings or where the grass is especially short. Here the males will perform a dance in front of the females to attract a mate. Raising their tufts and inflating their throat sacs, they produce a booming *oo-oo-oo* call, which sounds like air being blown across the mouth of a jug. All the while, with heads down, wings drooping, and tail erect, males stamp their feet in quick staccato, turn in circles, and occasionally jump into the air before charging at other males.[8] When a female prairie chicken sees a dancing male she's particularly impressed with, she'll choose him as her mate. She'll breed with him, then go off on her own to a spot on the prairie, build her nest, and lay a dozen or so eggs. She'll incubate them for nearly four weeks. If fortune favours her and the nest isn't raided by skunks, snakes, coyotes, racoons, or feral cats, there will be a big brood of new chicks to rear for the next six weeks, during which time she'll be on constant alert for hungry hawks and owls. It is an uphill battle.

In spite of the bird being listed under the US Endangered Species Act since the early 1970s, only 75 to 90 of them survive in the wild in three places: Attwater Prairie Chicken National Wildlife Refuge west of Houston, Texas City Prairie Preserve near Galveston, and at a private ranch in the Goliad prairie area north of Corpus Christi.

---

8. The North American Plains Indians knew a good dance when they saw one. One of their most familiar rites is the prairie chicken dance. Outfitted in ceremonial dress, men belonging to Cree, Blackfoot, Lakota, and other tribes have performed it for centuries, dancing in circles, stamping the ground, bowing, and turning. They imitate in honour of the mating display of male prairie chickens, whose own rite is as old as the plains themselves.

The population isn't small for lack of trying, though. The bottom line is that were it not for human intervention, Attwater's prairie chicken would be extinct. Although humans are responsible for their decline, we have also thrown them a lifeline in the form of captive-bred birds that continually replenish the small wild population. From modest beginnings when the first captive birds were hatched in 1992 at a private wildlife centre, they are today reared at five zoos and a university. Each captive-bred flock of Attwater's prairie chickens contributes to a pool that is used to boost the number of birds in the wild. Out of reach of predators, young prairie chickens are placed temporarily in protective enclosures surrounded by wild prairie. Once they are acclimatized to their natural habitat, they will be turned loose into one of the three sanctuaries, where they'll have to survive on their own. Although hundreds of captive-bred birds have been released this way, mortality—especially by birds of prey—is extremely high, so population growth in the wild is painfully slow.

The US Fish and Wildlife Service's recovery goal for the Attwater's prairie chicken is to eventually have 5,000 birds in three self-sustaining, geographically separate populations. If this is to be achieved, and if the population is to rebound beyond even this, we will need to overcome the most difficult challenge of restoring enough suitable native habitat—no small feat when you consider that less than 1 percent of it remains. It will no doubt take the protection of the Endangered Species Act, plus commitment on the part of government, conservation organizations, and private landowners if the Attwater's prairie chicken is to have a real fighting chance for a long future.

Puerto Rican Amazon

By dint of Puerto Rico's status as a US territory, this parrot too is fortunate enough to be protected under the four-decade-old US

Endangered Species Act. To understand how crucial such laws are for the survival of species, and perhaps even how we've evolved as a society, we need to look at what happened to another American parrot species a century ago.

Once found in the millions from the Gulf States to Ohio and even southern Ontario, the Carolina parakeet was a noisy, brilliant green, yellow, and orange bird that was done in by its own abundance and hunger. Because it turned to farm crops to survive after millions of hectares of its forest habitat were cleared, the small grackle-sized bird was slaughtered as a pest by farmers. It was also a victim of the millinery trade, the despicable 19th- and early-20th-century industrial killing of birds for feathers to decorate hats. The last Carolina parakeet in captivity died in 1918 at the Cincinnati Zoo in the same cage that Martha, the last passenger pigeon, had died four years earlier. The moral of the story? Without legal protection, it took only a matter of decades for two of the continent's most abundant birds to disappear. The same fate almost befell the Puerto Rican amazon. Also known as iguaca by the island's original Taino Indians, it is one of the most critically endangered parrots in the world. The 50 or so remaining birds are the last survivors of ancestors that were thought to have arrived from South America eons ago.

Like most members of the 30 strong *Amazona* genus, this noisy, green-bodied bird, with its scarlet forehead, blue primary (wing) feathers, and white eye-ring, is hard to miss. About 30 centimetres long and weighing in at under 300 grams, the Amazon eats mainly fruit, nuts, and nectar it gathers in the forest canopy. It isn't fussy, consuming more than 60 varieties of food. Mating for life, the iguaca nests in deep cavities in large trees, especially palo colorado trees, where it lays three to four eggs during the dry season from February to June, when its primary food, the fruit of the sierra palm, is most abundant. The female alone incubates the eggs for about 24 to 28 days until they hatch. Chicks stay in the nest for about two months before fledging.

Although the early indigenous Taino people hunted the amazon as food, their activities had little effect on the bird's massive population on the island, which may have been as high as a million, or 110 birds per square kilometre, spread throughout the island's forests and mangroves. It also appears to have lived on the smaller nearby islands of Antigua and Barbuda, as well as those of the Virgin Islands, where it has long since been extirpated.

It wasn't until Puerto Rico began to be heavily settled by the Spanish incursion in the 18th century that the parrot's numbers began to plummet (perhaps not coincidentally, this is also when the indigenous Taino people began to decline, devastated by the smallpox brought by the conquering Spaniards). Widespread clearing of the island's virgin forests for sugar cane, cotton, corn, and rice removed most of the old mature trees the parrot required for nesting. Furthermore, as its natural habitat was destroyed, the bird's enormous population was forced to forage on the very farms that replaced its native ecosystem just to get enough food to survive, like the Carolina parakeet decades before. This didn't sit well with the colonizing Spanish farmers. A campaign of extermination was waged against it. If that weren't enough, parrots of the genus *Amazona* are superb at mimicking human speech, so capture for the caged-bird trade may have also contributed to the species' troubles.

In 1972, only 16 birds survived, so the US Fish and Wildlife Service began a captive breeding program to try to boost the species' numbers. Just three years later, however, the iguaca had reached a low point. Only 13 birds were left on earth. But the breeding program would slowly begin paying dividends, and by 1989 the count went up to nearly 50 individuals, only to be slashed to just 23 birds later the same year as Hurricane Hugo ravaged Puerto Rico. In 2001, thieves stole several adult birds from the aviary where captive breeding was taking place. By 2004, the wild population had become fairly stable at 30 to 35 birds. Today, the species' stronghold is in the El Yunque National Forest in northeastern Puerto Rico, where its habitat covers a scant 16 square kilometres—just over one-tenth of 1 percent of its original range. Though it is fully protected, a population of about 30 birds means they are at a high risk of extinction. In 2006, some birds were released into the wild in Rio Abajo State Forest, establishing a second wild population for the species.

The good news is that more than half the newly released amazons are surviving, raising hopes that the population can be sustainably increased. This is not an easy task. Although the bird is well protected from human disturbances in its remaining tiny range, and its numbers are being augmented through a captive breeding program, the small population faces a slew of challenges from nature itself. Introduced alien species such as pearly-eyed thrashers (a large songbird) and European honeybees compete with the parrot for natural nesting cavities, and rats prey upon eggs and chicks. And the hard lesson of Hurricane Hugo can't be ignored: with such a small population, one catastrophic event can wipe out an entire species. The US Fish and Wildlife Service, working with the Puerto Rico government, the US Forest Service, the US Geological Survey, and Mississippi State and North Carolina State Universities, hopes to have two separate wild populations, each with a population of 500 birds, by 2020.

Enigmatic Owlet-Nightjar

Unlike parrots—colourful, noisy birds not easily missed when they are around—the owlet-nightjars, a very small family of just nine species, are among the most secretive and cryptically plumaged birds on earth. They are found only in the forests of the Australasian region. As befits their name, all species look like a cross between owls (with their large eyes surrounded by facial disks) and nightjars (with their short, gaping bills; relatively small weak legs and feet; and slender bodies). Strangely enough, recent evidence suggests they may be more closely related to hummingbirds and swifts than to either owls or nightjars. Like many nocturnal birds and other wildlife, there is an air of mystery about owlet-nightjars because they're active when it's dark. And one member of the family is particularly mysterious.

The 28-centimetre-long, enigmatic owlet-nightjar of New Caledonia has speckled grey-brown and black feathers; a long tail; short, rounded wings; a wide-gaping bill; and huge eyes for seeing in the dark. It's thought that the endangered bird, whose legs are longer than other members of its family, may hunt on the ground more often than other owlet-nightjars, which usually make short flights from a perch to capture flying insects. Its habitat is in humid evergreen forests and melaleuca (tea tree) savannahs. Although nobody has ever found a nesting enigmatic owlet-nightjar, the species probably breeds in tree holes. With an estimated population of fewer than 50 individuals, it is among the most endangered of the approximately 10,000 species of birds worldwide.

Located about midway between Australia and Fiji, in the South Pacific (and sitting on the same suboceanic ridge as New Zealand 1,500 kilometres to the south), the French territory of New Caledonia is made up of Grande Terre, a large mountainous island 350 kilometres long by about 60 kilometres wide, plus a few smaller islands. Formerly a chunk of the ancient supercontinent Gondwana, Grande Terre has been separated from other major land masses for 55 million years. Such long isolation has allowed a distinctive fauna and flora to evolve on the island, and many species, like the enigmatic owlet-nightjar, are found nowhere else. And this is indeed an enigmatic living thing: even local people residing in the area where the bird lives apparently have no knowledge of it.

Only two specimens of the bird are known, and it has never been photographed alive. It was first described in 1880 when one accidentally flew into a house in a rural village on Grande Terre. Not seen again for decades, it was thought to be extinct. That is, until there were unconfirmed reports of a dead enigmatic owlet-nightjar found in the 1950s, and another in the 1960s. For decades there had been little else to suggest its continued existence. Then, on November 5, 1998, professional ornithologists Jonathan Ekstrom and Joe Tobias of BirdLife International watched what appeared to be an enigmatic owlet-nightjar hunting insects as it flew in and out of the woods along a dirt road at dusk in Grande Terre's Riviere Ni Valley. Although nearly a week of further searching failed to find the bird, the credibility of the observers, who were sure of what they saw, meant the possibility of the species' existence simply couldn't be ignored. Currently listed as critically endangered on the IUCN Red List, it is not, as far as we know, yet extinct.

In a happy coincidence, the area where the bird was seen in 1998 already lies within a 7,500-hectare protected area, so at least here it should be safe in its habitat. Other than continued searching to find the species, both through organized surveys and by educating local people about the bird and asking them to report any sightings, there is little else that can be done to ensure its survival. However, New Caledonia's Grande Terre island has a central mountain range running its length, with five peaks over 1,500 metres high. Much of this area is inaccessible and poorly explored. Biologists are hopeful that additional populations of the enigmatic owlet-nightjar might be found here in the future.

RAVAGED AND RARE: REPTILES

Some endangered species fight a real uphill battle for good PR. Let's face it, if you're ugly—and in the eyes of many beholders, reptiles aren't the most lovable things imaginable—it's going to be tough. After all, many of them creep or slither along the ground and possess a scaly, toothy, dragon-like appearance. Moreover, we seem to tar them all with the brush of nastiness, owing to the usually un-deserved reputations of a few; the man-eating myth of the crocodil-ians and the belief that most snakes are venomous come to mind. When you add their cold-bloodedness, and the typically forbidding places they inhabit, it comes as no surprise that it's harder to en-gender support for their protection. The exceptions, of course, are the generally more appealing turtles, which nevertheless are widely endangered as well. Reptiles need good PR fast. Of the 3,000 or so assessed by the IUCN, 664 are threatened with extinction.

PHILIPPINES CROCODILE
Crocodiles have been around in one form or another since the age of dinosaurs. Some 65 million years ago, they survived the Cretaceous-Tertiary extinction event. This catastrophe, which killed off 65 percent of all species on earth, was likely caused by a 15-kilometre-wide asteroid slamming into the earth at 70,000

kilometres per hour, ringing it like a bell with a force equal to one billion Hiroshima bombs. Tyrannosaurus rex, triceratops, and the rest of the dinosaur pack perished, marking the end of their 160-million-year reign on the planet. Somehow crocodiles managed to squeak through. Although such survival skills in the past can't be argued, they may have less luck surviving the planet's current extinction event: the one being waged on the natural world by us.

The endemic Philippine crocodile is the rarest species of crocodilian in the world (a distinction for which it barely nudges out the critically endangered Chinese alligator of the dammed, dredged, and heavily polluted Yangtze River). Once found widely across the massive Philippines Archipelago, today fewer than 100 mature animals survive in a few scattered locations, most of them in one national park. An exploding human population, dynamite fishing, wetland drainage, habitat destruction for agriculture, and commercial poaching for crocodile skins have all taken their toll on the critically imperilled reptile.

The Philippine species is one of the smallest of the 14 crocodiles found worldwide. It grows to an average of only about two to two and a half metres long and weighs in at just 15 kilograms. Owing to its small size and relatively non-aggressive nature, it hardly fits the stereotype of a man-eater and isn't considered particularly dangerous by those who know the animal. Its diet is made up of fish, snakes, wading birds, pigs, civet cats, and the occasional domestic dog, while hatchlings eat everything from dragonflies to small fish. Females build a mound nest on a riverbank (sometimes they nest in holes) and lay about 20 eggs, which they incubate for over two months. The species also displays motherly care of her newly hatched young, a trait common to all crocodiles.

Largely a freshwater species, this rare croc lives in streams, creeks, rivers, lakes, and wetlands from sea level well up into the mountains, as high as 850 metres. It's also known to swim through salt water when it's moving from one freshwater creek to another. When it does, it crosses paths with the imposing saltwater crocodile species, which, at up to seven metres long and 1,000 kilograms, is the world's biggest reptile. Could this occasional commingling with its giant cousin be one of the reasons for the Philippine crocodile's current predicament? Is it possible that much of the historical persecution of the smaller species has its roots in a chronic case of mistaken identity? Given the significant size difference between the two species, locals have long mistakenly thought the Philippines crocodiles they saw were actually the young of the much-feared saltwater species. They killed them accordingly.

There was little interest in the Philippines crocodile until 1999, when one was found on the large island of Luzon, where it was thought to be extinct. This single, young animal, named Isabela for the provincial territory where she was found, was taken into captivity by Crocodile Rehabilitation Observance and Conservation (CROC), a project run by Filipino and Dutch conservationists, a local university, and the local government. After growing to maturity in captivity, Isabela was released back into the wild in 2007. By the time of her release, she had become somewhat of a media darling in the Philippines, a flag-bearer for her species who defied the odds and won the uphill battle for PR. Even so, Philippine crocodiles remained dangerously close to extinction.

The species wasn't given any actual legal protection by the national government until 2001, after which killing one would get you a minimum of six years in jail and/or a 100,000 pesos fine (about US$2,100). Beyond that step—admittedly an important one—the Philippines government showed little interest in helping the species to actually recover. That job was left in the hands of private and local organizations such as CROC.

Through public education and awareness campaigns, and by empowering local communities in the areas where the crocodiles survive, the Mabuwaya Foundation (which spearheaded CROC) has created three sanctuaries to protect the endangered reptile. What's more, in the summer of 2009, the foundation released 50 captive-bred subadults into promising lake habitat within the Philippines' largest protected area, Northern Sierra Madre National Park, on Luzon. The hope is that these animals will pioneer a self-sustaining wild population by 2012. Ten of them have been fitted with radio transmitters to monitor their movements and so that we can gain a better understanding of the species' natural history. Such information will be used in future conservation and reintroductions. In the hope of generating income for the local economy through ecotourism, nearby communities are taking pride in their stewardship of one of the world's rarest species. They are training guides and building local facilities for croc-watching, birdwatching, and other nature activities.

In addition to the small wild population, hundreds of captive Philippines crocodiles are being reared in breeding facilities both within the country and outside it. Although there haven't been any large-scale introductions into the wild aside from the one mentioned, these captive crocodiles are a "gene bank" for future reintroductions. Perhaps one little crocodile named Isabela has started a revolution.

LA GOMERA GIANT LIZARD

Sporting a name that's every bit as intimidating as a crocodile's, the critically endangered La Gomera giant lizard lives on one of the most sparsely populated of the seven Canary Islands, Spanish outliers located in the Atlantic Ocean about 100 kilometres off the coast of Morocco. The island of La Gomera is 370 square kilometres of rugged, volcanic-formed lava chimneys, mountains, and deep valleys—

an ideal place for lizards. Unfortunately for lizards, it's also been home to humans for millennia. People brought a hearty appetite for the easy-to-catch, slow-moving animals, as well as agriculture, grazing animals, and marauding rats and cats. It's not surprising that this half-metre-long lizard (not exactly a giant, despite its name), had all but disappeared. It was thought to be extinct for the last 500 years— that is, until the very end of the 20th century. Then, encouraged by the Lazarus-like reappearance in 1974 and 1996 of other presumed extinct giant lizards on El Hierro and Tenerife Islands, also in the Canaries, Spanish biologists began searching La Gomera. In 1999, they found a tiny surviving population of just six animals.

Desperate to escape the cats that preyed upon them, the last six lizards had been relegated to about a hectare of sparsely vegetated, crumbling rock ledge. They could only be reached on climbing ropes. Once found across the islands in large numbers—they had been abundant enough to be hunted, after all—the species was reduced to literally hanging on to the edge of a cliff. For centuries, nobody on the island knew of their existence.

Though the lizard's numbers may have declined historically owing to habitat destruction and hunting, today La Gomera is an unspoiled, rugged island, whose population of rural people is largely isolated from the rest of the world. Like natural evolution, cultural evolution can be very inventive on isolated islands; to wit, the unique whistled language invented by the people of La Gomera. Had the discovery of the giant lizard been made by La Gomeran natives instead of Spanish scientists from the mainland, news of the find might have echoed throughout the valleys of the island by means of Silbo Gomero, one of the few whistled languages anywhere. Known since Roman times, Silbo Gomero was probably developed by early shepherds who had to communicate across valleys and steep ravines. It works by mimicking the sound of the spoken language (Spanish nowadays, of course) and can convey information in complete sentences that can travel for several kilometres over the landscape. Though now largely replaced by the much less romantic cellphone, El Silbo lives on in La Gomera.

Soon after it was discovered, a plan for the protection and recovery of the La Gomera lizard was put in place. Although searches for the animal in other parts of the island have been fruitless, its habitat at the cliffs near Le Merica where it was rediscovered has been protected, and it's now illegal to kill the lizards. This has led to a significant growth in the species' population from single digits to about 90 animals in the wild. In addition, a captive breeding facility, located near the original habitat, was established in 2001 and officially opened two years later. Since then, several dozen lizards have been born there, and in 2008 six of the most suitable captive-reared lizards were released into the wild, with more to follow.

TURTLES

Night sweats. Hemorrhoids. Poor circulation. Low white blood cell count. Baldness. Male infertility. Menopause. Gum disease. Bad complexion. And more . . . These are just some of the ailments traditional Chinese medicine treats with concoctions made of the various body parts of turtles. What's tragic is that there's no scientific evidence that any of it actually works, so wild animals are literally being ground into powders for nothing. But there's more to it than folk medicine. To stop at the pharmacopoeia of turtle parts is to miss the cornucopia: turtle soup, turtle stew, and turtle jelly—dishes that still stir an appetite in Asia. Take turtle jelly, for instance (also known as guilinggao): this medicinal dessert soup, claimed to be good for the complexion, is made using any one of 89 Asian turtle species, 67 of which are on the endangered species list.

There's nothing new about grinding up turtles into unproven remedies or consuming them as food; it's been going on for centuries. Old habits are hard to break. What *has* changed is that now there are alternatives to such folk remedies that actually work. Moreover, there is a greater choice of how we get our protein. Most important of all, something else is different: precisely because of these old habits, many of the turtle species used in either folk medicine or as food are now plummeting toward oblivion, so it's illegal to kill them under various national laws and under the Convention on International Trade in Endangered Species. Unfortunately, these laws and the convention are usually ignored.

Need some numbers? They aren't available for all of Asia, but in Taiwan alone, 2,000 tonnes of shells only (the weight doesn't even account for whole animals) were imported for traditional medicine use between 1999 and 2008. That number bears repeating: 2,000 *tonnes* of shells into Taiwan alone. Turtles generally aren't very big animals, so this volume translates into millions of them being imported into one little corner of Asia in less than a decade. How many more must be used in China, with its 1.3 billion people? And this is just the medicinal use of the shell and doesn't include countless more turtles that are used as food. The consumption of these slow-moving, harmless animals throughout Asia defies the imagination.

YUNNAN BOX TURTLE

The Yunnan box turtle was first described to science in 1906, in southern Yunnan Province, China. It was already rare and wasn't recorded at all between 1940 and the new millennium despite intensive searching. By everyone's guess, this small, 15-centimetre-long, rather inconspicuous brown turtle would never be seen again. So, in 2000, the IUCN declared the turtle extinct.

Turtles are slow, not only in how they move but also in adapting to a changing environment. Despite surviving mass extinctions, ice ages, and other planetary upheavals for more than 200 million years, they can't adjust to the destruction of their natural habitat over short time scales. They can't just "up and move" to a new "neighbourhood" to escape human activities.

The Yunnan box turtle was in the wrong place at the wrong time. Though little is known about the species' original range, at the time of its discovery it was thought to inhabit only the swamps, streams, and ponds near the city of Kunming on the Yunnan Plateau, in southwestern China. Virtually all of this wetland has been swallowed up by the rapid expansion of the city. During the 20th century, its population has grown 60-fold, from about 100,000 to a sprawling metropolis of about six million today. What little wetland habitat that is left is severely polluted. This is affecting more than just turtles: a species of newt endemic to Kunming Lake has recently gone extinct. So perhaps it isn't all that surprising that the turtle hadn't been seen in six decades.

Then, in 2004, somebody from Kunming posted a photo on the Internet asking for help identifying a female turtle. It was a Yunnan box turtle, the first one seen since 1940. Remarkably, just a few months later, a local turtle expert found a male at a pet dealer in Kunming. He was able to buy both the "Internet" female and the male. Having been already declared extinct, however, there was a lot of doubt as to whether the animals were genetically pure Yunnan box turtles or hybrids with other species (hybridizing turtles is a common practice in breeding circles). Any doubt was soon erased as DNA analysis proved they were the real deal. And the good news didn't end there. Another female was found at a local market in 2006, and a few more live specimens have been found since then.

Discovering the elusive patch of Yunnan box turtle habitat in 2008 was the icing on the cake. Efforts are being made by the Kunming Institute of Zoology to protect it. With so few known individuals, the species was poised to quickly slide back into the extinction category, so the Kunming Institute set up a captive breeding program with support from the Turtle Survival Alliance, an international conservation organization. A tentative step toward the possible recovery of the species was made in 2010, when the first Yunnan box turtle eggs were laid at the breeding facility.

Unfortunately, supply and demand determines much of what happens in the world. In the criminal realm of the black market wildlife trade, extreme rarity all too often triggers the invisible hand of the market to land a heavy blow upon species teetering on the brink of extinction. With a supply next to zero, demand for the Yunnan box turtle on the black market may make it the most valuable turtle of all: it is estimated that the market price for the first one to become available for sale could be as high as US$50,000. Money like that will drive poachers to extreme measures to find any animals left in the wild. The Yunnan box turtle isn't the only one of its kind in Asia facing an uncertain future: seven other box turtles of the genus *Cuora* are also critically endangered.

BURMESE ROOFED TURTLE

While habitat destruction in China has driven the Yunnan box turtle toward extinction, it is consumer demand by that country's 1.3 billion people that is forcing turtles to extinction in places like Burma (or Myanmar, as it was unpopularly christened in 1989 by the new military government). An important centre of global turtle diversity, Burma is home to 28 species of tortoises and freshwater turtles, seven of them found nowhere else on earth.

The Burmese roofed tortoise of the Upper Chindwin River in the far north and the Arakan forest turtle of the great lowland forests of the west are both within a hairbreadth of extinction. And most of the other 26 species found in the country are endangered to varying degrees. As a locus of turtle habitat destruction, hunting for traditional medicine, and capture for the illegal pet trade, Burma is a microcosm of what is happening to the world's 328 known turtle species, over half of which are endangered.

An animal that spends its life quietly going about its business in obscure, mosquito-infested swamps, barely uttering a sound, eating mostly plants, and bothering nobody, is likely to go unnoticed. But an entire species going unseen from the 1930s to the 21st century can only mean one of two things: it was either extinct or vanishingly rare. Fortunately, it was the latter. In 2002, in the middle of Mandalay, the religious and cultural centre of Burma, among Buddhist monasteries and pagodas, scientists discovered three Burmese roofed turtles living in a small pond at a temple. Nobody knows how long they'd been there. The species was no longer presumed extinct.

Over the next couple of years, there were extensive surveys to locate the species in the wild, and by 2004 two tiny populations were found surviving—but just barely—in the Dokhtawady River and along the Upper Chindwin River, in northern Burma. As thrilling as the discoveries of a long-thought-extinct species are, it is estimated that only five to seven breeding adult female turtles remain. Once numbering in the hundreds of thousands, this is all that's left after centuries of hunting and egg collection have taken their toll.

Growing up to 60 centimetres long, this large terrapin, native to deep, slow-flowing rivers, is known for the brilliant green colour its head turns during the breeding season and for its rather cute upturned snout. The female lays its eggs in several separate clutches—each holding 3 to 10 eggs—buried in the sand of a riverbank. Since they're laid in winter and don't hatch until May, for several months they are vulnerable to any disturbance. Unfortunately, there is gold along the Upper Chindwin River, and miners use powerful hoses to wash the surfaces of sandbanks into the river to uncover traces of the precious metal. So, beginning in 2005, conservationists began protecting known nesting beaches along the river and have been removing hatchlings and transferring them to a captive rearing facility at the Yadanabon Zoo in Mandalay. (There's also another small group of eight breeding adults at this zoo that have produced a small number of young.) By 2010, nearly 400 of the baby turtles had been transferred to the safety of the zoo. And the number of young would be even higher if so many of the eggs laid in the wild hadn't been infertile. Scientists fear that there are too few male Burmese roofed turtles left to fertilize the eggs that are being laid by the last few females in the wild. So, the plan is to take some of the breeding-age male turtles reared at the Yadanabon Zoo and release them into the Upper Chindwin to breed with the females.

The turtles have more to worry about than gold mining. As a deep, slow-moving river, the Chindwin is popular for fishing, which in Burma could entail catching fish in traditional gillnets, electrocuting them by passing a powerful current through the water, or blasting them with dynamite. All of these techniques kill many river turtles also. However, as bad as the gold mining and the fishing are, they pale in comparison to the largest potential threat facing the Burmese roofed turtle and anything else that relies on the river. A large hydroelectric dam proposed for the Upper Chindwin has the potential to drown both the nesting beaches and the natural river channel under a large reservoir. Such a project only emphasizes the need to find suitable new habitat the species can be relocated to in the future. The saga of Burma's endangered species continues.

Arakan Forest Turtle

Living just a few hundred kilometres southwest of the range of the roofed turtle, the Arakan forest turtle of Burma sits near the top of the list of endangered turtles in Asia, or anywhere else for that matter. Previously thought to be extinct for almost nine decades, it was rediscovered by conservationists in 1994 at a local food market in China. It turned up at least one more time when, in 2001, workers for a conservation group bought two live specimens from a vendor at a Chinese market (both animals were subsequently sent to Zoo Atlanta in the United States for breeding). At this point, the species was known only by a few captive animals and museum specimens. This would soon change.

As one might expect with an animal so elusive and rare, its ecology and natural history are poorly understood. Less than 30 centimetres in length and sporting a brown shell with black mottling, the little turtle had been known in the past by the name *pyant cheezar,* local dialect for "turtle that eats rhinoceros shit." A poignant but obsolete name since the Sumatran rhino, the source of the turtle's gustatory treat, was wiped out decades earlier in the region.

The Rakhine Yoma Elephant Sanctuary in Myanmar is a 1,750-square-kilometre reserve of virtually impenetrable leech-infested forest and bamboo ecosystems. It's part of one of the largest remaining tropical lowland forests in Southeast Asia, a wilderness that stretches through the western part of Myanmar from Bangladesh to the Irrawaddy Delta on the Bay of Bengal. Enduring heavy rains here in the spring of 2009 (the season when turtles are presumably more active and easier to find), a team of conservationists from the Wildlife Conservation Society searched for the elusive animals and found five of them. They were the first of their kind ever recorded in the wild by scientists. They are verging on extinction.

Hunting for the traditional medicine trade and the food trade is a prime reason for their parlous state, but so have agriculture, logging, road building, and bamboo harvesting taken a toll. Even though the handful of wild turtles was found in an inaccessible sanctuary that is rarely visited by humans, its safety can't be assumed given the overwhelming commercial demand for the reptiles in Asia. As a precaution against poaching, conservationists have recommended that the Rakhine Yoma sanctuary's staff, plus scientists and conservation groups, be trained to identify and collect information on the species, which might be used in any future recovery plans for the turtle—currently no such plan exists. They also suggested that guards be placed on roads into the area to help prevent poaching.

And what of those two forest turtles taken in by Zoo Atlanta in 2001? Very difficult to breed, the slowly reproducing animals mate only once per year, and few offspring survive. The zoo, the only breeding facility for the species in the world, has produced just four Arakan forest turtles since receiving that lucky pair that narrowly escaped the mortar, the pestle, and the pot in 2001.

YANGTZE GIANT SOFTSHELL TURTLE

In contrast to the typically proportioned turtles discussed above, the Yangtze giant softshell (also known as Swinhoe's softshell) is the largest freshwater turtle species in the world, weighing up to 135 kilograms and measuring up to a metre in length. Once common throughout southern China and northern Vietnam, it lives in slow-moving rivers and murky ponds, where fish, frogs, crabs, and aquatic plants are its fare of choice. A pig-like snout, widely spaced eyes, and an enormous, deep head give it a somewhat doleful appearance. Instead of a hard shell (think army helmet), like a typical turtle, it is protected by a flexible, leathery carapace. With a slow metabolism and a relaxed lifestyle, a Yangtze giant softshell turtle can live for a century or more.

Perilously close to non-existence thanks to the pressure exerted on the land and water by a burgeoning human population in Asia, its population has been decimated mostly by habitat destruction and hunting for the food and folk medicine trade. In 2004, there were thought to be only four left, all males. One each survived in the Suzhou, Shanghai, and Beijing Zoos, and one in a pond in the middle of Hanoi, Vietnam (there is some dispute whether this one is the same species). But the population lurched abruptly toward zero when the Shanghai and Beijing animals died by 2006. Even had they survived, it looked like the end of the line for the giant turtle: a species that had been evolving for almost 250 million years was doomed without females. So, in a truly last-ditch effort, those working to save the turtle sent an urgent call out to hundreds of private and public zoos across China, asking for detailed descriptions of *any* large turtles they were keeping, on the slim chance that a previously unknown Yangtze softshell would show up. The odds were slim to none, and the odds of finding a female were half that.

But a reply from a zoo in southern China was intriguing enough that two conservation experts were sent to check out a large turtle living there. That turtle, in one of those odd twists of fate that can change the future, was a sideshow animal left to the zoo over half a century ago by a travelling circus as a payment for a place to perform. It's been living alone in relative obscurity in its dingy little pool in the Changsha Zoo ever since.

When the scientists laid eyes on the Changsha turtle, they couldn't believe their luck: it was a female giant softshell, previously unknown to the wider scientific community; and even better, it was still laying eggs—albeit unfertilized, since it had no mate to finish the job, but there were eggs nonetheless. She was the last known female of her species on earth. Although only the faintest hope flickered that one would be found, there she was, all 40 kilograms of her. She was about 80 years old. The zoo secured her pond with bulletproof glass, remote cameras, and a night watchman. She was too precious not to protect.

But a lone female does not a viable species make; her isolated spinsterhood would do nothing to ensure the propagation of her kind. She needed a mate. Enter the 100-year-old male that lives almost 1,000 kilometres away at the Suzhou Zoo. In 2007, an agreement was reached between the two zoos for the female to be transported to Suzhou to meet the male-in-waiting. In reality, he would at first only be contributing his sperm for artificial insemination—actual physical mating would be a last resort because the considerable weight of the animals could result in injury during contact.

Evidently adapting well to her new home, in 2008 the female turtle laid about 100 eggs that were then artificially fertilized with her suitor's sperm. Although the eggs were successfully fertilized, the embryos died during incubation. Further attempts since then have also been unsuccessful. Her lifetime of poor nutrition had resulted in a calcium deficiency, preventing the embryos from developing properly. Now, her diet is being supplemented with the hope that this problem will be remedied. Guarded optimism survives that the Yangtze giant softshell turtle might yet be artificially bred back from the brink of extinction. (As of mid-2011, no young had yet been produced.)

In the spring of 2008, local people reported seeing a previously unreported very large turtle in a pond west of the city of Hanoi. After years of searching unsuccessfully for this species in the wild, conservationists were skeptical at first. On investigating, however, they were able to photograph and confirm that it was indeed a Yangtze giant softshell turtle—the only one known to exist in the wild. It raises the possibility that there could be a few more of them out there, going about their turtle business as they have for eons, oblivious to the plight of their kind.

AMBUSHED: AMPHIBIANS

According to the International Union for the Conservation of Nature (IUCN), fully one-third of the approximately 5,000 species of frogs worldwide is threatened with extinction. Nearly 200 species have in fact been wiped from the face of the earth in the past few decades, most recently the Kihansi spray toad of Tanzania. It was declared extinct in the wild in November 2009.

No single factor is to blame for the perilous situation frogs are in. Habitat loss and degradation, climate change, UV radiation, chemical pollutants, and disease all play a part, individually or in combination. The great bulk of threatened frog species are found in the tropics.

ARCHEY'S FROG

What does a group of four small frogs, the tuatara lizard, and the southern beech tree have in common? They are all New Zealand originals and were evolving there 80 million years ago when the islands were still part of the southern supercontinent of Gondwana. But even the lizard and the tree are newcomers compared with the family to which the frogs belong, Leiopelmatidae.

Members of the Leiopelmatidae family are rightfully called archeobatrachia in scientific parlance, or "ancient frogs." Although the family contains but four species, all exclusive to New Zealand, it possesses an impressive provenance, diverging in an evolutionary sense from the rest of the frog world over 200 million years ago. What's more, they have changed very little in all that time and are virtually indistinguishable from fossilized frogs found in Australia (also part of Gondwana in early times) that have been dated to 150 million years ago. Such an early split from the main trunk of the frog family tree has given the *Leiopelma* frogs the distinction of being living fossils and, as such, they share some unique features.

The most obvious distinguishing trait of the *Leiopelma* species—or New Zealand frogs, as they are known—are their round pupils, rather than the typical slitted ones of more familiar amphibians, giving them an odd—some might say endearing—doe-eyed appearance. As well, look closely at a typical frog and you can't help but notice its conspicuous round ear drums. Well, New Zealand frogs don't have them and apparently don't need them, since they lack an inflatable throat sac and can't croak or sing like other kinds of frogs. All they can manage is a thin squeaking sound, but since it looks like they don't use it for communication, they don't need ears. Equally odd is that they have an extra vertebrae compared with other frogs, and although they have no tails, they possess vestigial "tail-wagging muscles" (in typically snappy scientific patter, they're called *caudalipuboischiotibialis* muscles). One of the New Zealand frogs' most unusual qualities is that the young skip the tadpole stage and emerge from the egg sac as almost fully formed frogs. Archey's frog, the most endangered and tiniest member of the Leiopelmatidae family, has all of the above, plus an unusual number of chromosomes.

Named for a New Zealand zoologist, Archey's frogs live in high-elevation forests and moist subalpine scrub habitats on New Zealand's North Island. Small, even by frog standards, they reach less than three centimetres in length. This diminutive stature, combined with nocturnal habits, a very effective greenish-yellow with dark mottling camouflage, and a silent disposition (remember, they can't croak), makes them very difficult to locate. At night, Archey's frogs move from the ground up into bushes and low trees, where they feed on small insects, worms, and other tiny invertebrates. Daylight hours are reserved for hiding out and resting on the ground under logs and rocks. Unlike most frogs, Archey's don't require a body of water to breed in and are apparently perfectly happy mating under logs and stones, as long as it's damp. Once hatched, the male will carry the young around on his back for several weeks and care for them until their transformation into the adult form is nearly complete. Once they've left the security of his back, it will take three to four years for the young to reach full adulthood—a very long time by frog standards.

Despite its 200-million-year role as a real survivor, Archey's frog is facing extinction. But going down the road of no return is nothing new for species of the ancient Leiopelmatidae family. Fossil records show that there were three additional family members (for a total of seven) as recently as 1,000 or 2,000 years ago. They may have been wiped out by the introduced Polynesian rat. Meanwhile, over the past decade, Archey's frog has seen its own population plummet by over 80 percent, a possible victim of the deadly chytrid fungus. The species, which already had a small range confined to just two tiny areas on New Zealand's North Island, has been decimated. Rats, which prey on frogs, are also likely to blame. Listed as critically endangered on the IUCN Red List, nobody knows exactly how many survive in the wild, but in one important study population, the frog's numbers declined from 433 to just 53 over a six-year period. The frog is extremely scarce and continues to decline; it is one of the planet's most endangered.

Virtually every step that can be taken to save the species from extinction is being taken. Their habitat is protected, and predatory mammals such as rats are being eradicated. Biologists are trying to learn how chytrid fungus affects the frog and are looking for a cure for the disease. And, as a pre-emptive measure, they've begun a captive breeding program. With a little luck, such conservation measures may help Archey's frog continue on its 200-million-year journey. In neighbouring Australia, another extremely rare frog struggles to continue its own unique evolutionary journey.

ARMOURED MISTFROG

Happy stories don't crop up very often in the sobering realm of endangered species. The news reports about threatened animals and plants are almost always dire and typically elicit a "here we go again" response. We've pretty much come to expect bad news. That's why the story of a little frog that lives in the rushing torrents of an Australian rainforest stream is so unusual.

First discovered in 1976, the armoured mistfrog is named for the male's spiny skin and its penchant for hanging out on spray-soaked boulders beside waterfalls, a specialized habitat known as the splash zone. At night, the little brown and grey mottled frogs, just over three and a half centimetres long, gather along the creek to enjoy the spray—and presumably sing a song that nobody's yet heard. During the day, they take refuge in deep cracks in the rocks around the cascade. Little is known about the frog's ecology, since it has been observed only a few times. However, based on the habits of a separate but very similar species known as the waterfall frog, it's thought the armoured mistfrog lays eggs under stream-bottom rocks and its offspring spend the tadpole stage living in the torrent.

Armoured mistfrogs are one of a group of amphibians ("amphibian" comes from the Greek *amphi,* meaning "two," and *bios,* "life"—in reference to their dual aquatic and terrestrial lives) known as torrent frogs. In Australia, they are found in northeastern Queensland—if you imagine that country's shape as resembling the head of a Scottie dog facing west, the area we're talking about is along the eastern edge of its northern pointy ear. Torrent frogs are adapted to breeding in and living beside tumbling creeks draining the highland rainforests of the region, known as the wet tropics. Several torrent frog species have suffered dramatic population crashes since the 1980s and 1990s, possibly due to chytrid fungus, the deadly pathogen that has ravaged frog populations around the world. The armoured mistfrog was found in an area of less than 130 square kilometres at high elevations in Cape Tribulation and Daintree National Parks. Note the past tense of the preceding statement. That's because after December 1991 the armoured mistfrog was never again seen in its known range. Experts thought it was extinct.

Fast-forward 17 years to July 2008. A doctoral student was searching for another species of torrent frog in an area more than 100 kilometres south of Daintree National Park. He happened to stumble upon what appeared to be several armoured mistfrogs in a stream. Rediscovering a long-lost species isn't an everyday occurrence, so tissue samples were sent to the Australian National University in Canberra to verify their identity. DNA analysis confirmed they were armoured mistfrogs.

Further investigations have revealed a tiny population of only 30 to 40 of the frogs at the site, where it lives side by side with the closely related waterfall mistfrog. Both species are infected with the same chytrid fungus that was thought to be the culprit for the armoured mistfrog's disappearance from its original range to the north. Oddly enough, despite the fungal infection, all of the frogs appear to be quite healthy and flourishing within their habitat. In a bid to understand the disease, scientists are trying to determine why the fungus has apparently had no effect on them. It's hoped that any new knowledge gained might contribute to the conservation of other amphibians afflicted by the deadly fungus.

As small as this newly discovered population is, it raises some hope that other populations of the species can be found. It has also encouraged a glimmer of optimism that some of Australia's other "extinct" frog species might be waiting to be rediscovered.

IRANIAN GORGAN MOUNTAIN SALAMANDER

Although the plight of the world's frogs has received much attention recently, the same can't be said of their amphibian cousins, the salamanders. Many of them are also threatened with extinction, particularly in Mexico and Central America, but you'd have to go to a cave in Iran to find what is likely the rarest one of all.

The world is so focused on Iran's politics that the country's rich and varied natural heritage is often overlooked. Its diversity of wildlife is impressive: over 8,000 species of plants, 1,900 of them found nowhere else; 500 species of birds, 160 species of mammals (including the endangered Asiatic cheetah, also discussed in this book), 219 species of reptiles, and 23 species of amphibians, not to mention nearly 200 freshwater, inland fish species.

Iran is included in two of the world's 34 biodiversity hotspots, the Caucasus and the Irano-Anatolian. Dr. Norman Myers, who created and developed the concept of the biodiversity hotspot, defines one thusly: "To qualify as a hotspot, a region must meet two strict criteria: it must contain at least 1,500 species of vascular plants (> 0.5 percent of the world's total) as endemics, and it has to have lost at least 70 percent of its original habitat." That it is part of two such hotspots shows just how important Iran and its natural treasures are to the biosphere as a whole and just how threatened those natural treasures are. That said, imagine a scene from the Iranian landscape and chances are sun-drenched desert or arid mountains come to mind. What doesn't come to mind is a cool limpid pool in a dark grotto. But that is precisely where one of the world's most endangered amphibians lives. Shir-Abad Cave, located in the eastern Elburz Mountains near the Caspian Sea, in northwestern Iran, is the only place on earth inhabited by the Gorgan Mountain salamander. Less than 20 centimetres long (most of it tail), with a body shape reminiscent of a lizard, this four-legged, four-fingered and -toed aquatic creature with smooth yellowish skin was unknown to science until 1979. That's when a single animal was collected and described. Thirty years hence and the small amphibian remains extremely rare: only about 100 adults are known to exist.

The Gorgan Mountain salamander's entire universe is limited to one small spring-fed, underground pool 100 metres long by 10 metres at its widest. Here, secreted away beneath the earth, generations immemorial of the small animal have been born and have died while on its evolutionary path, its existence unknown to the rest of the world until three decades ago. Perhaps its stay-at-home way of life isn't surprising for a water-loving species that is surrounded by dry mountain forest: it would desiccate and die if it tried to disperse. And although its larvae have occasionally been seen outside in the stream that drains the cave, mature salamanders have only ever been found in the cave pool itself.

The Gorgan Mountain salamander may have always been rare, a disjunct, far-flung species of the primitive 110-million-year-old Asiatic salamander family. Although the cave and surrounding forests are protected as a Natural National Place of Iran, the species faces several immediate challenges. Its extremely limited range and one-of-a-kind habitat, and a tiny, closed population, are like ticking time bombs of extinction. A single mishap, such as someone (the

TROUBLED WATERS: FISH

The largest group of vertebrates of all, there are about 20,000 species of fish living in the planet's salt and fresh waters (by contrast, birds, in second place, have half that number). According to the IUCN, one-fifth of them are threatened with extinction, including most of the sharks, which are surpassed only by the dwindling sturgeon family for the dubious distinction as the most endangered group of large animals on earth.

RIVER SHARKS

Of all the planet's creatures, none excite fear and awe like the sharks, yet we kill an incredible 270,000 of them every day. Many species might cease to exist within a mere 20 years. That's nearly half a billion years of evolution snuffed out in the blink of an eye.

The latest research shows that the collapse of the shark population is drastically upsetting aquatic food webs in complex ways not yet fully understood. For example, their decline is responsible for the death of coral on some coral reefs; and the removal of sharks from Chesapeake Bay has already resulted in the crash of the scallop fishery there. The main culprit for this state of affairs? A largely unregulated, unrestrained, unsustainable, and withal brutal global fishery. A major component of this is the finning industry, which chops off sharks' fins and tails to fill the demand for shark fin soup in Asia or to obtain cartilage for use in unproven natural health products.

Many sharks are threatened with extinction, but none more so than the members of the genus *Glyphis,* a group of freshwater species so rare that we don't even have names for some of them yet. Known as river sharks, they belong to the same family as iconic oceanic varieties such as the lemon, tiger, and reef sharks. Stocky, with a high, arching back; broad, rounded snout; and prominent fins, these grey-coloured fish are similar in appearance to more familiar sharks. What really sets them apart is where they live: in murky freshwater habitats. Sharks are synonymous with the deep blue sea, not the silt-ridden, warm fresh water of a meandering tropical river. Yet this is exactly the kind of environment in which species belonging to the *Glyphis* genus have adapted to.

Because they are so well hidden in the cloudy waters of southern Asia and tropical northern Australia, nobody knows for certain how many species of river sharks there are. Historically, they were largely known from a scattering of specimens and museum records from the 19th century. In the 1990s, though, the capture of specimens of the Ganges shark and the discovery of a hitherto unknown species in Borneo seemed to awaken interest and concern for this obscure group of underwater predators. Only four species have been named, three of which are listed as critically endangered on the IUCN Red List. There are, however, several more about which so little is known that they haven't been officially named yet. Instead, they are called *Glyphis sp. A, Glyphis sp. B* (the provisional name given the newly discovered species from Borneo), *Glyphis sp. C,* and so on. River sharks are exceedingly rare animals, and though their actual numbers are unknown, only a few individuals of each species have ever been seen.

Very little is known about their biology. Good vision is not much use in water the consistency of chocolate milk, so their eyes have become small. However, they have evolved a keen sense of smell, hearing, and electroperception for hunting (the ability to read weak electrical impulses given off by surrounding objects is common to all sharks, though this capacity may be heightened in river sharks). Once prey have been located, *Glyphis* sharks seize them with small, serrated teeth. They are thought to bear live young.

GANGES RIVER SHARK

It's hard to imagine a shark living in the turbid, polluted waters of eastern and northeastern India, but that's where this two-metre-long fish makes its home. In 1996, the Ganges shark re-emerged after an absence of a century and a quarter, when two of them were caught—the first since 1867. Little stands between the Ganges shark and extinction. Inhabiting the Ganges and surrounding rivers, along whose banks hundreds of millions of people live, the obscure shark has been fished for centuries. Moreover, pollution and the construction of dams have degraded its habitat.

It is thought to hunt by skimming along the bottom while looking toward the surface with its upward-facing eyes to pick out prey backlit by the sun. Because the Ganges and other northern Indian rivers are prone to flooding, the shark may also play an important ecological role by scavenging drowned livestock swept into the swollen rivers.

Strangely enough, this small shark has a reputation as a man-eater—in Bengali it is known as *baagh maach,* or tiger fish. Indeed, in the past it might have occasionally mistaken a human for a potential meal and taken a bite. But it's hard to imagine it as a killer, considering its relatively small size and its tiny teeth, so the Ganges shark may have gotten a bad rap. In fact, the real culprit is probably a much larger, much more aggressive species. The bull shark, at up to four metres in length and weighing over 300 kilograms, is known to swim up rivers around the world, often travelling far into the middle of continents. It has plied the Mississippi all the way to St. Louis and beyond, and made it 4,000 kilometres inland from the Atlantic to the city of Iquitos in the Peruvian Amazon. They are also found in some of the same rivers in India as the Ganges shark. (At this point it must be noted that bull sharks are not a freshwater species. They are a marine species with a tolerance for low salinity and a predilection for inland exploration.) All of this is by way of saying that given that bull sharks kill more humans than any other fish on earth—usually attacking in very shallow water—it's a good bet that the Ganges shark got its man-eater reputation by being confused with its nasty cousin.

There may be little that can be done to ensure the Ganges shark's survival, if indeed more than few dozen of them still exist. Although the Indian government has banned all fishing for the species, this measure is virtually impossible to enforce along thousands of kilometres of river populated by millions of independent fishers whose next meal might well be an endangered river shark.

IRRAWADDY RIVER SHARK

This river shark is known from just one museum specimen, a juvenile male about 60 centimetres in length that was caught in Burma's Irrawaddy River in the late 1800s. However, since the Irrawaddy shark lives in some of the murkiest waters on earth, it hasn't been presumed extinct by the IUCN—it could be easily missed swimming about in its chocolate milk–like environment. Everything we know about the species comes from that one specimen described in 1896 by Austrian scientist Franz Steindachner. Like others in the genus *Glyphis,* the Irrawaddy shark has very small eyes and small serrated teeth, which suggests that it hunts for small fish using smell, hearing, and electroperception. Based on its juvenile length, it's thought the species reaches a length of up to three metres. Little else is known about the fish.

Although probably never common, its virtual non-existence is probably the result of the same factors affecting the Ganges shark: fishing and pollution. The destruction of mangrove forests along the Irrawaddy River, potentially an important part of the shark's habitat, might also be an important factor in its decline, since some shark species use the shallows surrounding mangroves as nurseries.

NORTHERN RIVER SHARK

The northern river shark lives in a handful of rivers along Australia's north coast, including in Kakadu National Park, and in the area surrounding the port of Darwin. Growing to about two metres in length, it inhabits muddy, slow-moving tidal rivers, as well as possibly spending some time in shallow salt water near the river mouths. It appears that individual sharks are loyal to their home rivers. Although they are protected as an endangered species in Australia and listed as critically endangered on the IUCN Red List, they are at great risk of extinction thanks to being taken as accidental bycatch at the hands of local gillnet and hook-and-line fishers. Moreover, given their specialized, limited habitat, northern river sharks are vulnerable to pollution and development along rivers. Only those individuals living within the protected Kakadu National Park might have a real chance at survival. Fewer than 40 northern river sharks have ever been recorded.

In contrast to the river sharks, which are challenging to protect because they are always moving and we don't know the extent of their distribution in the typically murky waterways they inhabit, the Devils Hole pupfish faces the opposite problem: its entire world falls within a tiny, well-defined habitat that could be wiped out by a single catastrophic event.

DEVILS HOLE PUPFISH

On April 4, 2010, the 7.2-magnitude El Mayor-Cucapah earthquake violently shook Baja, Mexico, killing several people. Shock waves were felt hundreds of kilometres to the north in Death Valley National Park in Nevada, where US Geological Survey live-feed video cameras captured their effects on the tiny habitat of the highly endangered Devils Hole pupfish, a creature whose total known range is even smaller than that of the Gorgan Mountain salamander. The two-and-a-half-centimetre-long, guppy-like fish, with a population hovering around 100, lives only in Devils Hole, an otherwise inconspicuous pool of water deep within a crack in the Mojave Desert. The video footage shows the three-by-seven-metre pool sloshing violently back and forth, like a shaken bathtub (Devils Hole was once known as the Miner's Bathtub). The seething water rips algae off the two-by-four-metre rock ledge that the species uses for spawning and feeding. Beleaguered pupfish can be seen bolting into clear water from the churning cloud of vegetation and silt. A few minutes later, once the drama has ended, they return to a changed habitat. The scary thing is, it wouldn't take much to wreck the entire world of this species: living only in this little hole, it has the smallest distribution of any vertebrate on earth.

However, Devils Hole is more than simply a hole. Like the tip of an iceberg, the pool at the surface represents just a fraction of what's below: a vast, mostly unexplored, flooded cave system, whose absolute depth remains a mystery but reaches at least 150 metres. For 20,000 years, the cave's constant 34 degree Celsius water has provided a stable habitat for the iridescent blue pupfish. Little had changed in its environment until the 1960s. That's when the development of nearby alfalfa farms began to take off. Lots of sunshine and water are important for growing alfalfa. There was no shortage of sun in the desert, but water had to be drawn from the caverns beneath Devils Hole. Its level began falling. You might think a drop of a few centimetres really wouldn't bother a fish that lives in a practically bottomless shaft. But it does. That barely submerged, walk-in closet–sized rock ledge at the hole's entrance, so crucial for feeding and reproduction, would be high and dry even with a slight drop in the water: bad news for the pupfish.

The Devils Hole pupfish was declared an endangered species in 1967, at about the same time big agriculture was beginning to draw down the area's groundwater. At the time, its population was between 400 and 500. In 1973, while the battle between pupfish conservationists and developers was being waged, the US Endangered Species Act became law. Now the federal government was obligated to try to recover any species listed as endangered. The effort to save the pupfish would be a crucial early test for the act, the world's first comprehensive endangered species legislation. In 1976, four years after conservationists filed a suit against land developers and the state of Nevada, the US Supreme Court found in favour of the Devils Hole pupfish, mandating a minimum water level to protect the species from extinction.

Nature itself had provided a few problems for the little desert fish to contend with besides water-hungry alfalfa farms. In the 1970s, a flash flood washed debris into the hole, and an earthquake shook things up. Nevertheless, the population stayed pretty stable at around 400 until the 1990s, when the species' numbers began to mysteriously dwindle.

By 2006, it had hit its lowest count ever at only 38 individuals. As a precaution, conservationists began to supplement the fish's food supply to try to stem a further decline. This appears to have worked. Since then, though still only modest, pupfish numbers had been growing steadily for the first time in over a decade, though the number still fluctuates between more than 100 after young are born to below 100 later in the year.

Then, just when it looked like some headway was being made, the April 2010 earthquake hit. Nobody knows yet what effect the loss of algae in its habitat will have on the endangered fish. Surprisingly, a population survey in the week following the quake showed 118 fish, nearly 50 more than one year earlier. But would this number hold in light of the damage done to the pupfish's food supply? While there are no guarantees, biologists expect the algae will grow back. There may be another silver lining, too. It's possible the quake's sloshing washed away the accumulated fine silt that clogged up critical habitat between gravel particles where pupfish larvae find refuge. In fact, the survey done following the quake also showed more larvae than the previous survey.

We can only hope that the recent modest comeback of the Devils Hole pupfish continues and even accelerates. Our fingers should also be crossed that the US Endangered Species Act, so vital to the continued existence of the pupfish and a bevy of other species, will also persist strongly into the future.[9] The act, however, may have been too slow in coming to the rescue of the Alabama sturgeon, another of the world's rarest fish.

ALABAMA STURGEON

Some 200 million years ago, when the first sturgeons appeared on

---

9. In an ironic but not surprising twist in a country that has been deregulating itself wholesale at the behest of corporate America, today the US Endangered Species Act has itself become endangered. The legislation is being frayed around the edges by the constant attack of big business pro-development/anti-conservation forces in the United States. The recent de-listing of the still-endangered gray wolf in parts of the west is a good example of this.

earth, the planet looked nothing like it does today. There was no North America, Europe, South America, Asia, or Africa; in fact, there really weren't any separate land masses at all. The super-continent of Pangaea had just begun breaking up into the pieces that would eventually become the continents we know today. When sturgeons first appear in the fossil record, T-rex hadn't yet walked the earth, and flowering plants were still 100 million years in the future. By contrast, *Homo sapiens* have only been around for the last 200,000 years. If an animal deserves respect based on seniority alone, we should bow to the sturgeon, a thousand times our elder in the community of life.

Fossilized sturgeons look quite similar to their present-day descendants. They've changed little in the eons that they've been swimming the waters of the earth, a fact that has gained them the illustrious distinction of being living fossils. One of the oldest families among the fishes, sturgeons possess a skeleton of cartilage, as well as an elongated upper tail lobe, much like the sharks and rays. But unlike most fish, their body is covered with bony plates called scutes instead of the typical scales. At the business end, four sensitive barbels are found beneath an elongated snout, which is used to "snuffle" along the bottom in search of food.

Docile and slow moving, some sturgeon species are giants among fish. The largest species, *Huso huso,* grows up to five metres in length and can weigh 2,000 kilograms. Piscine methuselahs, a few can live for a century or more and may not breed until 20 years of age.

Slow growth rates, late sexual maturity, habitat destruction, and a high demand for the females of certain kinds for their caviar have pushed nearly all of the 26 sturgeon species toward extinction. The most threatened one of all lives in the southeastern United States.

Among the rarest fish in the world, the Alabama sturgeon was once found throughout the rivers of the Mobile Basin in Alabama and Mississippi. One of the smallest species in its family, the brassy-orange bottom-dweller reaches a length of only 45 to 75 centimetres and weighs in at about a kilogram. The species had been declining for decades owing to overfishing, dredging of its river habitat for navigation, and pollution. In recent decades it has become restricted to the Alabama River and its tributaries, where the construction of two dams in the 1970s is thought to be the real culprit in the species' recent precipitous decline: its age-old passage up and down the river had been blocked.

Although locals have known about the sturgeons for a long time—records from 1898 indicate an impressive commercial catch of 19,000 of them—the fish was only formally recognized as a distinct species in 1991. By then it was so rare that some questioned whether it even survived. This made it very difficult to have it protected under the US Endangered Species Act. Opponents asked, why protect a species that might not even exist? Resistance to having it designated under the act was strong. An alliance of business and industry claimed, among other things, that the listing threatened to harm the economy because it would result in restrictions on the routine dredging of the river and on barge traffic. As part of their strategy against listing it under the ESA, opponents also argued that even if it did still survive, the Alabama fish was one and the same species as the Mississippi River shovelnose sturgeon and therefore wasn't threatened with extinction. The US Fish and Wildlife Service (USFWS), the agency responsible for the act, abandoned its effort to protect the species in the early 1990s in the face of this opposition.

In 1993, a program began to captive-breed the Alabama sturgeon population back to health. One thing was missing: fish. So the search was on to capture breeding stock. By 1999, the state's fisheries department and the USFWS had netted tens of thousands of fish of various species in the search for sturgeons. Only six were caught, all males. A female was never captured. The last captive male died in 2002. End of breeding program. At the time, no more Alabama sturgeons were known to exist.

Just a couple of years earlier, in 2000, an Alabama environmental lawyer won a lawsuit against the USFWS, requiring the agency to finally list the sturgeon as a federal endangered species. Was the endangered designation too little, too late? Maybe not.

In the spring of 2007, state biologists captured a single Alabama sturgeon, the first of its kind to be seen in a half decade. It was the second-largest on record, so biologists believe it is very old and may have been one of the last to breed before those dams were constructed on the Alabama River in the early 1970s. This time, instead of putting it into captivity, biologists decided to implant the fish with a tracking device, release it back into the river, and follow its movements in the hope it would lead them to other sturgeons. By the spring of 2008, they'd been tracking it for a year and had learned where the fish likes to travel and where it likes to linger in the summer. A year later, biologists found another one in a different area. These remain the only two Alabama sturgeon known to exist.

In May 2008, some eight years after the designation of the Alabama sturgeon as an endangered species, the USFWS finally released its plan to protect the habitat of the beleaguered fish. Designation of part of the Alabama River and its tributary, the Cahaba River, as critical fish habitat is being proposed. As well, scientists are hopeful that the southernmost dam on the Alabama River could be opened for a short time during the spawning season, and that fish ladders might be constructed at the dam to allow free passage up river for any sturgeon. Even so, it may, after all, be too little, too late. With a known population that currently stands at two, and even if there are a few other individuals out there, it's quite possible that we may soon see the last of the Alabama sturgeon. Unfortunately, the same might be said of another bottom-dwelling river fish half a world away in China.

CHINESE GIANT PADDLEFISH

Struggling to survive in the same horrendous environmental conditions in the Yangtze River as the Baiji, the Chinese paddlefish is a giant among giants in the contest for the world's largest freshwater fish, reaching seven metres in length. It dwarfs the closest runners-up, the European catfish and the white sturgeon, neither of which reaches the five-metre mark. Locally it is known as the elephant fish, both for its size and for its long snout, which is one-third its body length. Though its appearance is reminiscent of a sturgeon, the two aren't closely related. The last confirmed sighting of one was back in 2003.

Living for up to 50 years, the Chinese paddlefish is one of only two species of paddlefish on earth, the other being the much smaller American paddlefish. Despite inhabiting the Yangtze River, where it has co-existed with millions of people for thousands of years, its habits remain obscure. Surpassed in size by few freshwater predators, it feeds on fish and crabs, and may also use electrical receptors along its long snout to help detect zooplankton in the water. Though it's never been confirmed, scientists suspect that Chinese paddlefish are anadromous, which means they live some of their lives in the marine environment before migrating up the Yangtze River to spawn (similar to salmon in other parts of the world).

Historically common, the fish's population had been steadily decreasing during the 20th century, mostly because of overfishing. The population plummeted after the Gezhouba hydroelectric dam was built in the mid-1980s. This giant barricade effectively severed the Yangtze into two rivers, an upper and a lower, thus separating the paddlefish's feeding grounds from its spawning beds. Fish trapped upstream by the dam might be able to spawn, but they'd starve. Those trapped below could eat but produce no offspring. The beleaguered fish couldn't have it both ways: its life cycle was cut in half. Another nail was added to its coffin with the construction of the world's largest-ever hydroelectric project.

Begun in 1994, the Three Gorges Dam is located just 50 kilometres up river from the Gezhouba project, further fragmenting the already truncated paddlefish habitat. The Three Gorges Dam has proven to be an ill-conceived behemoth. It has created a 600-kilometre-long reservoir that has displaced 1.2 million people, while submerging 13 cities, 140 towns, 1,350 villages, and countless archeological and burial sites under 100 metres of water. Hundreds of factories, waste dumps, and mines have also gone under, releasing untold thousands of tonnes of toxic waste into the river's ecosystem. And there are more dams to come: plans are afoot to build two additional ones upstream. The once-mighty Yangtze is becoming deadlier by the minute for anything that lives in it. Or beside it. Just ask any of the million or so environmental refugees whose homes now lie at the bottom of the Three Gorges' gigantic, polluted reservoir.

Despite all of this, and the fact that an extensive three-year search beginning in 2006 failed to find even a single Chinese paddlefish in the river, not everyone has given up on the species. It is still listed as critically endangered on the IUCN Red List, and scientists such as Qiwei Wei, China's foremost authority on the paddlefish, feels that sonar surveys and net-capture surveys might have missed fish that were hiding in "holes" or along rough bottom areas in the Upper Yangtze. Adding another glimmer of hope for the species is the reported capture and death of a large paddlefish because of illegal

UNEXPECTED ENDANGERMENT: INSECTS

The insects are the most abundant and diverse group of animals. Rough estimates of the number living at any one time is *10 quintillion* (that's about one and half billion of them for every human on earth). There are about 750,000 kinds described by science, or almost 20 times the variety of fish, amphibians, reptiles, birds, and mammals *combined*. Scientists who tally such things predict millions more species are waiting to be discovered. In spite of this, over 700 species of insects—and that's of just the 3,300 that have been assessed so far—are listed as threatened with extinction on the IUCN Red List.

FABULOUS GREEN SPHINX OF KAUAI

One of the largest insect groups with over 100,000 species, moths range in size from barely bigger than a pinhead to the giant Atlas moth of southeast Asia, whose wings can eclipse a good-sized dinner plate. Moths are everywhere—one glimpse at a streetlight on a warm summer night anywhere in the world attests to this. So though it might seem strange to utter the words "moth," "rare," and "endangered" in the same breath, it's not for the whimsically named "fabulous green sphinx of Kauai," a native Hawaiian moth hovering at extinction.

First observed in 1895 on the island of Kauai (it has been found nowhere else in the world), this exquisite large moth, with its bright green wings and orange antennae, wasn't seen again for another 66 years. After this second fleeting glimpse, a few more decades of absence was enough to convince scientists to list it as officially extinct in 1996. But species sometimes have a way of coming back from the dead and, during a search in 1998, a few fabulous green sphinx moths re-emerged Lazarus-like, moving it out of the gone-and-never-to-return category in 2003. Since then, only about a dozen of the moths have been seen, most of them drawn to powerful lights at a US Air Force tracking station that sits on a hill just above their habitat.

The fabulous green sphinx has only ever been observed in mountain forest in Kauai's Koke'e State Park, a cornucopia of rare plants and trees, many of which are found nowhere else. Degraded by introduced goats, pigs, and axis deer, this forest is one of the most endangered ecosystems in the world. Little is known about the green sphinx moth aside from where it lives. The species' caterpillars have rarely been observed, and its host plant (the one it lays eggs on as adults and feeds on as caterpillars) is still a mystery. Moreover, the exact reason for the moth's rarity is also unknown. Perhaps the introduced goats or invasive exotic plants have decimated the population of the moth's as-yet-unknown host plant? Maybe the ferocious Argentine ant, another invasive pest, is taking its toll by attacking the caterpillars? Nobody is sure. Ironically, because so little is known about this mysterious insect, it is still not protected.

Far to the south, across the vast Pacific Ocean, the future of a fellow six-legged creature looks just a little bit brighter.

LORD HOWE ISLAND GIANT STICK INSECT

If there is one group of creatures on this planet that we'd consider abundant, it is the insects. A thriving multi-billion-dollar pest extermination industry is testament to that. But you won't be needing pest control for the Lord Howe Island giant stick insect anytime soon. In fact, so rare is this bizarre organism that it was thought to have completely disappeared by 1930, done in by stowaway rats from a ship wrecked earlier in the century on the shore of this remote Australian island, about 650 kilometres off the coast of New South Wales.

Picture a typical stick insect, and a wispy, twiggy bug may come to mind—in fact, the largest, a species found in China, is practically all legs and 60 centimetres long! The Lord Howe species doesn't quite fit that mould. Not that it isn't strange with its chunky, cigar-shaped body (about 15 centimetres in length) and its short, stubby legs. It's also a heavyweight among insects, tipping the scales at 30 grams—that's heavier than many songbirds. A more fitting moniker for the big black insect is the "land sausage," another of its nicknames.

For decades nobody had seen the stick insect, until it was rediscovered in 2001 by Australian biologists. Oddly enough, it was found not on Lord Howe Island but 22 kilometres across the open Pacific Ocean on tiny Ball's Pyramid, a jagged, uninhabited 600-metre-high fang of volcanic rock, the world's tallest sea stack. According to geologists, Ball's Pyramid was never attached to Lord Howe Island, and giant stick insects can't swim. Nobody knows for sure how the insect got there. The best guess is that the first ones may have been accidentally carried in the nesting material of one of the thousands of seabirds that breed on the precipitous crag. Or maybe a female stick insect laden with eggs got washed into the sea during a storm and was lucky enough to drift over on some flotsam. However they got there, only about 20 individuals have survived on that desolate rock for the better part of a century. Even more remarkable is that all of the Lord Howe Island giant stick insects left on earth were discovered under a single bush growing in a cliff crevice a dizzying 90 metres above the crashing waves.

Once the biologists returned to the mainland, they got to work devising a recovery plan. The idea was to take a few individuals from Ball's Pyramid and captive-breed them into a population large enough to ensure the survival of the species in the wild.

Despite the precariousness of the tiny population, the biologists had to fight with bureaucracy to get permission to revisit the island and capture the animals. Two full years passed before their return in February 2003. That's a long time in the life of a species with just a handful of members left, so the scientists had no idea whether the beleaguered bugs still existed on Ball's Pyramid. They did. Two male and two female giant stick insects were collected for captive breeding back on the mainland.

Since then, the number of Lord Howe Island giant stick insects in the breeding program at the Melbourne, Australia, zoo has topped several hundred. Smaller numbers have also been bred at other zoos. Recently, 10 males and 10 females from Melbourne were returned to Lord Howe Island to live in a special enclosure. It is hoped that a full reintroduction can be made some time after 2011, once a rat eradication program is completed.

It isn't known exactly how many of the giant insects survive today on Ball's Pyramid, but the population is thought to be very, very small—likely fewer than 20.

LOST FROM THE FOREST:
TREES AND OTHER PLANTS

When we think of endangered species, it's easy to forget about the plants. Of course, they are every bit as alive as animals and are born, grow, reproduce, and die just like us, but their individual lives are generally thought to be less important. Nothing could be farther from the truth, really. Plants are primary producers, which means they can do something animals can't. Using photosynthesis, they trap the power of the sun, mix it with a little water and a few minerals, and create themselves. It's about as close as you can come to getting something from nothing. Good thing, too, since we in the animal kingdom ultimately depend on them for our food and would not exist without them. The key to photosynthesis is chlorophyll, life's magic green potion. Blood and chlorophyll have virtually the same chemical makeup, except for one important difference: at the hub of every haemoglobin molecule is an atom of iron, whereas in chlorophyll, it's magnesium.

Photosynthesis is fundamental to what is in effect a kind of planetary respiration, an elegant global symbiosis between the kingdoms of life. Plants breathe out the oxygen that we breathe in, and they breathe in the carbon dioxide that we breathe out. What's more, they help make the weather, are the foundation of our food

175

web, and are important sources of medicine and building materials. From plant's ancient fossils comes our petroleum. Without them we would perish by asphyxiation, starvation, dehydration, prostration. And, oh yes, they are beautiful to look at. To this last point, I could do no better than to add the words of naturalist Donald Culross Peattie: "True that a plant may not think; neither will the profoundest of men ever put forth a flower."[10]

The actual populations of plants and particularly trees is deceptive, however. As ubiquitous as they are overall, many individual species require very specific growing conditions and survive in quite small numbers; because of this, some have a very limited range, making them vulnerable to extinction. Nearly 1,600, or about half of all the critically endangered species on the IUCN Red List, are plants.

WOLLEMI PINE

For scientific accuracy, the landscape in the movie *Jurassic Park* might be clothed in forests of Wollemi pines. Fossil evidence suggests that 200 million years ago this wispy evergreen, with its knobby bark and fern-like spray of branches, was a dominant tree on the Gondwana supercontinent of the southern hemisphere and was eaten by many types of dinosaurs.

Until recently, Wollemi pines were thought to be extinct. Then, in 1994, while hiking in a remote gorge in Wollemi National Park north of Sydney, Australia wilderness explorer David Noble noted an unusual tree growing on a canyon ledge. Botanists soon returned to the site to confirm the identity of the tree. A species thought to be long gone wasn't. Unfortunately, there were fewer than 100 trees left, the last descendants of dinosaur-age precursors. The Wollemi pine was a living fossil hanging on by a thread.

---

10. Donald Culross Peattie, *Flowering Earth* (New York: G.P. Putnam's Sons, 1939), 4.

Growing up to 40 metres tall and with a trunk diameter of about a metre, this majestic tree is not actually a pine but a member of the ancient Araucariaceae family, which also includes the monkey puzzle tree of South America, the klinki tree of New Guinea, and the kauri of New Zealand. The famous stone logs of Arizona's petrified forest are eons-old members of the same family.

The exact location of the wild trees has been kept secret to protect them from the inevitably quick extinction that would result if collectors knew their whereabouts. Wollemi pines have also been propagated in greenhouses from the root cuttings of wild trees. These were made commercially available to the public through selected botanical gardens beginning in 2006. Proceeds from the sale of the cultivated trees help fund their conservation in the wild. It's also hoped this accessible, legal supply will reduce the value of the wild trees on the black market.

Almost all of the remaining wild trees are clones of each other (they have an identical genetic code), suggesting they passed through a population bottleneck at some point in the past when perhaps only a few individuals survived a close brush with extinction. So why is a tree that outlasted continental drift, dinosaurs, and ice ages barely hanging on now? One possibility is that because the species evolved at a time when carbon dioxide levels in the atmosphere were much higher than they are today (remember, trees need CO_2 like we need oxygen), they are now simply gasping for breath, so to speak, unable to adapt well enough to thrive in the present atmosphere. But who knows? If we continue to burn fossil fuels with abandon, maybe one day there will be enough carbon dioxide in the atmosphere for the Wollemi pine to thrive once again.

SICILIAN FIR

The Mediterranean region is a global centre of botanical diversity.

It's home to about 24,000, or 10 percent, of all vascular plant species, even though it covers less than 2 percent of the planet's surface. Half of these are endemic and are found nowhere else. Even tropical Africa, four times the size, is hard-pressed to surpass the Mediterranean's plant diversity. And a cooler region like Canada has only one-fifth as many plant species, despite being five times as big.

A 10,000-year history of human settlement and the development that entails, such as logging and agriculture, have resulted in many Mediterranean plants becoming endangered. An icon for the threatened botanical riches of the region is the endemic Sicilian fir tree. This 15-metre-tall Christmas tree–shaped species is considered the rarest tree in Europe. Just a handful survive.

At 200 people per square kilometre, the Mediterranean's largest island is densely packed with people. It's been that way for a long time. Sitting in the middle of the Mediterranean Sea, Sicily has been on important trade routes between Europe, North Africa, and Arabia for thousands of years. Few places have experienced as tumultuous a history. Greeks, Romans, Vandals, Byzantines, Arabs, Normans, Germans, French, Spanish, and Italians each ruled the island at some point over the last 3,000 years. Nature has played rough with the island, too. Earthquakes, volcanoes (Sicily's Mount Etna, Europe's largest and most active volcano, violently exploded in 1669, burying many villages under hot lava), and the bubonic plague are all part of its violent past.

When the Greeks colonized Sicily around 750 BC, they wrote that the mountains of the northwest were covered by firs. That would all change as the island's population and economy grew. After Arabs had taken control of the island in the early Middle Ages, Sicily experienced a population boom and many of its forests were cut for lumber to build houses. Later, rampant harvesting of timber for both naval and merchant shipbuilding not only depleted its forests but also resulted in severe erosion on the steep slopes of the island's mountains. It's hard for trees to grow when the soil has been washed away. Centuries of goat grazing only added to the problem. Not surprisingly, the Sicilian fir was becoming very rare. By 1900, it was thought to be extinct.

It was rediscovered in 1957, when a few trees were found in rocky soil on the slopes of the Madonie Mountains in north-central Sicily, in what today is a large regional park. Although surrounded by a 40,000-hectare protected area, a paltry 30 mature trees confined to a 100-hectare area are all that remain of the Sicilian fir in the wild.

Despite vigorous conservation efforts since the trees were discovered over five decades ago, the recovery of the population has been hampered by poor soil and rapid erosion where they grow and by the destruction of seedlings by grazing animals. To remedy this, protective stone walls have been built around individual trees to stabilize the soil, and each has been fenced to exclude grazing animals.

The number of naturally occurring seedlings produced by the firs has increased slowly in recent years, and the low genetic diversity (not unusual for such a small population) has been improved through the cross-pollination of mature trees. To determine the best locations for a future reintroduction program in the wild, nursery-grown seedlings were planted in various protected experimental plots by scientists from the University of Palermo. As well, thousands of locally produced nursery seedlings are now available to the public. Once mature, these trees will be a living seed bank to ensure the long-term survival of the species. Nurseries and botanical gardens outside Sicily have also produced inventories of seedlings.

The biggest potential threat to the Sicilian fir is global warming. Today, Sicily is facing desertification caused by hotter, drier weather and a badly eroded landscape. What's worse, the frequency of devastating wildfires on the island has been on the rise, so protecting the 30 mature firs against this menace has become an immediate priority.

VIRGINIA ROUND-LEAF BIRCH

Unlike the rocky, arid environment of the Sicilian fir's Madonie Mountains and its sparse vegetation, the moist ecosystem of the southern Appalachians of the United States boasts some of the highest tree diversity of any temperate region. This is where the first tree ever protected under the US Endangered Species Act is found.

Rediscovered in 1975 after an absence of nearly 60 years, the Virginia round-leaf birch is found along one minor creek in the southwestern corner of Virginia. A relatively small tree at about 12 metres in height, its round leaves and aromatic dark bark are unusual for a birch. It's also somewhat of an evolutionary mystery: scientists aren't sure whether it's a newly evolving species that had recently split off from a grove of similar sweet birch living nearby or the last survivor of a once-widespread species.

In 1975, there were 41 round-leaf birch, but by the early 21st century only 8 of the original wild ones remained, brought to the brink by illegal plant collecting, vandalism, cattle grazing, and competition from other vegetation. There has been a concerted effort by the US Forest Service, the state of Virginia, and independent conservationists to recover the population since it was listed as endangered in 1978. The goal was to have 500 to 1,000 trees in each of 10 self-sustaining populations. By 2003, there were close to 1,000 nursery-raised round-leaf birch saplings transplanted alongside the original 8 wild trees. On paper this looks good; however, none of the transplants has reproduced. And the last time one of the original wild trees reproduced was almost 30 years ago.

Very specific conditions must be met for the round-leaf birch to procreate in nature: the right size openings in the forest canopy above the trees (basically determining how much light they receive) must be present during the years they produce abundant seeds, which is only infrequently. In 1981–82, the planets had aligned for one particular tree and it produced 81 tiny seedlings. Things were looking up. That is, until vandals destroyed all of them.

Nevertheless, the Virginia round-leaf birch *is* better off today than it was a decade ago. Those hundreds of artificially grown trees that have been transplanted into the species' original habitat have reduced the threat of imminent extinction. This fact was recognized when it was up-listed from Endangered to the less serious Threatened category in 1994. But unless any of the last eight wild trees, or at least some of the nursery-grown saplings, can successfully reproduce, the round-leaf birch will remain rare.

On a desert island on the other side of the country, another tree lives by virtue of the US Endangered Species Act, this one with an even more precarious grip on survival.

Catalina Mahogany

It appears this tree has always been rare. When naturalist Blanche Trask first discovered it in 1897 growing in a single gully on Catalina Island, just 35 kilometres off the California coast from Los Angeles, she found only about 40 or 50 trees. The species grew nowhere else on the island. Over a century later, the mahogany's fortunes haven't improved. It is still found only in Wild Boar Gully, only now its population is in the single digits. What is remarkable is that just one new tree has been added (for a total of seven) to the population of six that existed when the species was first protected under the US Endangered Species Act in 1997.

One of the big worries for conservationists who are trying to save the Catalina mahogany is that it's hybridizing with the very closely related and much more abundant mountain mahogany. The seven endangered trees are outnumbered by its more populous cousins 10 to 1. The mountain mahogany looks poised to genetically swallow up the rarer tree. How does this work?

Species adapt to their changing environments through the continual process of natural selection through mutation. Genetic mutations usually have no real effect, and sometimes they're just plain bad, but every once in a while they are beneficial. For example, maybe a chance mutation of one or more genes results in a plant producing offspring that have slightly stronger roots. If this gives them a better chance of making it through the yearly windy season, relatively more of them will survive to pass this revised genetic code onto *their* offspring, and so on. Eventually the less fit, weak-rooted trees lacking the mutation will be replaced by the strong-rooted ones. A new species is born, an old one disappears. In time, another mutation will come along and the species will evolve again. But there's another way trees evolve: through hybridization.

The mixing of genes by breeding with a closely related, sexually compatible species is common among plants. Sometimes, whatever physical differences the genetically distinct offspring hybrid has compared with its two parent species will be beneficial. This results in a new species that out-competes both its parent species and eventually replaces them. So hybridization may end up dictating the fate of the Catalina mahogany. (Hybridizing is relatively rare among animals. When it happens, it usually results in sterile creatures such as the mule, the offspring of a horse and a donkey. There are exceptions. North America's eastern coyote, likely a recent hybrid between wolves and western coyotes, is a highly successful, fertile, and ecologically fit species.)

The dilemma is this: Should the mountain mahogany be removed from the vicinity of the endangered tree, leaving the last seven Catalina mahoganies to struggle on their own (something they're apparently not very good at)? Or, should the two species be allowed to mix their genes and create a completely new species? With hybridization, the Catalina mahogany will at least have some of its genes survive, enfolded into the genetic code of the mountain mahogany.

Though few other trees can claim to be as rare as either the Catalina mahogany or the round-leaf birch, three of them are found on one tiny island in the South Atlantic.

THE SHE-CABBAGE, HE-CABBAGE, AND EBONY TREES OF ST. HELENA

Most oceanic islands have never been part of a continental land mass. Instead, they are usually formed when an underwater volcano emerges from the sea. The ones that have been around for millions of years can be real factories of evolution. What they usually lack in land mammals, reptiles, amphibians, and often trees they make up for with birds, bats, and flying insects, along with plants with light-weight or salt-resistant seeds. All of these island-dwelling organisms have one thing in common: they've made it across open ocean from the mainland.

Such arrivals find empty niches on newly formed islands and over time evolve to fit them, creating new species. Unlike organisms living on continents that tend to have widespread populations, those on islands have much smaller ranges, so they are much more impacted by local human activities. This is why so many living things on islands are endangered.

Few islands fit this principle better than St. Helena, a British territory since the 1600s. A mountainous island of volcanic origin, it is located in the middle of the tropical South Atlantic, 2,000 kilometres from Africa. There are few places on earth more remote. Pondering what this seclusion meant for the biodiversity of the island, biologist E.O. Wilson wrote: "St. Helena was nearly a closed ecosystem, a biosphere functioning in great isolation, one step removed from a satellite colony in space."[11]

Aware of the near impossibility of escape, England took advantage of St. Helena's far-flung location by exiling Napoleon there in 1815, the Zulu king Dinizulu in 1890, and 6,000 Boer prisoners in the early 1900s. No longer in the exile business, today about 4,000 Saints, as they are known, make the island home.

St. Helena's human history is surpassed by its natural history. Many remarkable endemic species, from the beautiful to the bizarre, inhabit its 122 square kilometres. Take the St. Helena giant earwig. At eight centimetres long, it's the world's largest earwig and just one of 200 insects and other invertebrates on St. Helena that are found nowhere else on the planet. The wirebird—named for its skinny legs—is a species of plover exclusive to the island, and the national bird. The bug and the bird are critically endangered; the earwig hasn't been seen in decades and may already be extinct, while just a few hundred wirebirds survive. That said, St. Helena is especially well endowed with endangered botanical riches. Thirty-six of its plant species are found nowhere else.

Overgrazing by goats first introduced to the island in the early 1500s, the logging of native forests, and the introduction of alien plants over centuries of human occupation have decimated the once spectacular botanical life of St. Helena. Several species are already extinct: the dwarf ebony, the St. Helena heliotrope, and the St. Helena olive, to name a few. The bastard gumwood is down to

---

11. E.O. Wilson, *The Diversity of Life* (New York: W.W. Norton, 1993), 104.

one known individual. And much of the rest of the island's plant biodiversity hangs on by a thread.

She-Cabbage Tree

Free from competition with larger shrubs and trees, plants of the aster family (also called the sunflower or daisy family) have evolved into what are essentially "tree flowers" on St. Helena. This is exactly what the curiously named she-cabbage tree and he-cabbage tree are. In essence giant flowers, they're among the most endangered plant species anywhere.

The she-cabbage tree is named for its large smooth leaves, as opposed to the hairy he-cabbage. Like a long-stemmed flower, a slender, branchless trunk is topped by a clump of leaves and rosettes during one stage of its life cycle. Growing to only about seven metres tall, the once common tree was logged for its straight trunks, which were used for building houses. Invasive plants and the clearing of forest for pasture also took a toll.

The she-cabbage was thought to be extinct until 1976, when three mature trees were discovered along with a few seedlings on a high ridge. Another group was later found some distance away. These two subpopulations are considered to be genetically isolated—they're far enough apart that they can't reproductively mix under natural conditions. As a result, their ability to adapt to changing environmental conditions, pests, or disease may be compromised by what amounts to inbreeding within each separate population.

The she-cabbage isn't alone in its struggle to survive: once covered by lush tropical forests, today only about 10 percent of St. Helena is covered by trees. Now there are just a few wild she-cabbages left, all of them mature or in old age. Even nursery-raised trees cultivated to conserve the species number fewer than 50. Because it is so short-lived and enough new trees aren't growing in the wild to replace older ones, it's feared the she-cabbage could soon become extinct.

HE-CABBAGE TREE

Despite its similar name and similar appearance to the she-cabbage tree, the he-cabbage tree is a surprisingly distant relative and belongs to a different genus.

Found at the highest elevations of St. Helena, in Diana's Peak National Park and on High Peak, the he-cabbage tree was probably never common. An already scant population of fewer than 100 in the 1990s has shrunken even further due to a deadly infestation of moth larvae and competition from introduced plants. To stem this decline, invasive species such as New Zealand flax have been cleared from the tree's habitat, and between 100 and 200 cultivated he-cabbage seedlings were reintroduced in Diana's Peak National Park. Many of these have survived, but none is yet mature enough to produce seeds of their own. Despite these efforts at recovery, the population is very small and its habitat fragmented. Moreover, the percentage of viable seeds is low (many simply refuse to sprout), limiting the number of seedlings available for repopulation. Today, there are estimated to be fewer than 50 wild mature trees surviving on the island.

ST. HELENA EBONY

Once the dominant species on parts of the island, the St. Helena ebony was thought to be extinct for over a century. In 1980, two of them were discovered literally clinging to life on the face of a cliff near a geologic formation known as the Asses Ears. The ebonies survived because they were out of reach of the hungry goats that had wiped out the rest of their kind, along with many other botanical treasures. Two of the ebony's close relatives weren't so lucky: the St. Helena dwarf ebony is extinct, and the St. Helena redwood is extinct in the wild.

A member of the mallow family of flowers, the St. Helena ebony was historically described as a small tree of about five metres in height. The surviving wild plants, however (the only ones known in modern times), hug the ground as low bushes, its long branches covered in heart-shaped dark green leaves. Up to three beautiful white and purple flowers can bloom on the tree at any time of year if there's enough rain. The St. Helena ebony's wood is very dark, very hard, and very dense—so much so that it doesn't float, not unlike the commercially exploited, though unrelated mainland ebony. Demand for its fine wood helped push the island species toward extinction.

Although no additional wild plants have been found since the rediscovery of the species three decades ago, thousands of seedlings grown from root cuttings of the two survivors have been reintroduced to various wild sites on the island, as well as in local gardens. Nevertheless, because of the way these seedlings have been produced from cuttings, they are all identical clones of the two wild trees and are subject to the same problem that comes up again and again with tiny remnant populations: inbreeding. Such limited genetic diversity could result in susceptibility to diseases and pests in the future. To tackle this, scientists from Kew Gardens in the United Kingdom—also active in several other conservation projects on the island—are working with conservationists on St. Helena to develop seedlings with more genetic diversity. Seed banks are also being developed both on and off the island to ensure that the wild genes of the species will be available for future reintroductions.

NORFOLK ISLAND'S PHREATIA ORCHID AND PHILLIP ISLAND WHEATGRASS

Although on the opposite side of the planet, Norfolk Island, like St. Helena, is an extinct volcano hosting a number of extremely rare, endangered plant species. The small 35-square-kilometre Pacific island, lying between Australia, New Zealand, and New Caledonia, is best known for its most famous export, the distinctive Norfolk pine, a species occurring naturally nowhere else.

With its classic Christmas tree shape and wispy fronds, this beautiful evergreen was long ago cultivated and has been introduced to warmer coastal areas around the world. It's a close relative to the rare Wollemi pine of Australia. The Norfolk pine isn't the only unique evolutionary product of the island, though. An auspicious combination of climate, terrain, soil conditions, and isolation from other terra firma has blessed Norfolk with a diversity of endemic life. It is home to 15 species or subspecies of birds that are exclusive to the island (6 of which have already become extinct in modern times, including most recently the white-chested white-eye, a beautiful green and white warbler-like songbird, which hasn't been officially recorded in decades). But it is Norfolk's vegetation that is especially varied and fragile. Nearly 50 plant species grow here that are found nowhere else. About one-fifth of them have total populations in the wild of fewer than 50 individuals, making it one of the most endangered botanical assemblages in the world. The trouble is habitat destruction and invasive species—a familiar refrain on many of the world's far-flung oceanic islands.

NORFOLK ISLAND PHREATIA ORCHID

The Norfolk Island Phreatia orchid is the rarest of the world's 22,000 or so members of the family Orchidaceae living in the wild. Only five plants survive, all within the island's national park. These few tiny orchids eke out a life in Norfolk's last fragment of natural rainforest, which covers only about 500 hectares. Phreatia grow on the branches of trees as epiphytes, or air plants, where they take their water and nutrients from the air. It's a common lifestyle among tropical plants: about 24,000 species of the earth's plants are epiphytes. *Phreatia limenophylax* are only about five centimetres tall, with two-centimetre-long clusters of tiny greenish-white flowers; they're not the flashy, vividly coloured orchids we normally think of. Whether it was ever abundant isn't known, but it's a good bet the flower is so exceedingly rare today largely because of the destruction of 90 percent of the island's natural forest for farming and grazing, and for materials to build houses.

Living within the national park, the phreatia is well protected from direct human disturbance. Nevertheless, its tiny population makes it highly vulnerable to extinction. A disease or an unusually severe windstorm could take out the last five orchids in one fell swoop. As well, invasive plant species competing with the native trees on whose branches the orchid grows could have an impact on whether its population will increase. As insurance, the Norfolk Island Botanic Gardens stores *Phreatia limenophylax* seeds and is working on artificially propagating the plants. As well, there are ongoing efforts to identify and control invasive plant species, critical not only for the survival of the orchid but also for the world's most endangered grass, which lives on a little island just off Norfolk.

PHILLIP ISLAND WHEATGRASS

Of all the plants on earth, none is more ubiquitous than the grasses. From the equatorial rainforest to beneath shallow seas, from the high Arctic to the Antarctic (where only one native species grows, using a special protein to keep it from freezing), members of the 10,000-strong Poaceae family are everywhere. One grass must necessarily be the rarest, and given the perilous state of the Norfolk Island Archipelago's native vegetation, it isn't surprising that it's found here, on a tiny island six kilometres south of Norfolk.

Formerly covered by luxuriant vegetation, Phillip Island's 190-hectare ecosystem was rendered a treeless lump of volcanic basalt with little vegetation and heavy erosion by pigs, goats, and rabbits introduced when it was a penal colony during the 18th and 19th centuries. The removal of the pigs and goats in the early 20th century and finally the rabbits in 1988 allowed the island to undergo some natural regeneration of its flora. But for the Phillip Island wheatgrass, it was almost too late. This tufted, metre-tall perennial grass was thought to be extinct on the island until a handful of individual plants were discovered in the late 1980s living on cliff faces, where they had been inaccessible to the hungry introduced grazers of the past. Today, fewer than 50 Phillip Island wheatgrass plants survive here, with a small handful on Norfolk Island and another few dozen living about 1,000 kilometres away on Lord Howe Island.

Although the grass remains rare, Phillip Island has experienced a green renaissance. Many native plant species have made a comeback since the grazers have been removed. The island is also being reforested with Norfolk pines. This is not all good news for the Phillip Island wheatgrass subspecies, however. Improving growing conditions have also made it easier for non-native invasive species to become established, including kikuyu grass and buffalo grass, aggressive colonizers that compete with the native grasses for the best growing areas. Nevertheless, revegetation to prevent erosion and weed control are part of a continuing program to help the recovery of not only Phillip Island's endangered grass but its entire natural ecosystem.

PART TWO

LIVING BY THE GRACE OF HUMANITY: GONE FROM THE WILD BUT NOT EXTINCT

There's a truism that says "extinction is forever." You can't argue with that. But, as you'll soon see, extinction *in the wild* is not necessarily for all eternity. There are a few living things that have been erased from the natural world completely, with populations of zero in the wild, that still survive in small numbers under our captive care in zoos, aviaries, botanical gardens, laboratories, and breeding facilities, and within protective fenced-in habitat enclosures; they're like intensive care units for nature. And like a proper ICU, species or "patients" are given whatever acute attention they need to survive in the short term, while improving their situation enough so they can completely heal on their own after leaving. The primary goal of such *ex situ* (Latin for "out of place") species conservation is to increase their typically tiny populations back to some semblance of health, for future reintroductions back into the wild. And therein lies an even bigger challenge: there has to actually *be* a wild to return them to, a natural place where they can sustain themselves indefinitely, without our help. So protecting or restoring habitats is also critical for success.

Northern White Rhinoceros

The northern white rhinoceros, a subspecies of the white rhinoceros, once lived across much of central Africa. Its former range reads like a who's who of war-torn countries: Uganda, Chad, Sudan, the Central African Republic, and the Democratic Republic of the Congo all hosted populations of the animal in the past. It's an irresistible target: two tonnes of meat on the hoof sporting a horn practically worth its weight in gold living in countries saturated with firearms on a continent suffering widespread hunger. The outcome is painfully predictable. In 1960, there were 2,000 northern white rhinos left in the wild. Today, there are none. The last few animals, which survived in Garamba National Park in the Democratic Republic of the Congo, were gone by 2007. There was a report of three northern white rhinos in southern Sudan in 2008; though encouraging, it was unconfirmed. What's surprising is that the northern white rhino lasted as long as it did.

The Dutch first named the animal the "widje" rhinoceros, not for its colour but for its wide, square snout that is adapted for grazing. Misinterpreted, the English "white" has stuck. Surpassed in size only by the elephant and the hippopotamus, the white rhinoceros can weigh over 2,000 kilograms, reach almost two metres tall at the shoulder, and measure four metres in length. Northern white rhinos can live up to 40 years in the wild; in a healthy, secure habitat, they can enjoy a natural population growth of 7 to 9 percent per annum. The "Last Chance for Survival" project involves Fauna and Flora International, the Dvur Kralove Zoo in the Czech Republic, Back to Africa, the Lewa Wildlife Conservancy, Ol Pejeta Conservancy, and the Kenya Wildlife Service.

The entire global population of northern white rhinos is fewer than 10 captive animals, 4 living in the Ol Pejeta Conservancy in

Kenya, 1 remaining in the Dvur Kralove Zoo, and 2 at the San Diego Zoo's Wild Animal Park.

In December 2009, two male and two female northern white rhinos from Dvur Kralove Zoo were sent back home to Africa to try to save the subspecies. Travelling by air and road, on December 20 the travel-weary foursome arrived at their destination: Ol Pejeta Conservancy in Kenya, a wildlife conservation facility run by an organization that has already had success bringing back the endangered black rhinoceros.

Straddling the equator in the wild Aberdare Range of Kenya, Ol Pejeta is a healthy 360-square-kilometre patchwork of natural grassland, wooded plains, acacia scrub, and evergreen thicket. It is already home to elephants, giraffes, lions, black rhinos, and even some southern white rhinos—all well secured against poachers by guards and an electrified perimeter fence: heaven if ever there was one for the endangered northern white rhinoceros. Although technically they are still captive animals, it is hoped the natural surroundings in Africa will encourage more typical social and territorial behaviour (zoo animals rarely behave like those in the wild). The ultimate goal is to induce them to breed, something they've done little of in captivity: the last baby northern white rhino was born way back in 2000 at Dvur Kralove Zoo.

Though still early days, so far it appears the precious population of four northern white rhinos is doing quite well getting accustomed to a progressively more natural environment as the size of their enclosures are gradually increased. And there's more good news: in early 2011, the youngest male and female of the four have been showing real amorous interest in one another and may be close to mating. When and if they do, and if they produce a baby rhino, it will be a small first step in reaching the goal of reintroducing northern white rhinos into the wilds of central Africa within 20 years.

Success in bringing rhinos back is not without precedent. Happily, the closest living relative of the northern white rhino, the southern white rhino, has enjoyed a renaissance; through aggressive conservation, its numbers now approach 20,000, up from a low of fewer than 30 animals at the end of the 19th century. And further encouragement can also be found in the success of other large mammal species. Not far away in northern Africa, there has been a slow but steady resurgence of the scimitar-horned oryx, another currently extinct-in-the-wild hoofed animal. Will the northern white rhino follow suit? Never say never.

SCIMITAR-HORNED ORYX

The scimitar-horned oryx, with its white, muscular, horse-like body and tail and metre-long pointed horns (which can look like a single horn when viewed in profile) prompted Aristotle and Pliny the Elder to wonder whether it was the prototype for the unicorn. Tragically, since becoming extinct in the wild at the end of the 20th century, the sight of this antelope running wild today would be as much a figment of the imagination as would be a glimpse of the mythical horned horse itself.

Of course, it wasn't always this way. The scimitar-horned oryx is thought to have once been abundant across North Africa, with a million or more animals ranging from Tunisia south to Nigeria and from Mali east to Sudan. Living in semi-arid grasslands, acacia woodland, and rocky hillsides at the edge of the blistering hot Sahara desert, the oryx was superbly adapted to a bone-dry existence. To conserve water, this large 200-kilogram antelope raises its body temperature to nearly 47 degrees Celsius (that's 10 degrees higher than ours) to reduce its loss to sweating. It can also go without drinking water for up to eight or nine months, getting whatever meagre moisture it needs from a diet of grasses, herbs, roots, and buds. Its nearly white body reflects the heat of the intense desert sun, and specialized kidneys greatly limit urine production, keeping water inside where it's needed.

Each year, a wet season to the north beckoned and the oryx migrated, returning south again when it was over. Through most of the year they lived in herds of up to 40 animals, but during migration large congregations of 1,000 or more oryx were observed. This wouldn't last. The Sahara became hotter and drier and began to spread, reducing the scimitar-horned oryx's habitat and food supply and splitting the animals into smaller populations that moved into areas with enough forage.

Oryx in the northern part of their range were pretty much wiped out before the 20th century, owing mainly to overhunting. The southern population was able to hang on longer in sparsely populated parts of Chad and Niger, but even they were for the most part gone by the late 1980s—again victims of hunting. Just a handful survived out on the land. By 2000, the scimitar-horned oryx was listed extinct in the wild on the IUCN Red List. Although there have been occasional reports of the species in Chad and Niger since then, their presence has never been confirmed, despite intensive surveys.

It may be gone in the wild, but all is not lost for the scimitar-horned oryx. Today, there is a healthy population of over 1,500 captive animals in scientifically managed breeding programs around the world, largely the descendents of animals captured in earlier decades for zoos and private collections. They have become the gene bank from which a reintroduced wild population might one day emerge. Some of the biggest progress toward reintroducing the species into the wild has been made in Tunisia, close to where Pliny the Elder set up some of the first wildlife hunting reserves in the world about 2,000 years ago. It's also one of the earliest locations where the oryx was wiped out, in 1910. Within an 8,000-hectare fenced area in Tunisia's Dghoumes National Park, a small herd of scimitar-horned oryx, as well as endangered dorcas gazelles and Addax antelopes, are thriving in a semi-wild environment. In 2007, 17 of the oryx were released into this enormous compound. Eight were from another small Tunisian park. The other 9 were from US, French, and Irish captive herds specially chosen because of their distinct genetic lineage compared with the oryx already living in Tunisia. This step was taken to increase the overall genetic diversity of the Dghoumes animals, giving them a better chance at survival. The semi-wild reintroduction (they are still fenced-in) seems to be paying off. By early 2009, the original population of 17 had increased to 29 with the birth of a dozen baby oryx.

Once a viable, self-sustaining population is established, the goal is to someday remove the fences and let them range free and become migratory again. Similar programs for semi-wild, enclosed oryx populations are planned or are underway in Senegal, Morocco, Algeria, and Niger, all with an eye to the eventual release of the animals into the wild.

Perhaps one day the scimitar-horned oryx will once again range across North Africa, inspiring a whole new era of unicorn sightings.

MILU (PÈRE DAVID'S DEER)

If the oryx is a symbol of beauty and grace in the animal world (and how could a creature that inspired the unicorn be anything but?), the milu appears to be the archetype of improvisation. It has a long neck like a camel, cow-like hooves, the tufted tail of a donkey, and the antlers of a stag. This seemingly odd amalgam of four species was known to the Chinese as *sze pu shiang,* which means "none of the four." The sze pu shiang, or milu, is indeed an unusual deer. Living

in reedy, marshy areas, it loves to swim and frolic in the water, sometimes spending hours wading up to its shoulders. In summer its coat
is a rich ochre-red, and males carry spectacular, large antlers. Like
other members of the deer family, milu are social herding animals,
making them a prime hunting target for Chinese people throughout the centuries. This, combined with the destruction of its coastal
habitat, had the species sliding toward extinction by the 19th century.

While the wild population plummeted in the 1800s, a protected
herd thrived in the Nanyuang Royal Hunting Garden in Beijing (at
the time known as Peking). This enclosed 200-square-kilometre
reserve of wetlands surrounding the Yongding River was sealed off
from the outside world by a 70-kilometre-long wall. It had been
heavily guarded since it was built during the Yuan Dynasty in the
13th and 14th centuries. The public was never allowed access.

Enter Père Armand David, a French missionary and naturalist
who would eventually discover the giant panda and some 60 other
mammal species in China. Living in Beijing during Tongzhi's reign
as emperor in the mid-19th century, Père David likely passed the
walls of the forbidden royal hunting reserve many times before his
curiosity got the better of him. One day he finally persuaded the
guards to let him take a quick look over the barricade. He didn't
know it at the time, but this would end up being "the peek that
saved a species," for at just that moment, a herd of odd-looking,
unfamiliar deer walked by.

After much effort, Père David later got permission to take the skins
of two already slain deer back to Paris with him, where they were
subsequently described and named *Elaphurus davidianus* in his honour. Soon, the French government petitioned the Chinese emperor
to allow some live deer to be taken back to Paris. Eventually, a few
animals were sent to France, and later to England and Germany. The
deer thrived in their new European environments and reproduced

well. It's a good thing, too: during heavy rains in 1895, the Yongding River, which flowed through the royal deer sanctuary, burst its banks and destroyed part of the wall, allowing all but 20 to 30 of the deer to escape. All the escapees were soon killed and eaten by hungry peasants. To make matters worse, just a few years later, foreign troops occupying the park during the Boxer Rebellion (when the Righteous Fists of Harmony nationalists fought to banish Western influence from a China ruled by the waning Qing Dynasty) killed and ate the remaining deer. That left just a few tiny wild herds near the Yellow Sea, in eastern China. By 1939, the last of these were shot, making the milu extinct in the wild.

However, because of Père David's fortuitous peek over the wall and the subsequent European interest in the species, the story continued for what is now also known as Père David's deer. The news of the Boxer Rebellion slaughter prompted European zoos to pool their breeding deer at the vast English estate of Woburn Abbey. Here, the last milu in the world, a total of 18 animals, of which only 11 were able to breed, were assembled in the hope of saving the species. By the end of World War II, there were about 300 deer. Since then, as its population continued to increase, milu have been distributed to zoos around the world. In 1956, several were sent home, in a sense, to the Beijing Zoo. A few decades later, in 1985 and 1987, a total of 38 milu were flown to the Chinese capital to live in a new 60-hectare reserve located in an area that was once part of the Nanyuang Royal Hunting Garden, bringing the species full circle. At about the same time, a herd of nearly 40 animals was sent from the United Kingdom to a marshy coastal area near the Yellow Sea called the Dafeng Milu National Natural Reserve.

Today, over 1,500 of the deer live in Dafeng, and more than 50 herds have been established elsewhere throughout China. Most of the herds are very small, with just a handful of animals, but the species continues to show its resilience and reproduces well. None is yet considered wild, since all remain under captive management. Despite a current population of over 2,000 animals, genetic diversity remains worryingly low, leaving the deer vulnerable to disease. A major conservation priority is to improve the gene flow among the disparate populations of the species to avoid a further loss of genetic diversity.

With over 1.3 billion people, good wildlife habitat is hard to come by in China, especially in the traditional range of the milu near the Yellow Sea, so the Dafeng Milu reserve is critical. There is a strong sense of hope for the long-term survival of the deer.

ALAGOAS CURASSOW

Before it was connected to North America by the Isthmus of Panama about three million years ago, South America was a giant island separated from the rest of the world's land masses. Since breaking off the supercontinent Gondwana 130 million years earlier, its species were on their own to evolve in isolation. Combine this with its huge area (much of it equatorial) and its varied terrain and you have the richest variety of living things anywhere on the planet. For instance, nearly a third of the world's 10,000 or so bird species live in South America. There is a price to be paid for such great biodiversity, however: many individual species have small populations or small geographical ranges. The Alagoas curassow has both.

One of the earliest South American species to be described by science, the Alagoas curassow was first noted by the German naturalist Georg Marggraf in 1648 in northeastern Brazil in what was then a Dutch colony. As one of the pioneers of South American natural history, Marggraf would eventually record hundreds of species new to science. As a testament to its rarity, the Alagoas curassow wasn't seen again for over 300 years, until it was rediscovered in

1951. It then proceeded to disappear for another two decades, until the mid-1970s, when it resurfaced. In the late 1970s, several birds were taken from the wild to establish a captive breeding program as insurance against extinction. Only a few years later, there were an estimated 60 left in the wild.

A large, somewhat turkey-like ground-dwelling bird with a long tail, the Alagoas curassow grows nearly a metre long and lived in lowland Atlantic forest of Alagoas and Pernambuco States of Brazil. Its mostly black plumage with a purplish sheen is contrasted by its red legs, feet, and bill. The bird ate a diet of fruit and (judging from its habits in captivity) nested on the ground, where it likely laid two or three eggs. Owing to its rarity, little else is known about its ecology.

Two things caused the Alagoas curassow to disappear from the wild. By the late 1960s, rampant habitat destruction of its lowland forest and overhunting brought the species to its knees. Despite being well aware of the bird's perilous predicament, in the 1970s the Brazilian government sanctioned the destruction of most of the large forest remnants left in Alagoas State. This was done as part of a program to plant sugar cane to be used in the production of ethanol (an early precedent of the dangerous push to biofuels promoted by many governments today). Most of its forest destroyed, the bird ended up living in tiny slivers of habitat that were easily accessed by poachers, who simply finished the job begun by the loggers. By the late 1980s, the Alagoas curassow was pretty much history. It appeared on the IUCN Red List as being extinct in the wild for the first time in 1994.

The last hope for the species is a small population of around 100 captive birds, divided between two facilities in Brazil. Only a few genetically pure Alagoas curassows are left, and they are kept separate from the remaining captive population, most of which are hybrids with more common razor-billed curassows. The goal is to try to increase the number of purebred birds through scientific breeding with an eye to reintroducing them in the wild someday, while keeping the hybrid birds as a backup in case something goes horribly wrong with the "true" Alagoas curassows. Although there is little in the way of suitable habitat left in the wild for the birds, conservationists have nevertheless found a few relatively large fragments that might be suitable for future reintroductions.

SPIX'S MACAW

In the neighbouring northern Brazilian state of Bahia, just across the border from the erstwhile home of the Alagoas curassow, the Spix's macaw sits atop the list of the world's most endangered parrots.

The 17 macaw species of South and Central America are the giants of the parrot family, the largest of which, the hyacinth macaw, reaches a metre in length. There were once five species spread across the Caribbean as well, but they're extinct now. Among the most intelligent of all birds, macaws have a remarkable ability to mimic sounds and can manipulate fine objects with their dexterous feet. They form small social groups of 10 to 30 birds, which move noisily through their forested habitats searching for fruit. They are spectacularly beautiful birds with vividly coloured plumage, long tails, and big powerful beaks for breaking open seeds. Macaws are the iconic parrots and pay a dear price for it. In high demand by collectors, wild-caught specimens are a favoured commodity of the illegal worldwide bird trade, some species commanding prices in the tens of thousands of dollars on the black market. Unfortunately, conviction under laws such as the Convention on International Trade in Endangered Species seems to be worth the risk to local criminals, who can make a year's wages by capturing and selling a few rare macaws. This illegal activity has had a huge impact on the macaw population. Today, seven species, or 40 percent of the family, is endangered. At the top of the list is Spix's macaw.

Spix's macaw was first discovered in 1817 by German naturalist Johann von Spix in semi-arid forest known as caatinga woodland in Bahia. It wasn't until 1854, however, that the bird was assigned its current scientific name, by none other than Napoleon's nephew, naturalist Prince Bonaparte.

Growing up to 57 centimetres in length, this medium-sized macaw has a blue-grey body with bright blue wings and tail. Its blue-grey head sports a heavy black bill and a charcoal-grey skin patch around the eye. Probably always somewhat rare, Spix's macaw was considered extinct by 1938. Decades later, in 1985, three of the birds were found by biologists in the same area where Johann von Spix discovered it over a century and a half earlier. In the blink of an eye, Spix's macaw went from apparent extinction to critically endangered. Because very little had been learned about the species in the 168 years since it was first discovered, these birds were closely observed to ensure their survival and learn about their biology. There was a lot of catching up to do.

Spix's macaws live in open, dry woodland near rivers and streams dominated by caraiba trees, whose cavities they use for nesting. The female lays two to three eggs and incubates them for about four weeks, all the while taking food brought to her by her mate. Males continue to feed the mother and chicks once the eggs have hatched. Most of their diet consists of the fruit of just two local plant species. This pretty much sums up what has been learned about the lives of Spix's macaws in the wild. However, careful observation of the trio of macaws couldn't save them: they disappeared a few years after their discovery, possibly victims of poachers.

Another Spix's macaw wasn't seen in the wild until 1990, when a lone male turned up. He was dubbed by the media as "the loneliest bird in the world." Oddly enough, he was paired with a female blue-winged macaw, a closely related species, so amorous urges apparently hadn't diminished. Of course, it was an unproductive pairing: the two separate species couldn't successfully breed. Five years later, a captive female Spix's macaw was released in the male's territory as a potential mate. The two birds took a liking to one another and apparently paired up. It was to be a short romance: the female disappeared several weeks later, the victim of a suspected power-line collision. Alone again, the male then rekindled his Platonic relationship with the female blue-winged macaw. He was last seen in late 2000. He was the last of his kind ever seen in the wild. You can blame habitat destruction and the illegal bird trade. Africanized bees may have also played a small role, since the aggressive insects compete for the tree cavities that macaws nest in and will swarm the birds.

Because not all of its potential habitat has been surveyed, Spix's macaw is listed as critically endangered on the IUCN Red List, though the odds are strong that it is now extinct in the wild. There have been occasional unconfirmed sightings of the bird, particularly in the Serra da Capivara National Park, not far from where the last male was seen in 2000. This national park has a considerable area of caatinga dry scrub habitat that Spix's macaws are known to inhabit. It also happens to be the location of one of the earliest human settlements in South America at 25,000 years old. Despite such reports, doubt nevertheless remains that the bird survives in the wild there.

The fate of the species comes down to the success or failure of a captive breeding program. In 2010, the official number of birds in captivity stood in the seventies, most of them located in the Middle East at the state-of-the-art Al Wabra Wildlife Preservation in Qatar, while the remaining ones are divided among facilities in Brazil, Canary Islands, and Germany. The 20-year recovery plan for the species—out to 2030—hinges on a continued increase in the number of captive birds and the securing of suitable native habitat in

Brazil. The gradual release of birds back into the wild will eventually follow. Gathering more complete scientific knowledge of Spix's macaw and continuing to educate local communities about the endangered bird are important steps in the recovery. Happily, about 2,800 hectares of habitat have recently been acquired in two parcels in the last known stronghold of the bird, near Curaçá, Bahia State.

A hemisphere away, the Hawaiian crow also has a tiny population numbering in the seventies that is hanging onto existence by a thread.

HAWAIIAN CROW ('ALALA)

At one point, there was no place quite like Hawaii for crows. Fossil evidence shows that, over time, these large black songbirds evolved into separate habitat niches across the small archipelago, ultimately producing at least five species in a blossoming of adaptation nearly rivalling that of Darwin's Galapagos finches. Like the finches, each of these crows had a specialized bill adapted for a specialized feeding niche. Given the islands' small area of only 28,000 square kilometres (nearly identical to Massachusetts), the diversity of crows was remarkable. By comparison, the entire North American continent today has only six species of crows and ravens.

Unfortunately, the arrival of humans in Hawaii 1,500 years ago marked the beginning of the end of this flourishing diversity. It isn't known exactly what happened to the archipelago's crows, but by the time Europeans arrived in the late 1700s, there was only one species left, the 'alala.

One of Hawaiian culture's most sacred animals, the 'alala is believed to escort the dead to the afterlife. By the mid-20th century, it was well on its way there itself, surviving only in very small numbers in cloud forest on the slopes of the Mauna Loa volcano on the big island of Hawaii. Why the species' population dwindled so drastically isn't known, but diseases such as avian malaria and fowlpox are the likely suspects.

By the mid-1970s, with the 'alala approaching imminent extinction, biologists captured some of the last wild birds to begin a captive breeding program. Early on, the program had little success, producing few new birds. Also not helping the beleaguered crow's cause was an ill-conceived project in the late 1970s by biologists to learn more about the breeding and nesting behaviour of the species. Thinking it might help them solve the puzzle of its decline and better manage its recovery, they set up time-lapse movie cameras at several of the remaining 'alala nests to film them during their breeding season.

Any long-term intrusion into the private lives of wild species, especially endangered ones, is a risky business that should demand sober second thought before undertaking. Despite strong anecdotal evidence that the birds abandon their nests when closely observed, and an earlier case where a remote camera at a nest resulted in a nesting failure, the project went ahead. As it turns out, those red flags should have been heeded. Eleven pairs of nesting birds were filmed and, sure enough, several of the nests were abandoned. Only about 20 'alala were left in the wild by the time the study ended in 1980. Whether the film cameras' proximity to the nests and their noise were responsible for the nesting failures will never be known, but it seems a safe bet. Ultimately, it may have made no difference to the fate of the crow, but the lesson taken from the failed experiment is: Sometimes the road to oblivion is paved by good intentions. Conservationists are human, and occasionally in their haste to help, they do more harm than good.

A dozen years passed, and in 1992 there were only 11 'alala left in the wild. At this point, biologists wanted to capture some of those last few wild birds and place them in the captive breeding program.

Did the birds stand a better chance out in nature, or in captivity? It was both a scientific and a moral dilemma. The scientists already knew that the current captive breeding program, in place since the 1970s, didn't work very well (by 1992, only six birds born in captivity survived—not much to show for 16 years of work), but on the other hand, how could they stand by and possibly let the bird go extinct in the wild by letting nature took its course? As it turns out, they didn't have to decide.

Because the 'alala is on the endangered species list, and the US Fish and Wildlife Service was desperate to find a way to save the it, the service asked the independent Washington, DC–based National Research Council Board on Biology to make suggestions on what should be done. The board recommended not capturing the wild birds. Instead, they suggested removing their eggs and artificially hatching them in a better-staffed and better-funded breeding program. They would then be released back into the wild when they were old enough. Part of the plan was that once their first clutch of eggs were removed and artificially reared in captivity, the wild birds would lay a second clutch, thus doubling their reproductive output. (This approach was nothing new; it is similar to the technique used in the recovery of the endangered Chatham Island black robin and the California condor.) And it almost worked for the 'alala. By 1999, this new approach had added over 40 captive-hatched birds. Twenty-seven of them were released into the wild. All but 6 eventually perished because of poor habitat, disease, or predation by Hawaiian hawks. The rest of the introduced birds were recaptured. That was the end of the program. The recovery of the 'alala was proving intractable, despite best efforts.

By 2002, the last two 'alala in the wild, a mated pair, died, making the bird extinct in the wild. Not all is lost, however. In 2009, the US Fish and Wildlife Service announced plans to restore the 'alala back into the wild one day, primarily by protecting and improving habitat and by controlling threats to the species. By late 2010, owing to a lot of time and effort put in to a new and improved breeding program, the captive population of the 'alala stood at 77 birds. It is a move in the right direction for the eventual rewilding of this intelligent bird.

Guam Rail Ko'ko'

Like the 'alala of Hawaii, the Guam rail is protected under the US Endangered Species Act by virtue of Guam's status as a territory of the United States. Also known as the ko'ko' in the local Chammoro language, the rail is a small, chicken-like bird that was once so abundant on the small tropical island in the South Pacific that it was widely hunted for food with little impact on its population. Even as recently as the late 1960s, there may have been 10,000 of them left. Tragically, the Guam rail has nearly been done in by the same thing that wiped out the Mariana fruit dove, the Guam flycatcher, the rufous fantail, the cardinal honeyeater, the white-throated ground dove, the nightingale reed-warbler, and not quite yet the Mariana crow. That thing is *Boiga irregularis,* a native of mainland Australasia. The brown tree snake, a voracious, invasive species, first arrived in southern Guam hidden in ships' cargo. From there, it pushed its way north across the island. An efficient climber, it devastated bird nestlings and eggs not only on the ground but also up in the trees, leaving big holes in the avian ecosystem in its wake. It's not surprising Guam's forest birds had little defence against the marauder: until *Boiga irregularis* arrived in the mid-20th century, they had never seen a predatory snake.

By the early 1980s, there were only a handful of ko'ko's left. In 1983, a captive breeding program was begun, spearheaded by a Guam biologist named Bob Beck. Twenty-one birds were taken into captivity; the future of the species would depend on them. They were captured just in time, for just two years later, in 1985, the last wild-living rail was collected on Guam's Andersen Air Force Base. With that, the ko'ko' became extinct in the wild.

Rails are a group of birds that generally live in wetlands or grassy areas. The phrase "skinny as a rail" is in reference to the birds' narrow stature, which enables them to navigate among the tightly bunched reeds and grasses of their native habitats. The ko'ko' is a medium-sized ground-dwelling bird, about the size of a bantam chicken, with a brown head and neck and a black belly with bold white barring. Its eyes are a brilliant red. Although they are essentially flightless, ko'ko's are very quick runners; they were often seen early in the morning scurrying into the tall grass along roads, where they were feeding on a diet of insects, snails, geckos, skinks, and seeds. The rails were once abundant enough to be an annoyance to some people, as many of the birds would noisily chime in on a repetitive chorus of *kee-you, kee-you;* usually one bird would begin with an alarm call, only to trigger others within earshot. A year-round breeder, it generally lays between two and four speckled eggs in a shallow cup woven of grass and leaves. The downy chicks leave the nest after just one day, continuing to be fed by both parents. Of course, since the ko'ko' is a ground-nesting, flightless bird, its eggs and chicks are also vulnerable to other invasive species besides the tree snake—feral cats and monitor lizards, for instance. Both of these have also eaten their fair share of the rails, albeit nowhere near as many as the snake.

With no birds left in the wild, the recovery effort for the ko'ko' came not a moment too soon. Eventually, 17 American zoos were also involved in the program. Despite breeding at only four months of age, and laying up to 10 clutches of eggs per year in captivity, the actual increase in the number of rails would take time. It wasn't until 1989 that the first ko'ko's were introduced back into the wild

Bali myna » Mozart may have had a pet starling that he taught to speak, but it was nothing like the Bali myna (also a species of starling), with its snow-white plumage and its exotic song. Habitat destruction on the island of Bali and illegal poaching for the pet trade have made it among the rarest songbirds on earth. Collectors will pay thousands of dollars to own one. Only 24 birds are known to exist in the wild, with another several dozen in an increasingly successful captive breeding and release program.

Cat Ba langur » Irresistible with their heart-shaped faces and expressive eyes surrounded by ruffs of golden fur, Cat Ba langurs live in what's left of the tropical wet forests on Vietnam's Cat Ba Island. Illegal poaching and the loss of their forest habitat had reduced the population from some 3,000 in the 1960s to just 53 by the year 2000. Over the last decade, however, the dedicated effort of the Cat Ba Langur Conservation Project to pull the species back from the brink has had some success, and the population is slowly growing.

Greater bamboo lemur » The woolly and wide-eyed greater bamboo lemur eats pretty much only one thing: bamboo. And that's the problem: only 1 percent of their original bamboo forest habitat remains, so they're running out of both a place to live and their food supply. The good news is that a small new population of the highly social primate was recently discovered living in northern Madagascar, inspiring hope that the species still has a chance at survival. Even so, it's estimated there could be fewer than 100 greater bamboo lemurs left.

Iranian Gorgan mountain salamander » Perhaps it isn't surprising that the Iranian Gorgan mountain salamander wasn't known to science until 1979, living, as it does, in one tiny pool in a single cave in the mountains of northwestern Iran. Even now, little is known about this amphibian, except that it is critically endangered. Today, only about 100 breeding adults survive, threatened by the habitat damage and the disturbance caused by people visiting the cave.

Lord Howe Island giant stick insect » The Lord Howe Island giant stick insect, also fittingly known as the land sausage, is one of the larger species of insects, reaching 15 centimetres in length and weighing more than some small birds. Once thought extinct, in 2001 it was rediscovered on the world's tallest sea stack, the 600-metre-high spire of rock known as Ball's Pyramid, near Lord Howe Island, off the east coast of Australia. Only 20 of the bugs survived, clinging to existence under a single bush growing on the side of a cliff. Today, conservationists are captive-breeding the insect in a zoo for reintroduction to Lord Howe Island; however, for now the individuals on Ball's Pyramid remain the only ones living in the wild.

He-cabbage tree » Given such a masculine name because of its hairy leaves, the small he-cabbage tree survives on just a few sites in the high elevations of remote St. Helena in the South Atlantic, where Napoleon was exiled in the 19th century. Fewer than 50 mature wild trees remain. Fortunately, the species is being cultivated in the island's nursery, and some of these 200 seedlings have been planted in the wild, with the hope that they will one day mature and begin producing offspring of their own.

Pinta Island Galapagos giant tortoise » The last of the Pinta Island Galapagos giant tortoises is affectionately known as Lonesome George. He was discovered leading a solitary bachelor's life on that island in 1971 and was soon moved to the Charles Darwin Research Station on Santa Cruz Island to ensure his survival. Today, Lonesome George weighs 90 kilograms and is about 90 years old (members of the species are thought to live for 150 years or more). It's hoped that he will breed with one of the two Isabela sub-species females he's penned with, passing his Pinta Island genes on to future generations.

Nene goose » The nene goose is a success story of endangered species conservation. As many as 25,000 of them thrived in Hawaii when Captain James Cook arrived there in 1778, but these numbers were later decimated by habitat destruction, hunting, and introduced mammals. Only 30 birds survived by the middle of the 20th century, when three of them were sent to a breeding facility in England in a last-ditch effort to save the species. After 10 years of successful breeding, 100 were returned to Hawaii, beginning the recovery of the nene in the wild. Today, there are more than 1,500 wild nene geese in Hawaii.

on Rota, a small, snake-free island about 70 kilometres north of Guam.[12] The release of rails on Rota took place over a 10-year period. Today, it's thought that there are between 60 and 80 birds living on the island, yet questions remain whether they can sustain themselves over the long term.

Unfortunately, attempts at getting the birds back to the wild on Guam itself have met with failure. The survival of 16 and later 44 birds released on parcels of land protected by snake barriers on Andersen Air Force Base in 1998 and 2003 was thwarted by feral cats, which eventually killed all the rails. But the ko'ko' and the people trying to save them aren't giving up easily.

As it currently stands, there are about 100 ko'ko' at the breeding centre on Guam and 35 additional birds in US zoos (these numbers do not include the wild-living birds on Rota).

In November 2010, 16 birds, individuals known to be strong breeders, were released onto snake-free Cocos Island, a 34-hectare atoll located two and a half kilometres off southwest Guam. This island— one-third state park, the rest a privately owned resort whose owners are working in cooperation with the government on the project—is already home to several reintroduced Guam species that have been extirpated from the main island. It is hoped that initially at least six pairs of rails will breed on the island.

Pinta Island Galapagos Giant Tortoise

"I frequently got on their backs, and then giving them a few raps on the hinder part of their shells, they would rise up and walk away—but I found it very difficult to keep my balance."[13] Even

12. Rota is also home to the only wild Mariana crows in existence, another Guam native species ravaged by the snakes.
13. Charles Darwin, *Voyage of a Naturalist Round the World in the HMS Beagle* (London: George Routledge & Sons, Limited, 1860), 394.

the most serious Victorian naturalist became playful in the midst of the otherworldly wildlife on the Galapagos Islands. This image of a giddy Charles Darwin broncobusting a giant tortoise speaks volumes about how novel these remarkable animals are.

Among the largest reptiles in the world, Galapagos giant tortoises can weigh over 225 kilograms and possess a shell that spans over one and a half metres. The subtle physical differences between the 11 closely related subspecies, which are distributed among varied islands and habitats across the archipelago, would play a future role in Darwin's theory of evolution.[14]

Years after leaving the islands, Darwin saw the differences in the tortoises as adaptations to the unique environment of each island. For example, tortoises living on low-lying, relatively barren islands with little vegetation had to reach high overhead to get what few leaves there were. The shells of these animals flared upward at the front to provide clearance for the long, upward stretching neck (in 1574, Abraham Ortelier named the islands for the shell of this particular tortoise subspecies, which resembled a Spanish saddle called a galapago). Meanwhile, on larger islands whose high volcanoes captured moisture from the air, vegetation thrived closer to the ground. Here the tortoises evolved unflared, dome-shaped shells and shorter necks.

Darwin was obviously taken with the giant tortoises when he made his famous visit in 1835. They were holdovers from the age of dinosaurs. As many as 250,000 of them were distributed among

---

14. Darwin wasn't the only person to discover that life evolves by the process of natural selection. Alfred Russel Wallace, an unrecognized naturalist and specimen collector, came up with the same idea independently at roughly the same time as Darwin while collecting animal specimens in the jungles of Indonesia—at the time known as the Malay Archipelago. In fact, Darwin's and Wallace's papers on evolution were presented together at a meeting of the Linnean Society of London in 1858. Popular history has largely neglected Wallace, and Darwin got credit.

the archipelago's islands then, though it was just a fraction of the population of earlier centuries. Today, the story is much different. Estimates put the combined number of all the subspecies in the islands at about 15,000. (The only other place on earth with a completely wild population of native giant tortoises—though members of a separate genus—is on the remote atoll of Aldabra in the Indian Ocean, where 152,000 still survive.)

The exploitation of Galapagos tortoises began soon after the islands were discovered by accident in 1535 by the Bishop of Panama, whose ship drifted off course while en route between Panama and Peru. Such early visitors to the Galapagos recognized the value of the trusting, livestock-sized tortoises—they could live aboard ships for months with no food or water, an ideal way to store meat for ocean voyages centuries before refrigeration. Over the ensuing centuries, tens of thousands of the docile creatures were loaded onto ships by visiting whalers, fishers, and buccaneers. Although there was no room on the *Beagle* to take on any adult tortoises for meat, we know from his writings that Darwin did enjoy tortoise meat while he visited the islands.

The tortoises faced more than hungry sailors, however. In the early 1800s, the first permanent settlers of the islands brought dogs, pigs, goats, and cats. By either destroying habitat or preying on the eggs and young, these domestic animals played their part in decimating tortoises' numbers. Moreover, the lumbering reptiles were hunted by settlers for the valuable oil that was produced by rendering their fat.

Today, the 11 subspecies of Galapagos giant tortoises are found on six islands (two or three other subspecies are thought to have already gone extinct). The largest population is the Alcedo Volcano subspecies on Isabela Island, with an estimated 5,000 individuals. The rarest is *Geochelone nigra abingdoni*, a saddleback tortoise that originally lived on the small island of Pinta in the northern part of the archipelago. Tortoises are no longer found on Pinta, however. The plants that provided their sustenance had been munched into oblivion by introduced feral goats. But for one individual, affectionately known as Lonesome George, the Pinta Island giant tortoise would be little more than a memory.

This solitary animal was discovered in 1971 by American biologist Joseph Vagvolgi and was soon moved to the Charles Darwin Research Station on Santa Cruz Island. Lonesome George has been the poster boy for the entire endangered Galapagos ecosystem ever since. As Galapagos tortoises go, he is mid-sized at 90 kilograms and middle-aged at about 90 years old—they are thought to live for 150 years or longer.

The plight of the Pinta Island giant tortoise is as dire as it gets for a species. Although George is apparently completely alone, there is still a flicker of hope that his species might be saved. He's kept in a pen with two females from neighbouring Isabela. Although the females are of a different subspecies from George, hopes were that he would breed with one of them and pass his Pinta Island tortoise genes to a new generation. There was a problem with this plan. George hadn't shown even a glimmer of interest in the fairer sex in decades. That is until 2008, when his libido finally clicked into gear.

That July, George mated with one of his companions. Even though the female belonged to a different subspecies, any offspring would at least carry half the genes of the Pinta Island tortoise. The female laid about a dozen eggs. Excitement grew in the conservation community. But as time went by, it became apparent that the eggs weren't developing as they should and were beginning to lose mass. Alas, in December 2008, it was announced the eggs failed. Another attempt in 2009 also was unsuccessful. Nobody knows for sure why. Was George infertile, or was the female? Or was it some-thing else? In case the failure of the eggs has something to do with the female, there's a $10,000 reward for anyone who finds George a suitable mate. The problem may be genetic incompatibility with the Isabela females. Based on DNA comparisons, scientists now think the Espanola Island subspecies may be more compatible with George. Two females were brought to live with him in 2011 in the hope that he will breed with them.

In the meantime, other scientists are taking a different tack in their effort to ensure the survival of the Pinta Island subspecies by looking for members of George's subspecies among the large popu-lation of tortoises on Isabela Island. Although the island hosts dif-ferent native subspecies, people have translocated tortoises from island to island over the centuries, so it's hoped that at some point in the past, Pinta Island tortoises may have brought to Isabela. In 2007, DNA analysis revealed a male tortoise with half Pinta Island genes. It's been determined that this animal is a first-generation hybrid offspring of an Isabela and a Pinta Island tortoise. So, there's a chance that one of its parents, a pure subspecies of Lonesome George's kind, might still be alive. Thus far, only a fraction of the 2,000 tortoises on the island have been tested. There's still a chance more pure Pinta Island tortoises might exist.

Yet another possibility: Hundreds of Galapagos giant tortoises are found in zoos throughout the world. It's possible that one or more of them might have been taken from Pinta Island a long time ago and shipped off to be put on display somewhere. It could be a tall order finding one, however, since there are thousands of zoos worldwide, as well as several saddleback tortoise subspecies, all of which look pretty much alike. Even with the help of DNA testing, this might be like finding a needle in a haystack.

RABB'S FRINGE-LIMBED TREE FROG

Frogs have been around for more than 300 million years, eclipsing the age of even the ancient cold-blooded reptilian order to which Galapagos giant tortoises belong. Not surprisingly, to get to where they are today, they've survived many of planet earth's most violent doomsday events. First up was the Permian extinction that wiped out 95 percent of life in the oceans and 70 percent of life on land about 250 million years ago. Known as the "mother of all mass extinctions," this low point in the history of life appears to have been caused by an asteroid slamming into the earth or global volcanic activity, or both. Then, beginning just a little later in geologic terms, the tectonic shift of the earth's land masses caused the coming together and later splitting up again of the supercontinent Pangaea, 250 million and 175 million years ago respectively. After that, a momentous meteor impact ended the reign of the dinosaurs 65 million years ago. And last but not least, just 10 millennia past, the planet was shivering through a massive ice age. Somehow, frogs got through all of this, and today there are nearly 5,000 species to prove it.

But, for all their staying power in the face of such global cataclysms, frogs may have met their match in the form of a much smaller foe: a fungus whose diameter is about half the thickness of a human hair. First identified only in 1998, this mortal enemy of frogs, known as chytrid fungus, infects their unique skin, a highly porous membrane that helps them breathe and hydrate. The fungus blocks these functions, especially when infecting an area on the belly known as the "drink patch" where frogs take in water and essential nutrients known as electrolytes (sodium, potassium, magnesium, and so on). This often results in the quick death of the animal, though curiously, for some reason, certain species seem to have resistance to the fungus and are able to survive.

Scientists think chytrid fungus may have started to gain epidemic proportions at least as early as the 1970s and might be responsible for more than 100 extinctions of frog species since then. The disease is found in South, Central, and North America, the Caribbean, Australia, and Europe. Today, over 350 kinds of frogs are confirmed to be infected worldwide, with another 1,000 or so that are susceptible. That's nearly one-third of all species. Although habitat destruction is still the largest threat to the survival of frogs worldwide, this disease is such a serious problem that an International Union for Conservation of Nature report in 2007 stated that chytrid fungus may be "the worst infectious disease ever recorded among vertebrates in terms of the number of species impacted, and its propensity to drive them to extinction."[15]

Perhaps unsurprisingly, climate change might be involved in the severe nature of the epidemic and its spread, because warmer temperatures may be playing a role in weakening the resistance of frogs to the disease. Unfortunately, despite much research, nobody yet knows (as of early 2011) how to effectively stop the spread of chytrid fungus or how to treat those species already infected.

The frogs of Central America have been especially hard hit. The genus *Atelopus*, for example, a group of beautiful toads living in rainforests, has already seen 71 of its 113 species become extinct. Then there are the bizarre-looking fringe-limbed tree frogs, also victims of the fungus.

The Oaxacan fringe-limbed tree frog and Rabb's fringe-limbed tree frog are large (up to 10 centimetres in length), arboreal frogs with oversized webbed feet, flat disks on the ends of their toes, and scalloped fringes of skin on their forearms. Both have been ravaged

---

15. *Amphibian Conservation Action Plan*, proceedings of the IUCN/SSC Amphibian Conservation Summit 2005, ed. Claude Gascon et al. Gland, Switzerland: World Conservation Union.

by the disease. The Oaxacan species hasn't been seen for years in its southern Mexican habitat and may already be extinct. Rabb's fringe-limbed tree frog, however, still hangs on by the slenderest of threads.

This amazing frog, though strange in appearance, is even stranger in habit. Using its big webbed feet and hands as air brakes, it can glide safely to the ground from high up in the forest canopy, where it spends most of its time. Its breeding habits are also bizarre. After the female has laid 60 to 200 eggs in a water-filled tree hole, the male takes over from her, first to incubate, then to rear the tadpoles. While taking care of the little ones, he allows them to engage in a bizarre form of cannibalism—on his own body. The tadpoles nibble on him, eating little flakes of his skin while he sits half submerged in water inside the tree hole.

Alas, it may be too late for this remarkable animal in the wild. It was already rare when first discovered as a brand-new species in 2005 at a few small sites in the mountainous cloud forests of central Panama. Chytrid fungus showed up the following year. The Rabb's fringe-limbed tree frog may have already succumbed to the fungus by the time it was scientifically described, officially named, and its specieshood confirmed in 2008. At sites where the males were once heard singing in their habitat, they sang no more.

Fortunately, some frogs still exist in captivity. As insurance against the loss of the species, the El Valle Amphibian Conservation Center in Panama captured several of the frogs for captive breeding while a few could still be found. Zoo Atlanta and the Atlanta Botanical Garden are also involved in the program in the hope that the species' population can be increased enough to stock former wild habitats in Panama. It's likely the last chance of survival for the frog. Since there is only one female Rabb's fringe-limbed tree frog in captivity, however, there is only one known female

Rabb's fringe-limbed tree frog on earth, so survival might be too much to expect.

In the meantime, the search continues, so far without success, for the species in its wild, native habitats in the mountains of Panama.

WYOMING TOAD

Like Rabb's fringe-limbed tree frog, the Wyoming toad is also struggling to survive chytrid fungus. A relative newcomer to the world of frogs, it evolved when a population of Canadian toads was separated from its parent species by a glacier during the Pleistocene era about 10,000 years ago. "Set adrift" on their own, isolated from the larger population by an ice sheet hundreds of kilometres wide, the toads continued to evolve in their southeastern Wyoming habitat. In doing so, natural selection had changed them enough genetically so that when the glaciers retreated 10 millennia ago, they could no longer breed with Canadian toads. But it didn't matter. The nearest Canadian toad was 800 kilometres away. The Wyoming toad had become its own species.

This grey-brown, warty species was probably never widespread, living only in the Laramie Basin region of Wyoming. Nevertheless, the toad was quite common until the mid-1970s, when its population suddenly and inexplicably plummeted. It was listed under the US Endangered Species Act in 1984, and was thought to be extinct just a year later.

Happily, there is another chapter in the amphibian's story. That's because in 1987 a small population was found living in shortgrass habitat along the shores of Mortenson Lake, an alpine body of water located 24 kilometres from the city of Laramie. Apparently, the inconspicuous five-centimetre-long toads had been going about their little lives unnoticed here as they always had, eating beetles, ants, and other insects, burrowing into the soft dirt, and hibernating in abandoned ground squirrel holes. Because its mating trill is quieter than the familiar stentorian chorus of the familiar American toad, it isn't surprising the Wyoming species wasn't noticed earlier at Mortenson Lake. The beleaguered amphibian may have been down to just a dozen individuals by the time the lake became a small National Wildlife Refuge (NWR) in 1993, its sole purpose to protect the toad under the Endangered Species Act.

Although chytrid fungus, a deadly pathogen sweeping amphibian populations worldwide, is seen as the primary threat to the Wyoming toad's survival, an important factor contributing to the early decline of the species appears to have been spraying for mosquitoes around the lakes of the Laramie Basin decades ago. Perhaps it's no coincidence that Mortenson Lake, the species' last refuge, is one of the few wetlands that wasn't being dowsed with the insecticide fenthion—a chemical known to be deadly to frogs. Global warming may also be affecting this species, as droughts cause the evaporation of water from area lakes, making them saltier, something amphibians generally do not adapt to.

Mortenson Lake NWR continues to be the only place where Wyoming toads live outside a controlled, captive environment. In spite of this, the species is listed as extinct in the wild on the IUCN Red List, since, owing to the presence of chytrid fungus, the population at the lake can't yet sustain itself through natural reproduction. So its survival there depends on the periodic injection of new captive-bred toads into the population. Today, thousands of young Wyoming toads are produced in captive breeding programs in zoos and wildlife research centres across the United States. However, until the secret of how to prevent wild Wyoming toads from being affected by chytrid fungus can be learned, and more suitable, safe habitats can be found in southeastern Wyoming, this little relict species from the last ice age might well remain extinct in the wild.

THERMAL WATER LILY

Although saved from *complete* extinction by a German botanist, the thermal water lily, in contrast to expectations for the Wyoming toad and several other extinct-in-the-wild species, may never have the option of returning to its native habitat someday.

Discovered in 1986 by biologist Eberhard Fischer of Germany, the tiny water-loving plant, whose little white flowers and pads are a mere one centimetre in diameter (the largest water lily, native to the Amazon, has pads three *metres* across), lived around a single 40 degree Celsius hot spring in Mashyuza, southwestern Rwanda. It grew only along the damp edges of the spring, occupying just a few square metres. Its total world population was as few as 50 plants.

Fischer, seeing how much local people used the hot spring, thought the water lily was in jeopardy, so he collected some specimens just in case its only habitat was destroyed. The specimens ended up back in Germany at the Bonn botanic gardens. It turned out that Fischer's concern for the future of the plant was well founded: people in Mashyuza exploited the hot spring heavily, ultimately diverting it to irrigate crops. This prevented water from reaching the water lily's habitat, which soon dried up. By 2008, the IUCN declared the species extinct in the wild.

But a few of Fischer's plants still hung on at the Bonn botanic garden, where they survived for over 10 years, though horticulturists there were unable to propagate any new ones. It appeared the thermal water lily was doomed to disappear for good. Then, in 2009, when only a single plant survived, a handful of seeds from the seed bank at the botanic garden were sent to Kew Gardens in London. Maybe *they'd* have better luck cultivating the world's smallest water lily. This weighty task—the fate of a species—would be in the hands of Kew horticulturist Carlos Magdalena.

Unlike other water lilies, this species didn't root in deep water;

instead, it lived in muddy areas warmed by the hot spring. As a result, Magdalena, described by Kew Gardens as a top "code-breaker" when it comes to figuring out how to cultivate unusual or rare plants, worked for months to find the secret of propagating the thermal water lily. He finally cracked the code by placing the seeds and seedlings in moist soil surrounded by 25 degree Celsius water. They began to grow. A turning point was reached in November 2009 when the first cultivated plants flowered. Now, with its propagation technique established, dozens of new plants have been cultivated.

Magdalena hopes to one day return the species to its original habitat in Rwanda so that it might grow wild again. The question is, will there be any habitat left to return it to? So saving the organism itself from oblivion is only half the battle because, like every other species on the planet, it needs a place to live.

PART THREE

COMEBACKS: UNDER 100 AND BACK AGAIN

The stories that follow tell us that extinctions aren't preordained. They show what can be accomplished when the best human qualities express themselves: knowledge, foresight, effort, optimism, perseverance, and, most importantly, selfless love and compassion that transcends species boundaries. It took all of this, plus the necessary economic resources, to reel these animals back from the brink of extinction. Although each one of them might have been considered by many as a lost cause (hearken back to the fatalistic and false belief that the dodo went extinct because it was unfit for survival), a few conservationists refused to give up on the futures of these living things whose histories are much older than ours. And they succeeded despite the odds. After a lot of hard work, every one of these endangered animals has been wrested from oblivion, from populations in the wild as low as 5 individuals to over 100 today; in some cases, well over that number.

WISENT (EUROPEAN BISON)

Prehistoric Europeans took early notice of the wisent (pronounced *vizent*). It should come as no surprise that an animal hefting enough meat to feed an entire village for a week would pique their interest. Its value to early inhabitants is evident in the 17,000-year-old paintings of it (or a very similar species) on the cave walls of Lascaux in southwestern France.

Weighing up to nearly 1,000 kilograms and measuring over two metres in height, the wisent is Europe's largest land animal. Closely related and similar in appearance to the American bison, the slightly smaller European species is a forest dweller rather than a strictly grassland animal like its better-known cousin. It is more similar, in fact, to the less-well-known wood bison of Canada's boreal forest. Living in small herds of about 10 to 30 animals, the wisent inhabits deciduous and mixed deciduous-evergreen woodland, with a bit of grassy meadow mixed in. In contrast to most large hoofed mammals, which are grazers, the wisent are largely browsers, eating leaves, twigs, bark, saplings, and the berries of several hundred plant species, along with just a little grass.

Heavy hunting over thousands of years and the accelerating destruction of its forested habitats by an expanding European population had decimated the population, creating perfect conditions for extinction. The species was already gone from the British Isles, Sweden, and the Iberian Peninsula by the 1500s. The remaining stronghold of the wisent was in the Bialowieza Forest in Poland, the last primeval forest wilderness left in central Europe. Fortunately for its wildlife, Bialowieza was owned for centuries first by Polish kings, then by Russian royalty (Catherine the Great took control of this part of Poland in the third partition of the country in 1795). In the first recorded edict protecting the forest, Polish king Sigismund I in 1538 decreed the death penalty for anybody poaching a wisent.

Naturally, the nobility's motivation in protecting wildlife wasn't altogether altruistic: they simply desired a large stock of animals for them and their friends to hunt. These aristocratic wildlife "owners" employed large contingents of indentured guards to protect the animals from poachers. In spite of this, by 1812 only 300 to 500 bison remained, along with another very small population of a separate mountain subspecies in the Western Caucasus Mountains of Russia.

Under increased protection, the Bialowieza Forest population gradually increased to nearly 800 animals over the next century. Then World War I happened. German troops occupying the region killed almost 600 bison for their meat, horns, and hides, reducing the population to about 200 animals. A German naturalist warned the army that the species was on the brink of extinction, but in the end his warnings weren't heeded: the rate of hunting may have slowed for a while, but in the atavistic spirit of sore losers throughout history, the defeated Germans wanted to make a statement, so they laid waste to the forest's wildlife at the end of the war. All but nine wisent were killed. By 1919, the lowland subspecies was extinct in the wild, a fate that would befall the Western Caucasus Mountains subspecies less than a decade later. Fortunately, 54 wisent were living in zoos throughout Europe at the time of the species extinction in the wild. This small captive population had descended from just 12 original founder animals. They nevertheless represented the only hope for the survival of a magnificent species.

Reintroductions of wisent into Bialowieza began in the early 1950s. The species has done well. A strictly protected habitat and a high survival rate of newborn young has enabled the species to come roaring back. Its numbers continue to grow, despite serious concerns about inbreeding after the species passed through that genetic bottleneck of a dozen individuals (low genetic diversity makes the wisent susceptible to hoof-and-mouth disease). Thanks to those Polish kings and Russian monarchs, a remnant of wild Europe remains. Today, about 800 wisent live in the 1,500-square-kilometre Bialowieza Forest straddling the border between Poland and Belarus. This lowland mosaic of deciduous and mixed wood-land, bogs, marshes, thickets, and meadows is one of the continent's most important biodiversity hotspots. More than 10,000 species of animals and plants live here, including wolves and European lynx. Some of its giant oak trees are over 500 years old and have trunks more than six metres around. In addition to the reintroduced wild population in the Bialowieza Forest, another 1,000 or so live wild in nature reserves in Russia, Lithuania, Slovakia, and Ukraine. Most recently, a small herd was sent to Moldova—where the wisent appears on the country's coat of arms—for reintroduction. There are about 1,400 living in zoos in 30 countries around the world as well.

Some 2,000 kilometres to the east on the Mongolian steppe, another species with a Polish connection, the Przewalski's horse, is also enjoying a new lease on life as the result of an intensive, long-term captive breeding effort.

PRZEWALSKI'S HORSE

Only two species of wild horse survived into modern times, both living in central Asia. (Zebras, onagers, and asses, though mem-bers of the equine family, aren't considered horses, whereas mus-tangs and other "wild" varieties are feral animals descended from escaped domestic horses.) One of them, the historically abundant tarpan, lived on the steppe grasslands of southern Russia. It was hunted to extinction for its meat in the late 19th century. The other is Przewalski's (pronounced *shuh-vall-ski's*) horse.

The only wild ancestor of the domestic horse alive today, Przewalski's horse has a slightly different genetic makeup than the current domestic species, although the two can still mate and produce fertile offspring. It was named for Nicholai Przewalski, a Russian geographer and explorer of Polish ancestry who noted the unique horse in 1879 as he passed through China on his way to Tibet as part of an expedition for Alexander II.

It's thought the species once lived on grasslands through-out eastern Europe and Asia, from Germany across the steppes of Russia to Mongolia and China. This stocky, little horse—it weighed only about 300 kilograms and was just 13 hands, or 132 centimetres, high at the shoulder—with its golden-brown coat, long black tail, and stiff black mane like a Mohawk haircut, lived in small groups of up to 10, called harems. It was the quintes-sential patriarchal arrangement: one dominant male bred with all the breeding-age females. Bullied by the alpha stallion, other males didn't get to breed. By the time Przewalski saw the species in the late 19th century, its numbers were already thinning, the vic-tim of meat hunting, pressure from agriculture, and competition with domestic grazing animals. It would survive on the vast Asian plains for less than a century longer.

In the late 1960s, the very last Przewalski's horse in the wild died in Mongolia's Gobi Desert. But that wasn't the end of its story. Seventy years earlier, a small number of the horses had been col-lected for zoos around the world. The process of capturing such high-spirited animals was difficult. Foals provided the best "return on investment" because they were still young and would live a long time in a zoo environment. Often captured at the expense of the rest of the harem, which would be shot, foals were left undefended, confused, and more easily taken by barbaric collectors.

Ironically, these captive animals would ultimately save the Przewalski's horse as a species. But extinction threatened even the early captive horses. Spread among zoos and collections across the globe, there was no single herd large enough to effectively increase the population. To make matters worse, an early group of captive animals in the United States didn't survive and another important herd living in the Ukraine was shot by German soldiers during their occupation of the country during World War II. By 1945, about 30 captive Przewalski's horses survived around the world. Only 13 of these were capable of breeding.

In 1959, new breeding programs were established in Europe and the United States. These efforts were coordinated through the use of an international studbook to keep track of which animals bred with which. By the mid-1970s, there were 250 Przewalski's horses living in captivity, despite passing through a genetic bottleneck of just 13 breeding animals a few decades before. Every Przewalski's horse in existence today can thank the contribution made by that baker's dozen of ancestors. It was a very close call.

In 1992, a program to reintroduce Przewalski's horses back into the wilds of Mongolia was begun. It was a success. The species is now protected across its range. Today, there are over 300 of these wild horses running free in three grassland reserves in Mongolia. Although it is still critically endangered, Przewalski's horse is no longer listed as being extinct in the wild. Another 2,000 or so live in zoos and breeding facilities throughout the world.

Vancouver Island Marmot

Przewalski's horses and wisents are large, distinctive hoofed mammals. Sharks and tigers are powerful and dangerous predators. Peregrine falcons and cheetahs are fast. Mountain gorillas and bonobos seem so human. These animals grab our attention. Then there's cuteness. This is the realm of lemurs, pandas, marmosets, and monk seals. These animals endear us. You can add another to the list: the almost irresistibly adorable Vancouver Island marmot.

It is hard to imagine anything cuter. In fact, it was one of the mascots of the 2010 Vancouver Olympics.

These rotund, 70-centimetre-long members of the squirrel family are reminiscent of a giant woodchuck, but with chocolate brown fur and the added panache of a white nose, crown, and belly. They are generally thought to be a species unique to Vancouver Island that has evolved rapidly since the last ice age 10,000 years ago (although a few scientists have questioned whether they are a different species from their mainland British Columbia cousins). Found only in the island's alpine meadows, they live in burrows, survive on a diet of plants, and undergo a long winter hibernation that lasts upward of six months. Probably never abundant, Vancouver Island marmots began plummeting toward extinction in the early 1980s—clear-cut logging; predation by wolves, golden eagles, and cougars; and possibly other environmental changes are to blame.

Alpine areas, such as the kind the marmot inhabits, are known to be particularly sensitive to climate change. Montane environments around the world are expected to be impacted by warming temperatures more than almost anywhere else. Their typically high-altitude, subarctic-like ecosystems are at risk of getting swallowed up as more temperate species move up mountains into cooler temperatures to escape a warmer climate. But marmots and other species already living in the alpine zone near the tops of mountains have no such luxury: they have nowhere to go.

Less than a decade ago, there were only about 30 Vancouver Island marmots left in the wild, giving them the dubious distinction of being Canada's rarest mammal. But conservationists have been working tirelessly to ensure their survival. Since 2003, when a program to capture, breed, and reintroduce the animals into the wild began, their numbers had increased dramatically—to 300 at the end of 2010. The goal of the Marmot Recovery Foundation is to have a sustainable population of 600 marmots in the wild by 2012.

BLACK-FOOTED FERRET

The black-footed ferret, a svelte, buff-coloured, 40-centimetre-long member of the weasel family, with black feet, tail tip, and "bandit" mask is another cute burrowing mammal that refuses to disappear. It has lived for thousands of years on the North American plains in close association with its primary prey species, the prairie dog, a type of ground squirrel.

Prairie dogs once thrived with numbers in the hundreds of millions, living in colonies that literally covered 10 to 20 percent of the Great Plains. Individual colonies, known as prairie dog towns, were sometimes dozens of square kilometres in area and consisted of a complex burrow and tunnel system for shelter and protection from predators, storage of food, and the rearing of young. Black-footed ferrets not only rely on the prairie dog colonies as their primary source of food (an adult ferret will eat one every three days, on average) but they also use their burrows as ready-made homes to provide shelter from the elements and the owls and coyotes that prey on them.

Once human settlers arrived in the region, the prairie dog became a target of farmers and ranchers who saw the rodents as destroying valuable agricultural and grazing lands. A century-long war of poisoning and shooting prairie dogs ensued; it continues to this day in places. The result? Ninety-five percent of their population has been wiped out and with them went the black-footed ferret. By the 1950s, the ferret was thought to be extinct.

But to everyone's surprise, that wasn't the end of the little predator's story. A small colony was discovered in South Dakota in 1964. Unfortunately, this colony had disappeared by 1974. One ferret, captured earlier as part of an unsuccessful captive breeding program, survived in a wildlife facility in Maryland until it died in 1979. The species was presumed extinct, again.

Jump forward two years to 1981, when a farmer in Meeteetse, Wyoming, was led by his dog to a colony of a black-footed ferrets. The species had risen from the "dead," Lazarus-like, for the second time. Unfortunately, canine distemper broke out in the colony, killing many ferrets and threatening to wipe out the species' last population. So all of the survivors were taken into captivity in the mid-1980s as a precaution. It is a good thing they were, because today's entire black-footed ferret population is descended from just a handful of these animals that were able to successfully produce offspring in captivity.

In 1987, one of the most concerted efforts in history for the recovery of an endangered species began. Since then, about 7,000 ferret kits (as the young are known) have been produced. Of these, 2,600 have been released into the wild as part of 19 reintroduction projects spread across eight US states, northern Mexico, and most recently Canada, where, in 2010, ferrets poked their bandit-masked, whiskered faces from their burrows to gaze on the Saskatchewan prairie for the first time in more than 70 years.

As encouraging as its progress has been, today's black-footed ferrets face two great challenges: disease and habitat availability. As unlikely as it may seem, sylvatic plague, caused by *Yersinia pestis,* the same bacteria that killed millions of Europeans during the Black Death of the 14th century, is a major threat to the species' survival.

Since arriving in San Francisco in the early 1900s on fleas living on ship rats—there's those damned ship rats again—the disease has slowly spread eastward across the Great Plains, killing black-footed ferrets, prairie dogs, and other wildlife that becomes infected (and since you asked, yes, it is still deadly to humans if not quickly treated). One hundred percent of infected ferrets die of the disease. The largest outbreak yet happened in Conata Basin, South Dakota, site of the most successful reintroduced colony. About 100, or one-third of the total ferret population there, died in 2008. Plague also killed nearly two-thirds of the prairie dogs in Conata Basin.

Recently, a vaccine has been developed that protects the ferrets against the disease. All captive animals are now injected with it before they are released into the wild. However, those already living in the wild must be captured to be given the vaccine, a difficult and expensive task for conservationists and stressful for the animals, but absolutely necessary. Yet vaccinating the ferrets is only half of the equation.

Prairie dogs also suffer a high mortality from sylvatic plague, which may be the most serious hurdle to clear if black-footed ferrets are to survive in the long term, since they depend on their long-time prey species so intimately for survival. If prairie dogs decline even further owing to the disease, it will be increasingly difficult to recover the population of black-footed ferrets in any sustainable way. Unfortunately, there is currently no vaccine that works with prairie dogs, whose population is already reeling with the disease. So, in the short term, prairie dog burrows near ferret colonies are dusted with an insecticide to kill the fleas that transmit plague. This helps prevent infection but is expensive. A vaccine that is delivered in bait has been used successfully in the laboratory, and it is hoped that it will be ready for widespread delivery to prairie dogs in the near future.

Today, in addition to the 290 in captivity, there are about 250 wild-born and 750 captive-reared ferrets spread among the various reintroduced colonies throughout the North American plains, including the newest one in Grasslands National Park in Saskatchewan. All in all, not a bad comeback for a species thought to be extinct as recently as 1981. But owing to the vicissitudes of nature, including cold winters, predators, disease, and the challenge of obtaining enough prey, only about half this number will survive to breed in the wild each spring, and just 3 of the 19 reintroduced colonies have self-sustaining populations. So the injection of a steady stream of captive-bred animals into the wild is currently required to simply maintain, never mind grow, the population.

Nevertheless, it is hard to argue that the resurgence of the blackfooted ferret isn't a success, for its current situation is immensely better than it was a few decades ago and continues to improve. On the other side of the world, in Australia, the northern hairy-nosed wombat, yet another endangered burrowing mammal (this one a marsupial), is making a comeback of its own.

Northern Hairy-Nosed Wombat

Some stories have staying power. None is older than those of the Indigenous people of Australia, who arrived on that southern land mass 40,000 to 50,000 years ago—some say over 100,000 years— when gigantic marsupials still roamed the land.

The aboriginal story of the bunyip, Australia's most famous legendary creature, may have its origins in a real animal known as the giant wombat, the largest marsupial that ever lived. Though it became extinct 30,000 to 40,000 years ago, there is a chance it co-existed with the earliest Indigenous people. That's a long time for a culture to remember something, but a rhinoceros-like, two-metre-high, three-tonne behemoth carrying a human adult–sized baby in a pouch (it was a marsupial, after all) would be hard to forget. The bunyip legend is as popular Down Under today as it ever was, and wombats, though much smaller now, still live in the Australian wilds. One of them has been almost sucked into the vortex of extinction itself.

Among Australia's rarest mammals, the northern hairy-nosed wombat is one of three surviving members of the Vombatidae family, which it shares with the less endangered southern hairy-nosed and common wombats. Though it pales in comparison with its megasized ancient predecessor, the northern hairy-nosed wombat is nevertheless a chunky, muscular animal, weighing over 30 kilograms and reaching more than a metre long. With its plush-toy look, fuzzy muzzle ("hairy-nosed"), silky brown fur, and roly-poly gait, this long-lived species rivals the distantly related koala for the title of cutest Australian mammal. And although it may look as slow as a koala, wombats can hit 40 kilometres an hour in a sprint, carried along on stubby legs with powerful feet tipped by long digging claws.

And do they like to dig! Among the world's largest burrowing mammals, the northern hairy-nosed wombat bucks the trend of other marsupials by having a backward-facing pouch for its young. This keeps dirt out as it excavates complex tunnel networks that can reach 20 metres in length and delve three and a half metres underground into multiple rooms. Up to 10 individuals might live in a single tunnel complex, known as a warren. They've adapted to the brutally hot temperatures found in their native habitat along dry creek beds in the semi-arid grasslands and open woods of central Queensland State by living in cool burrows during the day and coming out at night to feed on grass.

The northern hairy-nosed wombat was once common, living in several locations in the states of Queensland, New South Wales, and Victoria before Europeans arrived in Australia. After centuries of habitat destruction owing to cattle and sheep grazing and predation by introduced dingoes and red foxes, the endangered wombats are today confined to just one small 500-hectare area within Queensland's Epping Forest National Park, set up in the early 1970s specifically to protect the last few members of the species. Although its population began to slowly rebound, only 35 wombats survived by the 1980s.

In 2000, between 10 and 15 percent of the wombats were killed by dingoes. To make sure this wouldn't happen again, a 20-kilometre-long fence was built around the wombat habitat in the national park in 2002. Other measures were also taken. The fence is monitored twice daily by volunteers to make sure dingoes and foxes are kept out. Feeding and watering stations were set up for the wombats to use when they need it. Introduced plants, which out-competed the native grasses eaten by the animals, were removed. Prescribed fires eliminated excess fuel that might result in destructive natural wildfires. And even though a captive breeding program tried in 1996 was a failure, there are plans to try again in the future using knowledge gained during a successful breeding program for the closely related southern hairy-nosed wombat.

So far, the recovery of the species has been a qualified success. While the increase in numbers has been slow, the last full census of the animal was encouraging. DNA analysis of hairs captured on special tape placed at the entrances of wombat burrows showed a total population of 138, a fourfold increase since the 1980s. But it's still too early for a sigh of relief. Although the historical causes for the species' decline have been largely removed, the very small population size and single location make the wombats vulnerable to natural catastrophes such as severe drought, flooding, or disease. As insurance against this, a multinational mining company donated money to set up a second location for the species. Located about 700 kilometres south of the current population, the Richard Underwood Nature Refuge in Queensland State received its first few southern hairy-nosed wombats from Epping Forest National Park in late 2009. If successful—and there's no telling how wild animals will adapt to a new habitat—up to 24 wombats will be moved here.

For the time being, it appears the northern hairy-nosed wombat will avoid the fate of its giant Pleistocene-age predecessor.

IBERIAN LYNX

Wildcats. They range from animals smaller than a typical tabby to the great lions and tigers. They all evolved from the same ancestor in Asia and over millions of years spread across the earth. Of the 36 species on the IUCN Red List, 25 are threatened with extinction. The most endangered large cat of all is the Iberian lynx of Spain: it could be the first one to go extinct since the sabre-toothed tiger disappeared at the close of the last ice age.

In his foreword, Stuart Pimm wrote of an Iberian lynx he saw beside a Spanish lake: "It looked at me just as cats do, with complete contempt, for it belonged there and I didn't." Contempt for humans, or whatever the cat equivalent of contempt might be, would be completely justified in the case of this southern European wildcat. In 1900, there may have been 100,000 across the Iberian Peninsula. By 1960, there were only about 4,000 of them left. From there it went quickly downhill: three decades later, about 1,100 remained. Dozens of separate lynx populations were erased from the peninsula in the 1990s. By 2005, there were fewer than 100 adult animals hanging on in two tiny patches of habitat in Spain's Doñana National Park and the Sierra Morena in Andalusia.

At about 60 centimetres at the shoulder and weighing in at 13 kilograms, the Iberian lynx is smaller than the more northerly and more numerous Eurasian lynx, and about the same size as the Canada lynx of the boreal forests of North America. While it shares the trademark ear tufts, bobbed tail, and long ruff of fur under the chin of the other lynxes, it is distinguished by a much shorter coat, an adaptation to the warmer climate where it lives. The pale orangey-grey fur is adorned with distinctive black spots like a leopard. Its long legs and lithe, feline body are guided through the world by fiery yellow eyes and large ears, the search and detection sensors of a deft nighttime predator.

Typical for a lynx, the Iberian species is a solitary, largely nocturnal hunter whose primary prey is rabbits. Nearly 100 percent of its natural diet is made up of the quickly reproducing rodents, which it stalks in an ecosystem of open woodland and dense shrub thickets. This near-total dependence on one prey species for survival is a risky way to get a living, though, and has been the downfall of many a highly specialized predator. For example, snail kites in the Everglades and black-footed ferrets on the Great Plains are both teetering on the edge of oblivion because of the dwindling of their exclusive prey species—apple snails and prairie dogs respectively. Likewise the lynx. The rabbit population on the Iberian Peninsula has collapsed dramatically since the 1950s, itself the victim of overhunting and habitat destruction, but mostly owing to the misguided, one might say intensely stupid, actions of one man.

Paul Felix Armand-Delille, a doctor and bacteriologist, had a problem with rabbits in the gardens on his estate in northern France. After reading about the success of the myxoma virus in killing off hundreds of millions of destructive introduced rodents in Australia, Armand-Delille thought he'd use the virus to get rid of his rabbits, even though they were part of the native wildlife. In 1952, the doctor deliberately and illegally—he was later convicted and heavily fined—infected two rabbits with myxomatosis and loosed them upon his estate, hoping they would spread the disease to others. It worked: Armand-Delille was quickly rid of his long-eared garden irritants. Unfortunately, the story doesn't stop there. Did he release the disease, not expecting it to go beyond the confines of his own land? It is hard to believe a scientist wouldn't know better. A little over a year later, the virus had spread clear across France, killing 90 percent of the country's rabbits. By the following year, it had spread to the rest of western Europe, including Spain, where it was decimating the wild rabbit population, the primary food source for Iberian lynx. This marked the beginning of a precipitous decline of both the rabbit and consequently the lynx populations. But the dominoes didn't stop falling there. The Spanish imperial eagle, once a fixture in Iberian skies, specialized in hunting rabbits too. Its population reached a low of about 30 pairs in the 1960s, also owing largely to starvation caused by a dearth of its primary prey. Fortunately, the eagle's story might still have a happy ending: after decades of intensive management, the majestic raptor's current population is about 400, and it has been downlisted from endangered to vulnerable on the IUCN Red List.

A female lynx with her two or three cubs need to eat three rabbits per day for nearly a year until the young are independent. With so few of the rodents surviving the epidemic of myxomatosis and another more recent deadly disease, Iberian lynxes were forced to turn to mice, rats, waterfowl, partridges, and deer to survive. But there just wasn't enough of this kind of prey to sustain thousands of large wildcats, and the lynx's population crashed. Lynx also killed red foxes and feral house cats, not to eat but to eliminate as competitors for an ever-diminishing supply of food.

The reasons behind any potential extinction are rarely simple. The decline of the Iberian lynx—albeit at a much slower rate— began long before Dr. Armand-Delille's crime nearly wiped out Europe's rabbits. Centuries of overhunting; the loss of almost all of its natural woodland-scrub habitat to agricultural, pine, and eucalyptus plantations; the building of vacation homes; road construction; road kills; and habitat flooding by dams had also taken a heavy toll on the cat. As recently as 1960, the Iberian lynx ranged across about 60,000 square kilometres, or 10 percent, of Spain. Today, just a half century later, its entire world breeding range is just 124 square kilometres, an area no bigger than New England's Nantucket Island. What's more, this area is divided between two widely separated parcels, splitting an already tiny population into two even smaller, reproductively isolated ones.

This is not to say all hope is lost for the lynx. After all, another endangered predator, the Iberian wolf, today boasts a population in the thousands after a sustained recovery effort by conservationists. It too stood on the brink of extinction, and in 1970 just a few hundred remained. They suffered severe habitat loss as well, not to mention "wolf persecution," an irrational hatred of wolves among European peoples that has historically triggered widespread poisoning, trapping, and shooting, often for no more than the "sport" of it. (How can such acts of violence against the wild counterparts of our beloved domestic companions be justified? They can't.) Although Iberian wolves didn't face starvation like the lynx—because they evolved eating a wide variety of foods and weren't dependent on any one species—they overcame tough odds and came back. Their story and the recovery of the Spanish imperial eagle must spur on those who work for the lynx.

Indeed, the Iberian lynx has made some progress. The species is now fully protected from hunting, although individuals are still occasionally killed illegally. In 2005, the first cubs were born in captivity to a female named Saliega, a positive start to the breeding program. By 2010, there were nearly 80 animals in captivity (though many of them have contracted a serious kidney disease), living at three facilities in Spain and at a new breeding centre in Portugal, a country where the species was wiped out decades ago. Former lynx habitats have been set aside for repopulation. In 2009 and 2010, seven animals were translocated from Sierra Morena in southern Andalusia to a wilderness in the state of Cordoba to the north; they were the first Iberian lynx ever to be reintroduced into former habitat. The goal is to add another 20 over the next several years, while also releasing cats into a second, separate habitat. As well, an attempt has been made to conserve and recover the wild rabbit population in Doñana National Park, and although as yet unsuccessful, it represents an important part of creating sustainable conditions for the cat. Today, about 200 Iberian lynx live in the wild, up from a 100 or fewer in 2005.

CALIFORNIA CONDOR

An icon of endangered species, this magnificent bird is a reminder of a very different time long past when great throngs of wildlife roamed throughout North America.

During the Pleistocene age, about 13,000 years ago, North America's vast savannah-steppe ecosystem was alive with big animals. Camels, large-headed llamas, long-horned bison, Columbian mammoths, four-horned pronghorns, giant ground sloths, dire wolves, short-faced bears, American lions, and scimitar cats roamed the plains in great numbers. The scene rivalled the great legions of animals on today's African Serengeti.

Among the Pleistocene megafauna was the California condor, which appears to have been relatively common from the Pacific Ocean across the vast plains and almost to the east coast. It shared the sky with two even more massive condor-like species, known as teratorns. The largest, dubbed the "incredible teratorn" by paleontologists, had a wingspan of five metres. Expert scavengers, the three condor species thrived on the carcasses of large mammals. Many of these giant animals went extinct some 10 millennia ago, likely overhunted by humans or wiped out by a massive event such as a meteor impact (the latest evidence, a large crater recently found in western Nova Scotia, suggests the latter). With no more megafauna, the teratorns' food supply was greatly reduced, and they soon died out themselves. But the California condor lived on, its range shrinking to the far west of the continent, where it survived by feeding on the carcasses of marine mammals along the Pacific coast. Today, its remaining range is made up of scrubby desert, canyons, and open grasslands in very limited areas of the southwestern United States. Though still around, the condor barely survives—but with the help of caring people, it is fighting back.

This dark bird with its bare orange head soars hundreds of metres above the earth on steady wings that stretch nearly 300 centimetres from tip to tip, scanning the ground for dead animals. Despite its size, it takes no live food. It is only occasionally the first species at a carcass, usually locating its food from the air by watching for turkey vultures, ravens, and golden eagles feeding on the ground. The condor doesn't use its sense of smell to find carrion. This is in contrast to its smaller cousin, the turkey vulture, which possesses the keenest sense of smell of any bird. Because of their enormous size, condors will drive other scavenging birds away from a carcass—that is, except for golden eagles, which, despite being only half as large, keep the giants at bay. Such timidity toward eagles is reserved only for scavenging situations, however: a condor will vigorously chase away eagles and any other birds that approach its nesting area.

Listed as critically endangered on the IUCN Red List, the population of California condors reached an all-time low of just 22 birds in 1981. Habitat destruction, overhunting, and persecution by ranchers had pushed the species to the edge. And a scavenging lifestyle caused many condors to die of lead and strychnine poisoning after eating bullet- and shot-ridden carcasses or from eating coyotes and other animals that were deliberately poisoned. By 1987, the last six condors in the wild had to be taken into captivity in a last-ditch effort to save the species under the US Endangered Species Act. They did well in captivity, with numbers growing to 150 by 1998. In the early 1990s, a program to release captive-bred condors into the wild was begun.

By 2003, the first California condor chick to be born and reared in the wild since 1981 took flight, and since then several more wild chicks have fledged. In late 2010, there were almost 400 birds in total, 200 of them in captivity. And the species' horizons are widening beyond its initial southern California and Grand Canyon strongholds. A pair of condors recently attempted to nest in northern California's Big Sur for the first time in a century. In Mexico, the second reintroduced condor chick to be born in that country hatched in 2009.

With about $35 million spent so far by the US government, the California condor's has been one of the most expensive endangered species recovery programs in history. It has its critics. They say that the bird should be left to its own devices, that too much is being spent on it at the expense of other endangered species, and that it may be doomed to extinction anyway. Valid arguments, perhaps. But in an age when Hollywood blockbuster movies routinely cost over $100 million to make and elite professional athletes sign contracts for $50 million, is it too much to ask for some generosity for one of the most magnificent species of birds this good earth has ever produced?

WHOOPING CRANE
Coming close to the California condor in the amount of effort and money spent to ensure its survival is another majestic North American species. Imagine a bird with a snow-white body, black wing tips and a red crown, standing as tall as a man's chest, with

wings that could span a small room. The whooping crane—named for its powerful bugling call—is a most spectacular and extremely rare bird.

Once numbering as many as 10,000 birds, this species had become a mere ghost of its former self. Historically found across much of North America, from the subarctic to northern Mexico, merciless hunting and habitat destruction in the 1800s and early part of the 20th century almost drove the whooping crane to extinction. In 1941, only 21 "whoopers" were left: 15 migratory birds and 6 in a sedentary population in Louisiana. By 1949, the Louisiana birds were gone, wiped out by severe weather.

The few surviving birds still had to run a perilous 4,000-kilometre gauntlet of migration as they followed a centuries-old route down the middle of the continent in the fall, only to retrace it again in spring. On the way to their Texas Gulf Coast winter home from breeding grounds at Wood Buffalo National Park in Canada's North (it wasn't until 1954 that this, the species' last nesting place, was finally found) they would encounter the gunfire of farmers, whose few bits of grain they might nibble on. Somehow this tiny population of cranes dodged a bullet for another two decades, until the late 1960s, when an intense cooperative recovery program between the United States and Canada gradually brought the species back from the brink. Whooping cranes dodged yet another bullet in 2010 when their wintering site at the Aransas National Wildlife Refuge on the Texas Gulf Coast was spared the effects of the infamous BP Gulf of Mexico oil spill.

One of the most publicized species recovery campaigns of the 20th century has had marked success: today, there are 263 migratory birds plying the skies between Wood Buffalo National Park and the Aransas National Wildlife Refuge. Moreover, a small non-migratory Louisiana population has been re-established, and the species has been reintroduced into a former breeding area in central Wisconsin. These two populations account for about 140 birds. Add another 167 birds in captivity and the whooping crane's total population is approaching 600. Though the current population is still small, and their long-term survival remains firmly in the hands of humans, this majestic bird's rise from near ashes inspires hope for those working for other imperilled creatures.

SHORT-TAILED ALBATROSS

The fact that the impressively sized California condor, whooping crane, and short-tailed albatross are among the most endangered birds on earth, yet are now on the comeback trail, suggests a paradox: though we seem particularly inclined on the one hand to destroy the most remarkable of living things, on the other, we fight the hardest to save them.

Ten *million* short-tailed albatross once glided above the waves across 35 *million* square kilometres of North Pacific Ocean, from Japan to North America, from the Sea of Okhotsk to the Hawaiian Islands. These large, eight-and-a-half-kilogram white birds with a generous bubble-gum pink bill and a wingspan reaching over two metres, were once the most abundant albatross and the largest seabird in all the northern hemisphere.

The defining characteristic of the true seabirds, like the short-tailed albatross, is their nomadic, oceanic life. They are as much marine creatures as are whales and fish. Species such as albatrosses and shearwaters, which spend most of their lives foraging on the high seas, can travel great distances with minimal effort by taking advantage of the winds. Next to food supply, wind probably effects their movement and distribution more than anything else, especially between 35 and 60 degrees latitude, where it blows almost continuously. On long, slender wings, short-tailed albatrosses soar just above the water, beating their wings only occasionally to maintain lift, taking advantage of updrafts created as air currents deflect off the faces of waves. This uses much less energy than flapping flight and enables the birds to travel the vast distances they need to gather food. An individual bird might routinely cover hundreds of thousands of square kilometres during the non-breeding season in its search for surface-schooling fish and squid.

Even though they spend much of their lives far from the sight of land, every October, at the beginning of the nesting season, breeding-age short-tailed albatrosses, drawn from all over the North Pacific, leave their solitary life of wandering behind to satisfy the urge to reproduce on Torishima, a tiny 500-hectare speck, part of the Izu Island chain, in the Philippine Sea south of Tokyo. They had been doing this for thousands of years on Torishima; millions of them once created a bustling city of brilliant white birds where each pair claimed its tiny patch of ground on which to build a nest, lay, and incubate an egg, then rear its solitary chick. Breeding adults returned every year. New offspring, however, would take to the high seas for up to 10 years before coming home for the first time to breed themselves once they were sexually mature and paired for life with a mate.

There is going to be trouble whenever a species factors into an economic equation. The short-tailed albatross was no exception to this rule, possessing as it did more than 10,000, soft, airy feathers. The bad news was that people in the United States and Europe needed feathers, lots of feathers, to stuff their mattresses and pillows. The birds were also collected for their meat, oil, and eggs. There is no such thing as an unexploited chance to make a buck, so the short-tailed albatross, which has no defences on its breeding ground (it had evolved over the millennia in the absence of humans and other predators), was clubbed into near non-existence by Japanese feather collectors. Black rats, stowed away on their ships, also invaded the island, adding to the decimation of the bird's population. During the peak of the exploitation, in the late 19th and early 20th centuries, five million short-tailed albatross were killed in just over a decade and a half. By the 1930s, when a ban imposed earlier by the Japanese government against killing the birds was finally enforced, the population of the species had plummeted to fewer than 50. A decade later it was presumed extinct.

Then a remarkable thing happened. In the early 1950s, a handful of first-time breeding birds that had been away at sea maturing finally returned home to Torishima to nest. Their reappearance after being at sea for years saved this magnificent species from extinction. By 1954, there were 25 birds on Torishima, including at least six mated pairs.

Given half a chance, the short-tailed albatross has shown that it has remarkable resilience for a species that was all but extinct. Today, there are nearly 3,000 of them, the great majority returning to Torishima, with the remainder nesting on Minami Kojima, in the Senkaku Islands. Unfortunately, it's hard to really know what the status of the birds are on this second island, since it lies in a hotly disputed area claimed by Taiwan, China, and Japan since the 1960s and is therefore difficult for scientists to access.

Despite its brilliant comeback, the North Pacific's largest seabird is still far from safe.

Much work has been done to enhance the nesting habitat on Torishima, including revegetation to prevent erosion, the setting of decoys to attract birds to nest in new areas on the island, and designating it as a national wildlife protection sanctuary of Japan to which only scientists are permitted access.

What's more, important strides have been made in the past couple of decades to reduce the accidental drowning of albatrosses on longline fishing gear, currently the major threat to their survival while at sea. Brightly coloured banners to deter them from landing near the gear and weighted lines that sink the baited hooks out of the reach of albatrosses have reduced the death toll significantly. In fact, two short-tailed albatrosses killed by longlines in the Bering Sea in late 2010 were the first recorded by the Alaskan Pacific cod fleet since 1998. Of course, this is just one fishery, albeit a large one; however, other North Pacific fisheries are also working to reduce the death toll.

But there's one thing nobody has control over. The centre of the short-tailed albatrosses' universe, Torishima, happens to be the exposed top of an active volcano. Eighty-five percent of the species' entire population nests on the flanks of an actively seething caldera. In 1902, a violent eruption wiped out the entire population of 125 people who lived on the island. Humans never returned to live there. One hundred years later, in August 2002, another eruption occurred, fortunately at a time of year when all the birds were at sea.

Nobody knows when the next eruption will be, of course, but if it happens during the nesting season, it would be catastrophic for the species. As insurance against this, a small group of chicks is being translocated to a non-volcanic island in Japan's Bonin Islands, where the albatross formerly bred. It's anticipated that the chicks will "imprint" on the island and return there one day to breed as adults, creating a "backup" population free from the threat of volcanoes.

In 2010, two pairs of the species were also discovered nesting on the US National Wildlife Refuges at Midway Atoll and Kure Atoll in the northwestern Hawaiian Islands. Although it has a long way to go, the short-tailed albatross looks like a species that is determined to once again rule the winds of the North Pacific.

CAHOW (BERMUDA PETREL)

A true ocean-going seabird like the albatross, the cahow has been struggling for its survival for more than four centuries now.

> "I have been at the taking of three hundred in an hour . . . Our men found a pretty way to take them . . . standing in the rocks or sands by the sea side . . . making the strangest outcry that possibly they could . . . the birds would come flocking and settle upon the very arms and head of him that made the sounds, answering the noise themselves . . . and so our men would take twenty dozen in an hour. There were thousands of these birds and two or three of the islands were full of their burrows."[16]

The abundance of this seabird (named for its haunting call) is evident in this passage written in 1610 by William Strachey, just a year after the British settled Bermuda. The subjects of King James I weren't the first to discover this diminutive landfall in the North Atlantic, though. The Spaniards beat them to it in 1515. But they were so terrified by the *cahow-cahow* nighttime calls of a million birds, believing they were demons, that they would never permanently occupy Bermuda. What the Spanish did, however, was release pigs onto the island as a living food store for passing ships. This likely marked the beginning of the end for the cahow, as the porcine invaders overran the breeding colony, collapsing countless nesting burrows underfoot. It's likely the cahow's population had suffered a significant decline by the time of British settlement.

The cahow, or Bermuda petrel, is a medium-sized seabird with brownish-grey upperparts, white underparts, a black cap, and a hooked black bill with external nostrils (a common feature of the

---

16. William Strachey, *A True Reportory of the Wreck and Redemption of Sir Thomas Gates, Knight, upon and from the Islands of the Bermudas* (London, 1625).

"tube-nosed" seabirds, which also include albatross and shearwaters). Sporting long, slender wings a little over a metre across, the cahow is able to navigate through the stormiest North Atlantic conditions. Most of its life is spent at sea, where it captures small squid and fish near the surface. During the January-to-June breeding season, it will fly hundreds of kilometres over the ocean during the day to capture food to bring back to its nesting mate and single chick at night, under the cover of darkness.

By 1614, escaped rats from arriving ships had become a plague on Bermuda. The exponentially multiplying rodents devoured the eggs of seabirds, including the cahow's, adding to the already serious damage caused by the pigs brought earlier by the Spanish. Moreover, the rats ate all the crops, leaving the starving people of the island with no choice but to eat seabirds to survive. In just a decade or so, the cahow's population plummeted from hundreds of thousands to nearly zero: it was thought to have disappeared by about 1621, earning it the dubious distinction of being one of the first extinctions in recorded history. Or so it was thought.

During World War I, after it had been "extinct" for about three centuries, a Bermudan naturalist found a bird he claimed was a cahow. At the time, nobody seemed to pay him any mind; there was a war on, after all. Then, in 1935, a mysterious bird was discovered dead on the ground at the foot of the lighthouse on St. David's Island, at the eastern end of Bermuda. It was sent to American Museum of Natural History ornithologist Robert Cushman Murphy in New York, who confirmed it as the long-lost cahow. The prodigal seabird had returned. But where did it breed? That question wouldn't be answered for another 16 years. In 1951, Murphy; Louis Mowbray, naturalist and founder of the Bermuda Aquarium; and a 15-year-old Bermudan boy named David Wingate found a tiny colony of 18 pairs nesting on barren rocky islets in Castle Harbour at the eastern end of the island. The nesting territory was tiny, covering barely a hectare. The breeding cahows had somehow gone about their business while eluding detection for all those centuries, even though they were within just a few kilometres of several villages.

The 1951 discovery had a profound influence on the young David Wingate. After returning from Cornell University in 1958 with a freshly minted ornithology degree, he began to work full time for the critically endangered seabird. He held the official post of conservation officer for the Bermuda government from 1966 until his retirement in 2000.

Special nesting burrows were constructed on the cahows' islets, and partial covers, known as baffles, which restricted the size of the openings, were placed at the entrance to the existing nest cavities to prevent larger white-tailed tropicbirds from taking the sites. Rats were removed and native vegetation was planted on the breeding islets as well as on other potential nesting islands. The number of breeding cahows began to grow, but their islet colonies offered very limited room for the expansion of the species' population.

In pre-colonial times, cahows nested all over Bermuda in burrows they dug in the soft soil of the forest floor, but any restoration of former breeding habitat on the main island was impossible. It was simply too developed and too populated to be an option. Nonsuch Island, located at the eastern entrance to Castle Harbour, however, had potential. At six hectares it was much larger than the islets the breeding birds were confined to. When David Wingate moved there to live in 1962, it was a barren rock. A disease had earlier killed the native cedar trees, and introduced pigs stripped it of the rest of its vegetation. Wingate's goal for the island, which he dubbed the "Nonsuch living museum," was to restore it to its pre-colonial ecological state in preparation for the reintroduction of the cahow. After decades of work, Wingate and his family removed introduced plants and animals, planted 100,000 trees and shrubs on the island, and restored freshwater ponds and a salt marsh. Nonsuch hadn't seemed so natural in centuries.

All the work spearheaded by Wingate is paying off. The cahow is really and truly coming back to Bermuda. Breeding success has gone from 5 percent in the 1950s to 50 percent in 2010. The nesting islands in Castle Harbour have become a national park. Over 100 fledgling birds were translocated to Nonsuch Island between 2005 and 2008, four decades after Wingate began restoring it. In 2009, the first cahow chick in nearly 400 years was born on the island and a new nesting colony had taken hold. By 2010, there were a total of 95 breeding pairs, plus scores of non-breeding cahows throughout Bermuda.

Yet, despite its success, the species is still highly endangered. A large unknown is the effect climate change and more severe hurricanes will have on nesting sites. For the first time in living memory, the islets were flooded during recent hurricanes. Fortunately, it happened during the non-breeding season when no cahows were present. Although the species ranges across a vast swath of the North Atlantic, from the North Carolina coast to the Azores, it appears to spend most of its time gathering food in or near the Gulf Stream. Some oceanographers predict the Gulf Stream will weaken as more and more cold water from melting Arctic ice disrupts it. What effect will this have on the distribution of marine life in the world's most powerful ocean current? Will it result in a decline in food availability for seabirds in the North Atlantic? And how would this effect a species like the cahow that still sits at the edge of extinction?

CHATHAM ISLAND BLACK ROBIN

Like the cahow, the recovery of the Chatham Island black robin is one of conservation's most celebrated triumphs. Not long ago, this sparrow-sized bird was considered by most biologists to be functionally extinct, meaning its disappearance was all but inevitable. Fortunately, some refused to accept such a verdict for the species.

In the 1970s, the entire population of black robins lived on Little Mangere Island, a small sea stack in the Chatham Islands about 1,200 kilometres off the coast of New Zealand. By the 1800s, the species had been wiped out in the rest of the island chain by cats and rats that arrived with European settlers. But Little Mangere was uninhabited and surrounded by 200-metre-high cliffs, so introduced predators never made it there. But the island was a prison, too. With a dying forest and a harsh climate, the birds were unable to thrive. And, the catch-22 was that evolving in an environment where strong flight to evade predators wasn't needed meant their wings were too weak to carry them off the island to another place to live.

In 1972, this remnant population was discovered by Don Merton, a New Zealand biologist and conservationist. There were only 18 birds left. Keeping a close eye on the fate of the hapless species, Merton continued to return to the island, watching the population dwindle to only 7 birds by 1975. Something clearly had to be done. So, in a risky last-ditch effort, Merton and his small team relocated the remaining few birds to two larger islands with better habitats—and hopefully a better chance at survival. However, this didn't seem to help, and the species continued its slump toward extinction.

By 1979, the fate of the black robin rested on the tiny wings of the sole breeding female, named Old Blue, plus three males and a non-breeding female. It also weighed on the shoulders of Merton and his helpers. At this point, the bird's survival must have seemed hopeless, but both birds and humans refused to give up.

Merton decided to take drastic action: when the lone female robin laid her eggs, they would be moved to the nests of other birds—

abundant Chatham Island tits, to be precise—so that these surrogate females would incubate and hatch the robin's eggs as their own. Why? It is well known that many songbirds will lay a second clutch of eggs if the first is lost. So it was hoped that taking Old Blue's first clutch of eggs would force her to lay another. Indeed, she did lay a second clutch and hatched them. But what to do with those baby robins that were being reared in the nest of the surrogate Chatham Island tits? They were put back into the black robin's nest and added to the young from her second clutch—the ones she hatched herself—to double her family size. To help feed all these extra mouths, Merton and his team provided additional food to supplement what was being brought by the parents. It worked. This proved to be a successful strategy for the Chatham Island black robin.

Today, they number around 250, living on South East Island and Little Mangere Island, all of them descended from that lone female. The technique of placing the eggs of one species with a surrogate of another to increase the number of clutches laid is known as cross-fostering. It has since been emulated around the world in the recovery efforts for other species of endangered birds.

Old Blue lived for an amazing 13 years—that's twice the normal lifespan of the species. She may have been the saviour of her kind, but she couldn't have done it without dedicated conservationists, especially Don Merton, who would go on to play an important role in other endangered species success stories, including that of one strange parrot.

KAKAPO

Think of a parrot. What comes to mind? If it is a squawking, brilliantly coloured bird perched in the midday sun on a branch eating a piece of fruit in the tropical jungle, you'd be right. But there are a few parrots that are distinctly different from that stereotype, and

New Zealand's endemic kakapo is one of them. A Maori word for "night parrot," the kakapo is the most unusual species in a spectacular family of birds. How unusual? It is heavier than any other parrot. It is flightless and lives largely on the ground. Its face is as much owl-like as it is parrot-like (in fact, the kakapo's genus name is *Strigops*, from the Greek *strix* for "owl" and *opsis* for "face"). It is also commonly known as the owl parrot—a name that's even more suitable considering its nocturnal habits. If all that isn't enough, it's one of the longest-lived animals on the planet, reaching 100 years or more.

The ancestor of the kakapo arrived in New Zealand thousands of years before humans came on the scene. With the exception of a few species of bats, there were no mammals there at the time, so the kakapo eventually became flightless to fill an ecological niche that would have been occupied by a similarly sized herbivorous mammal. The species flourished in this environment and lived on both the North and the South Islands, as well as on Stewart Island. The abundance of fossils indicates that at one time it was New Zealand's third most common bird. Their cryptic green plumage made them exquisitely adapted for hiding among the vegetation to avoid the only predators they had: four species of raptors and the laughing owl. But evolution, as effective as it is in adapting life to its surroundings, needs time to do it. Things began to change too rapidly for the kakapo to keep up its defences once the first humans arrived around AD 1000.

Not only did the Maoris hunt them for food, skins, and feathers, the dogs they brought with them made short work of the kakapo, a bird with a very strong scent (easy to locate), a habit of freezing rather than fleeing when danger threatened, and an inability to fly (easy to catch). As well, the Polynesian rats that also arrived with the Maoris decimated kakapo eggs, which were laid in ground nests.

The species had already been wiped out across most of its former range by the time Europeans landed in the 1800s. Massive clearing of forests for timber and agriculture, hunting, the introduction of weasels and ferrets (a misguided effort to reduce an overabundance of introduced rabbits), feral house cats, and specimen and egg collecting for zoos, collections, and museums drove the kakapos' numbers perilously low.

By the early 1970s, many thought that the bird was extinct. In fact, it *was* extinct on the more highly populated North Island. But in 1977, a population of 100 to 200 birds was found by an expedition to remote Stewart Island, which lies off the southern tip of South Island. This last population survived only because of the inaccessibility of its habitat. But even on this lonely outpost, the long reach of humans was having an effect. Feral house cats, introduced earlier (deliberately or accidentally) by humans, were killing almost 60 percent of the birds every year. The population wouldn't last long at that rate, so a cull of Stewart Island's marauding cats was carried out. Although the cats were successfully eradicated from the island, in the 1980s conservationists decided to begin moving the remaining birds to predator-free islands where they would be safe. By 1992, 65 kakapos had been successfully relocated to their new island homes. Today, they live on two predator-free islands: Codfish Island and Anchor Island. Here they are carefully monitored by biologists to ensure breeding success.

Even if they're safe, building the population back to self-sustaining levels has not proven to be easy. Since females normally don't breed until they are about nine years old and generally do so only every second year, the road back to full, independent specieshood is going to be a long one. In early 2011, there were a total of 120 kakapos. That is almost twice the number of two decades ago, but there is still a long way to go before they're able to survive on their own. No doubt it will be difficult road to recovery for the kakapo, but the success of the crested ibis shows us how much can be accomplished when rescuing an endangered species.

CRESTED IBIS

From the 17th to the 19th century, the crested ibis was officially protected in Japan. The Tokugawa shogunate (the samurai rulers of the time) revered the species and forbade any hunting or capture of these large wading birds.

Their abundance under shogun protection would quickly cease after the Meiji Renewal in 1868. This ended military control and restored imperial rule to Japan. The shoguns lost power, and many of their edicts were repealed, effectively ending protection for the ibis. From then on, the species went into serious decline. A combination of widespread poaching to collect its long crest plumes for the millinery trade, destruction of its forest and wetland habitats, and the heavy use of pesticides had reduced the crested ibis to just a handful of birds by the 1960s. Only five individuals remained in all of Japan in 1981. Something had to be done, for at the time, these were the only known crested ibis left anywhere, and the fate of the species was thought to be at hand. In January of that year, the five were captured and kept in the Sado Japanese Crested Ibis Conservation Center on Sado Island, on the west coast of Japan. The intent was to breed them in captivity to bring the species back from the edge. It was not only Japan that lamented the decline of the crested ibis. Once ranging across much of eastern Asia, by this time the species had already become extinct in Taiwan, South Korea, North Korea, and apparently China.

But later in 1981, to everybody's surprise and delight, the crested ibis was found surviving in a remote, mountainous area of Yangxian County, Shaanxi Province, China. The tiny population of four adults and three chicks was the first of the species to be seen in that country in a half century.

With a wingspan of 140 centimetres, the crested ibis is a spectacular, large wading bird. Snow-white plumage in the non-breeding season (its head, neck, and back turn dark grey in the breeding season) and a large shaggy crest of long plumes contrast with its brilliant red patch of facial skin, red legs, and long down-curving black bill tipped in red. Like many freshwater wading birds, the species has a varied diet that includes small fish, frogs, crabs, snails, molluscs, and insects. It gathers these by probing its bill into the water, mud, or long grasses along riverbanks, ponds, and rice paddies. Tall trees are a key part of its breeding habitat. Mated pairs build a flimsy nest, high up in the crotch of a large tree. Both sexes incubate up to five eggs and both feed the newly hatched young.

By 1990, less than a decade after the seven Chinese birds and their habitat were stringently protected, the population had grown enough that 25 ibis chicks were captured for a captive breeding program, a cooperative effort of both Chinese and Japanese conservationists. Within a decade, that number had increased to 130 birds. The species was well on its way to a comeback in China. By 2002, there were 140 birds in the wild and 130 in captivity. The story was not so rosy at the Sado Island conservation centre in Japan. Those five ibises captured in 1981 failed to produce any young, and the last survivor of the group, a female named Kin, died in 2003 at the ripe old age of 36 years.

Chinese birds were sent to Japan in an attempt to repatriate the species to a land where they were now absent. Fortunately, years of experience had taught scientists a thing or two about how to successfully breed captive crested ibis. Armed with this knowledge, the Sado Island facility would once again host the magnificent birds. Today, there are over 100 crested ibis in captivity at the conservation centre, all awaiting eventual reintroduction into the wild. In 2008, a dozen or so ibises, gifts from China, were released into the Japanese wilds. For the first time in decades, a wild-living crested ibis laid eggs in Japan in 2010. Although they didn't hatch, it marked a watershed for the species there.

According to the Chinese government, the official number of crested ibis living in that country in 2010 stood at 1,617—997 of which lived in the wild. The crested ibis is a success story, yet the species is still in great danger of becoming extinct. Remember the four adult birds (along with their three chicks) whose 1981 discovery in China led to the ultimate rescue of the species? Every crested ibis alive today can trace its genetic roots back to two of those four birds. This has resulted in very, very low genetic diversity for the species. In fact, the ibis has one of the smallest gene pools of any endangered bird. Serious problems are already cropping up as the population grows. Some chicks are born with deformities, possibly owing to inbreeding, and the species as a whole is thought to be more susceptible to disease than it would be if it was genetically diverse. Intense management to try to improve the genetic diversity is now a critical component of the recovery effort.

The growth of the crested ibis population itself creates a catch-22 situation. The larger the population of a species, the more suitable habitat it requires. It was hard enough to ensure the protection of habitat for an isolated population of 7 or even 100 birds, but now there are many times those numbers in the wild. This will probably bring the inevitable conflict between wildlife and the rural people who also depend on the land. In China, conservationists have been spreading the species around, reintroducing it to suitable habitat in diverse parts of the country, trying to avoid having the entire population concentrated in one area. The birds have also been spreading themselves around: in April 2008, a crested ibis was spotted along the southern Yangtze River for the first time in half a century.

All in all, despite the obstacles faced, the resurgence of the crested ibis from practical extinction to nearly 2,000 birds is a conservation success story, though like most others, one whose final chapter has yet to be written.

SEYCHELLES MAGPIE ROBIN

In contrast to a widespread species such as the crested ibis, whose original range may have spanned much of a continent, the Seychelles magpie robin probably never had more than a few dozen square kilometres to call home.

This lovely songbird is neither a magpie nor a robin. It is so named because of its plumage (like a magpie) and its tame, bold behaviour (like the European robin). Found only in the beautiful tropical Seychelles Archipelago in the Indian Ocean, it is the size of an American robin and clothed in black plumage with a dark blue iridescence, with large white patches on its wings. Its song is a jumbled, melodic outpouring, often sung from a tall tree, and its strange call sounds like an electric pencil sharpener. Inhabiting coastal lowland forests across the Seychelles Archipelago, the magpie robin used to follow now extinct giant tortoises while plucking insects, spiders, worms, and even little lizards from ground disturbed by the passing reptile. A quick study, it learned from its association with tortoises that following other large, slow-moving animals might be profitable, so when humans arrived on the Seychelles in 1770, the tame songbird became a frequent companion. It was commonly found foraging in yards and gardens, even hanging around dinner tables and waiting for scraps of food. The Seychellois, as the islanders are known, came to love their magpie robins. But there were aberrations: in the 19th century, a Frenchman reportedly shot 24 of the birds in one day, a thoughtless act that would have been impossible a century later, when there simply weren't that many magpie robins left to shoot.

Unlike its two abundant namesake species, the Seychelles magpie robin came close to disappearing for good when it had dwindled to just a dozen birds in 1965. Although much of its forest habitat across the archipelago was earlier destroyed for banana plantations, the biggest culprit for the magpie robin's drastic decline was predation by introduced house cats and rats.[17] Though it once inhabited eight islands in the Seychelles, the species was finally relegated to Frégate Island, a tiny two-square-kilometre privately owned atoll that is known for its exclusive luxury resort. Although the island was cat-free by the 1980s after a successful eradication program, the magpie robins' situation didn't improve.

With its tiny population still not growing and being restricted to just one island, a full recovery program run by BirdLife International and funded by the Royal Society for the Protection of Birds began in 1990. Habitat improvements, a ban on pesticide use, cat and rat eradication, the provision of artificial nesting boxes, supplemental feeding, and the control of the introduced barn owl (a predator) and common myna (a nesting site competitor and nest marauder) were all essential pieces of the puzzle to pull the magpie robin back from the edge of extinction.

In 1994, after Frégate's magpie robin population had experienced a fourfold increase to 48, the first of the reintroductions to other islands began as two birds were translocated to Aride Island. In 2000, the islands of Cousin and Cousine received their first magpie

---

17. One of the most serious threats to songbird populations worldwide is domestic and feral house cats. In the United States alone, estimates range from 500 million to over 1 billion songbirds are killed every year by nearly 100 million house cats. It's a good idea to keep Fluffy indoors, for the sake of the birds.

robins. The total population stood at 86, almost double what it was six years earlier. Another six years on and the population had doubled again to 178 birds in total, living on Frégate, Cousin, Cousine, and Aride. In 2007, a watershed was reached when the species was downlisted on the IUCN Red List from critically endangered to endangered, signalling a distinct improvement in prospects that few threatened species enjoy. And the progress continues as the species' range has been expanded farther to include Denis Island, where 20 birds were successfully reintroduced in 2008–09. Today, about 200 magpie robins exist on five Seychelles islands. Their future is far from certain, however. As a nation of small islands, many of them low-lying atolls, the Seychelles are seriously threatened by sea-level rise caused by climate change. Its beaches have already begun to disappear, being slowly swallowed by the sea. With their already limited area, small islands such as the ones where magpie robins live are especially vulnerable.

Nene (Hawaiian Goose)

Although they too are oceanic islands, the mountainous Hawaiian Archipelago is fortunate not to face the real threat of disappearance under a rising sea like the low-lying Seychelles Archipelago, the home of the magpie robin. Hawaii's native biodiversity is among the world's most severely challenged nevertheless. Yet there have been a few endangered species success stories on the islands (the Laysan duck, Hawaiian coot, and Hawaiian stilt come to mind), none more impressive than that of an unusual goose.

Perhaps it isn't so ironic that the nene, Hawaii's official state bird, started life as an immigrant from a cold, northern land. Who can blame the first Canada geese that ended up on that far-flung Pacific archipelago for escaping the nasty winters of their homeland, as many Canadian people do today?

The nene goose (pronounced *nay-nay* after the Hawaiian word that describes the bird's soft voice) and four other geese on the islands that have since gone extinct had all evolved from a pair or a flock of the well-known North American birds that somehow made it (perhaps blown off course in a storm) to the archipelago about a half million years ago. They never left. Adapting to empty ecological niches, they evolved into a variety of species over time, including an extinct giant goose that stood 1.2 metres tall and weighed nearly nine kilograms. Today only the nene survives. Despite the passage of thousands of years, the nene remains closely related to the Canada goose genetically. In fact, it is a closer kin than some subspecies of Canada goose are to each other. But you wouldn't know it to look at it.

Being isolated on an oceanic island with no predators and little competition has had a profound effect on how the species evolved. First of all, because it has exploited the variety of Hawaii's terrestrial habitats over the millennia, the nene spends less time in water than other geese. Instead, this average-sized goose, with its heavily striped buff, black, and white plumage and distinctive diagonal neck barring spends its time in grasslands, shrub lands, lava plains, and coastal dunes; only occasionally does it use freshwater environments. So, it's not surprising the nene has lost most of the webbing between its toes (it doesn't need to swim much), has long, strong legs for manoeuvring on rough terrain, and a more upright posture than other geese for browsing on leaves, grass, fruits, seeds, and the flowers of shrubs and trees. Moreover, living as it does in a tropical paradise where food is available year round, the nene lost the urge to migrate, making it the most sedentary species of goose, with the smallest range.

When Captain James Cook arrived in Hawaii in 1778, the nene was still common, with an estimated 25,000 spread throughout the archipelago, and may have been even more abundant before Polynesians arrived a millennia or so before that. That has changed. Habitat conversion for agriculture and building, hunting, and predation by introduced mongooses, pigs, cats, and rats conspired to decimate the population, which hit a low of just 30 birds by the middle of the 20th century. The nene was poised to follow other native Hawaiian geese species into extinction.

Then, Sir Peter Scott, British naturalist, filmmaker, conservationist, and founder of the Wildfowl and Wetlands Trust (WWT) took up the bird's cause. In the 1950s, three nene were sent from Hawaii to the WWT facility in Slimbridge, England. After 10 years of careful and intensive captive breeding, the population there had grown to 126 birds. These were sent back to Hawaii to replenish the beleaguered wild population. The slow recovery of the nene had begun. Since then, further captive breeding, both in England and on Hawaii, coupled with habitat protection on the islands, has helped bring the nene back. Today, over 1,500 birds are divided among the islands of Hawaii, Kauai, and Maui. Although the population is a far cry from the handful of birds that remained in the 1950s, several obstacles still have to be overcome to ensure the long-term survival of the species.

Reproductive success in the nene is low, with possibly as few as 10 percent of females successfully rearing offspring. This may be due to the loss of eggs and chicks to introduced predators. Also worrying is inbreeding depression, or low genetic diversity, a phenomenon that occurs after a species passes through a very small population bottleneck (in this case, 30 or fewer individuals, depending on how many of the birds bred). Such a loss of genetic diversity can result in poor resistance to disease and less resilience in adapting to changing environmental conditions. Another concern is road kills, which account for the deaths of a significant number of adult birds.

In addition to the nene that are found in their native Hawaii, a population of captive birds lives half a world away in Wildfowl and Wetlands Trust sites throughout England. Even St. James Park, near Buckingham Palace in the middle of London, has a small resident flock of nenes. The story of Hawaii's state bird, an erstwhile Canada goose long since transformed, is a qualified success. Though its long-term future is still unclear, it is infinitely better off than it was a half century ago.

BLUE IGUANA

It takes a lot of work and commitment to wrest a species from immanent oblivion: intense planning; countless hours, days, and months of labour; and money are critical. But it can be done. Perhaps it isn't too surprising that, so far, all of these success stories are of mammals or birds; after all, they are the most popular kinds of living things. However, on Grand Cayman Island, they have a different favourite.

Best known for its stingrays, sharks, and coral reefs, this Caribbean island boasts of another distinction: it has successfully rescued one of the most endangered reptiles on earth from extinction.

Once abundant, according to fossil evidence, the blue iguana's numbers began to decline after the arrival of Europeans on Grand Cayman about 300 years ago. By 2003, a scant 5 to 15 of them were all that were left in the wild. The population of the defence-less, meaty lizards was decimated largely by cats, dogs, and rats that arrived with settlers, as well as by habitat destruction as land was cleared for homes, agriculture, and cattle grazing. In more recent times, real estate development has taken its toll. By 2005, the blue iguana was considered to be functionally extinct, which meant its population was too small to sustain itself.

Originally thought to be a subspecies of the Cuban iguana, it wasn't until 2004, through careful comparisons of the animal's scales and through DNA analysis, that scientist Frederic Burton established the Grand Cayman animal as a unique species that had long ago diverged from its Cuban cousins. The blue iguana has low genetic diversity, suggesting it may be evolved from a single pregnant Cuban iguana female that was washed into the sea during a storm a few million years ago, only to drift across to Grand Cayman.

With a lifespan that is comparable to human's—the record is almost 70 years for a captive animal—the blue iguana is Grand Cayman's longest-lived and largest land animal at a metre and a half long. It can top the scales at a chunky 14 kilograms. Stubby spines run all along its back, giving it an air of dinosaurian ferocity, although like many lizards it is harmless and quite docile. In spite of its name, its skin is usually grey to match its rocky surroundings, but once in the presence of other iguanas, males turn a gorgeous Caribbean-sky blue. Add to this jewel-like ruby and gold eyes and you've got yourself one handsome lizard. And there's something else really neat about these animals: they actually have a third eye on the top of their heads. Not some superstitious ability to see what nobody else can, but an actual eye with a rudimentary lens and retina. Apparently, it may not be able to see that well, but it can detect light and dark and movement—probably not a bad thing to have if you want to avoid being eaten (even though its only natural predator on Grand Cayman is a snake that preys solely on subadult lizards).

Active during the day, blue iguanas live in rocky areas in dry scrub habitat in the interior of the island, where they find shelter in holes between rocks and in tree cavities. They used to also live near the coast, but that habitat has been eaten up by hotels and houses. Leaves, seeds, and flowers account for almost its entire diet; only rarely are small invertebrate animals eaten. About 50 of Grand

EPILOGUE

Do not forget your brethren, nor the green wood from which you sprang. To do so is to invite disaster . . . One does not meet oneself until one catches the reflection from an eye other than human. —LOREN EISELEY

The once-abundant little Franklin's bumblebee lives in an area between northern California and southern Oregon, sandwiched betwixt the Sierra Cascade and the Coast Mountains. It has the smallest geographical range of any bumblebee anywhere, and the smallest population. In 1998, only 94 Franklin's bumblebees were counted across their range. By 2004 and 2005, none were seen, despite extensive surveys. The year 2006 brought a glimmer of hope for the species with the sighting of a single bee. The promise was short-lived, however, for no Franklin's bumblebees have been seen since. Other bee species are still relatively common in the areas where the Franklin had once lived, so the cause for its decline is a bit of a mystery.

Because pesticide use and habitat destruction don't appear to have severely affected other bees in the area, the sudden collapse of this species may be owing to an exotic disease imported into the country on commercial domestic European bumblebees. Used for pollinating greenhouse tomatoes and peppers, some of these insects may have escaped into the wild, transmitting the disease to the native Franklin's bumblebee, which would likely have little resistance to it.

Some might say that, as dreadful as the loss of any single species would be, it wouldn't have any real, tangible impact on us. This may be true, for *one* species. But think of an airplane wing. Lose one of its rivets and the plane won't crash. Yet a little water seeps into the empty hole, then freezes and expands, forcing apart a little bit of the sheet-metal joint, putting extra strain on surrounding rivets until they break. And so on. The process continues until sooner or later the wing falls off and the plane crashes. Species are like rivets, wings ecosystems, planes biospheres. In the words of ecologist Aldo Leopold, "The first rule of intelligent tinkering is to save all the parts." The possible loss of Franklin's bumblebee, one of these "rivets," tells just this story.

While dinosaurs were thundering across the land 130 million years ago, the flowering plants had just begun their rapid ascent to the throne of the plant kingdom. This "grassroots" revolution would change the face of our planet forever. The flowering plants, or angiosperms as they are known, would quickly wrap the globe in a multi-hued cloak of green. In a geological blink of an eye, they became the dominant life forms on land. Broad-leafed trees, herbs, flowers, shrubs, bushes, and grasses dominated the earth by the time dinosaurs vanished 65 million years ago.

Scientists are still puzzled over exactly why angiosperms came to dominate so quickly. Even Charles Darwin said they were "an abominable mystery." The latest thinking, however, is that the flowering plants only took off once they had evolved a pollinating relationship with bees, butterflies, beetles, birds, bats, and many others.

This gave angiosperms an efficient way to reproduce, and a leg up on the more primitive conifers and ferns, which depended on the random movement of wind and water to distribute their seeds.

Darwin may not have figured out why flowering plants had taken over the world so quickly, but he did understand the unique relationships between plants and pollinators. In 1862, he saw a museum specimen of the Madagascar star orchid. This flower was unusual in that it had a tube, 25 centimetres long, at the bottom of which sat a pool of rich nectar. He predicted there must be a moth living in Madagascar with a proboscis of roughly the same length that pollinated the orchid. Forty-one years later he was proven right when the moth wielding such an appendage was discovered. There are many such exclusive bonds between one plant and one pollinator species. Most pollinators aren't choosy at all, however, and will visit a variety of flowering plants. Wild bees, the most important group of pollinators on earth, are mostly generalists.

Watch any bumblebee buzzing in a meadow. She (the workers are always females) feverishly zips from one flower to the next, poking her body into each in search of nectar. Every time she does this, some pollen sticks to the fuzz on her body. This gets delivered from the last plant's male stamen to the female stigma of the next flower, completing the reproductive cycle. This act is repeated countless times every day around the world and keeps the engine of life humming along.

Although we've exploited domestic honeybees for thousands of years to pollinate our crops, wild pollinators are an unappreciated economic engine of our civilization. Their "free" contributions to global ecosystems are estimated to be worth tens of billions of dollars every year, worldwide. But this is about something much more important than money.

Banish pollinators from your garden and your flowers won't

bloom; remove them from the fields and there'll be no vegetables, from the orchards and we go without fruit; wipe them from a region and the ecosystem will collapse; exterminate them completely and the lives of 75 percent of all flowering plants would soon grind to a halt. And what ultimately depends on flowering plants? Most terrestrial organisms, including us. What's more, this symbiosis between pollinators and plants is only the most obvious of the interdependencies among living things and the environment. More and more, we learn of an ever-widening web of mutually necessary, but often subtle, distant, and unseen linkages between the earth's organisms.

We must—quickly—appreciate our kinship with the world's myriad living things to engender a wider compassion that includes active concern. Albert Schweitzer expressed such a relationship with animals and plants in his philosophy of "reverence for life" when he wrote, "I am life, which wills to live, in the midst of life, which wills to live."[18] Ultimately, the realization of such empathy for the non-human living things that are members of the earth's community may be the only way to engender the compassion we need to save them. And even if, by chance, *Homo sapiens* somehow physically survive in the absence of Franklin's bumblebees, fabulous green sphinx moths, Pacific right whales, Amur leopards, Devils Hole pupfish, California condors, Sulu hornbills, Cayman blue iguanas, Yunnan box turtles, Wyoming toads, Catalina mahogany, and the millions of other species that crawl, creep, fly, run, swim, and flower around us, could we survive the loneliness?

If Franklin's bumblebees are still pollinating flowers in the meadows of northern California and southern Oregon, and we try our best to save them, at least we'll have made another decision in favour of the future of life.

---

18. Albert Schweitzer, *Civilization and Ethics: The Philosophy of Civilization II*, 3rd ed. (London: Adam and Charles Black, 1946), 242.

In this book, you've read about just a small sample of what has been accomplished by people the world over who have shown genuine compassion for the non-human living things we share this planet with. People whose goal is to prevent them (and by extension, maybe even ourselves) from becoming extinct, a finality so powerfully described by Father Thomas Berry, the late American Catholic priest and eco-theologian:

> Extinction is a difficult concept to grasp. It is an eternal concept. It is not at all like killing individual lifeforms that can be renewed through normal processes of reproduction. Nor is it simply diminishing numbers. Nor is it damage that can somehow be remedied or for which some substitute can be found. Nor is it something that simply affects our own generation. Nor is it something that can be remedied by some supernatural power. It is rather an absolute and final act for which there is no remedy on earth or in heaven. A species once extinct is gone forever.[19]

---

19. Thomas Berry, *Dream of the Earth* (San Francisco: Sierra Club Books, 1990), 9.

HOW YOU CAN HELP

GENERAL

These organizations are involved in saving species and endangered ecosystems:

Encyclopedia of Life: **www.eol.org**
Nature Canada: **www.naturecanada.ca**
Saving Species: **www.savingspecies.org**
Wildlife Conservation Society: **www.wcs.org**
World Wildlife Fund: **www.worldwildlife.org**

MAMMALS

Cat Ba langur—Cat Ba Langur Conservation Project: **www.catbalangur.org**
Eastern North Pacific right whale—Save the Whales: **www.savethewhales.org**
Gilbert's potoroo—Gilbert's Potoroo Action Group: **www.potoroo.org**
Greater bamboo lemur—Institute for the Conservation of Tropical Environments: **http://icte.bio.sunysb.edu**
Hainan gibbon—Fauna & Flora International: **www.fauna-flora.org**
Iberian lynx—SOS Lynx: **www.soslynx.org**

Iriomote cat—International Society for Endangered Cats Canada:
   www.wildcatconservation.org
Javan rhinoceros—International Rhino Foundation: www.rhinos-irf.org
Maui's dolphin—World Wildlife Fund: www.worldwildlife.org
Mexican wolf—Lobos of the Southwest: www.mexicanwolves.org
Mountain bongo—Bongo Surveillance Project:
   www.mountainbongo.org
Northern hairy-nosed wombat—The Wombat Foundation:
   www.wombatfoundation.com.au
Northern sportive lemur—Madagascar Biodiversity Partnership:
   www.madagascarpartnership.org
Northern white rhinoceros—Ol Pejeta Conservancy:
   www.olpejetaconservancy.org
Scimitar-horned oryx—Sahara Conservation Fund:
   www.saharaconservation.org
Seychelles sheath-tailed bat—Nature Seychelles:
   www.natureseychelles.org
South China tiger, Amur leopard, Asiatic cheetah—Panthera:
   www.panthera.org
Vancouver Island marmot—The Vancouver Island Marmot Recovery
   Foundation: www.marmots.org

BIRDS

For bird species not specifically listed below visit BirdLife International:
   www.birdlife.org

Amsterdam Island albatross, short-tailed albatross—Royal Society for
   the Protection of Birds: www.rspb.org.uk
Bachman's warbler—National Audubon Society: www.audubon.org
Bali myna, Floreana mockingbird, Madagascar pochard, mangrove
   finch—Durrell Wildlife Conservation Trust: www.durrell.org

Black stilt, Campbell Island teal, Chatham Island black robin, kakapo—
  TerraNature Trust: **www.terranature.org**
Cahow—Government of Bermuda, Ministry of Public Works,
  Department of Conservation Services:
  www.conservation.bm/bermuda-petrel-cahow
California condor, white-collared kite—Peregrine Fund:
  www.peregrinefund.org
Echo parakeet, Mauritius kestrel, pink pigeon—Mauritian Wildlife
  Foundation: **www.mauritian-wildlife.org**
Eskimo curlew—Bird Canada: **www.birdcanada.com**
Hawaiian crow, Molokai thrush, nene, Oahu creeper—American Bird
  Conservancy: **www.abcbirds.org**
Niceforo's wren—ProAves: **www.proaves.org**
Spix's macaw—Parrots International: **www.parrotsinternational.org**
Whooping crane—International Crane Foundation:
  www.savingcranes.org

REPTILES

Grand Cayman blue iguana—Blue Iguana Recovery Program:
  www.blueiguana.ky
Philippines crocodile—Cagayan Valley Programme on Environment and
  Development: **www.cvped.org**
Turtles—Turtle Survival Alliance: **www.turtlesurvival.org**

AMPHIBIANS

Amphibian Ark: **www.amphibianark.org**

FISH

River sharks—ReefQuest Centre for Shark Research:
  www.elasmo-research.org

INSECTS

Xerces Society for Invertebrate Conservation: **www.xerces.org**

TREES

Catalina mahogany—Catalina Island Conservancy:
  www.catalinaconservancy.org
He-cabbage, she-cabbage, and St. Helena mahogany—St. Helena
  National Trust: **www.nationaltrust.org.sh**
Virginia round-leaf birch—Center for Biological Diversity:
  www.biologicaldiversity.org

ACKNOWLEDGEMENTS

There are many people whom I would like to thank, listed here in alphabetical order by first name: Alan Lewis, Alan Sanders, Dr. Bradley Wilson, Christopher Sheehan, Dr. Dan Mennill, Daniella Schrudde, February Balbas, Fred Burton MBE, Glenn Dodge, Gregory Cairns-Wicks, Janos Olah, Jon Hornbuckle, Leonora Enking, Liz Mwambui, Lynn Labanne, Maiko Lutz, Martin Hale, Dr. Martina Raffel, Merlijn van Weerd, Patricia Paladines, Dr. Patricia Wright, Paul Calle, Dr. Rebecca Cairns-Wicks, Dr. Rick Hudson, Sandra Valderrama, Sergio Seipke, Simon Colenutt, Dr. Thomas Geissmann, Vicky Sawyer-Somma, Victoria Jackson.

Thank you to the IUCN for permission to quote the endangerment categories for species listed on the IUCN Red List of Threatened Species.

I am very grateful to Dr. Stuart Pimm for writing the book's foreword. And thanks to Leo MacDonald, Sarah Howden, and my editor Brad Wilson, all at HarperCollins Canada.

A heartfelt thank you to all the people, everywhere, who work tirelessly to protect and save our irreplaceable natural world.

Last but not least, my deepest appreciation must go to my wife, Paula.

SELECT BIBLIOGRAPHY
AND RECOMMENDED READING

Ackerman, Diane. *The Rarest of the Rare.* New York: Vintage, 1995.

Askins, Robert A. *Restoring North America's Birds.* New Haven, CT: Yale University Press, 2000.

Audubon, John James. *Audubon's Birds of America.* Popular ed. New York: Macmillan, 1950.

Beletsky, Les. *Collins Birds of the World.* London: HarperCollins, 2006.

Berry, Thomas. *The Dream of the Earth.* San Francisco: Sierra Club Books, 1988.

Bodsworth, Fred. *Last of the Curlews.* London: Longman, 1955.

Cornell Lab of Ornithology. *The Birds of North America Online.* http://bna.birds.cornell.edu/bna/.

Darwin, Charles. *The Origin of Species.* New York: Penguin Putnam/New American Library/Mentor, 1958.

———. *The Voyage of a Naturalist Round the World in H.M.S. "Beagle."* London: George Routledge & Sons, Limited, 1860.

Dawkins, Richard. *The Blind Watchmaker.* London: Penguin, 1988.

———. *The Greatest Show on Earth.* New York: Free Press, 2009.

Day, David. *Noah's Choice.* London: Penguin, 1991.

Ehrlich, Paul R. *The Machinery of Nature.* New York: Touchstone, 1986.

Ehrlich, Paul R., David S. Dobkin, and Darryl Wheye. *The Birder's Handbook*. New York: Simon and Schuster, 1988.

Eldredge, Niles. *The Miner's Canary*. New York: Prentice Hall, 1991.

Farrand John, Jr., ed. *The Audubon Society Encyclopedia of Animal Life*. New York: Clarkson N. Potter, 1982.

Feduccia, Alan. *The Origin and Evolution of Birds*. 2nd ed. New Haven, CT: Yale University Press, 1999.

Fortey, Richard. *Life: An Unauthorised Biography*. London: HarperCollins, 1997.

Gill, Frank. *Ornithology*. 2nd ed. New York: W.H. Freeman, 1995.

Goodenough, Ursula. *The Sacred Depths of Nature*. New York: Oxford University Press, 1998.

Hirschfeld, Erik, ed. *Rare Birds Yearbook 2009*. Shropshire, UK: MagDig Media, 2008.

International Union for Conservation of Nature. *International Union for Conservation of Nature Red List of Threatened Species*. http://www.redlist.org.

Leopold, Aldo. *A Sand County Almanac*. New York: Oxford University Press, 1949.

Livingston, John A. *Rogue Primate*. Toronto: Key Porter, 1994.

———. *The Fallacy of Wildlife Conservation*. Toronto: McClelland and Stewart, 1981.

Lovejoy, Thomas, and Lee Hannah, eds. *Climate Change and Biodiversity*. New Haven, CT: Yale University Press, 2005.

Luther Martin, Calvin. *The Great Forgetting*. Santa Fe, NM: K-Selected Books, 2010.

Marzluff, John M., and Rex Sallabanks. *Avian Conservation*. Washington, DC: Island Press, 1998.

Matthiessen, Peter. *Wildlife in America*. New York: Viking Press, 1959.

Mountfort, Guy. *Rare Birds of the World*. London: Collins, 1988.

Nielsen, John. *Condor*. New York: HarperCollins, 2006.

Novacek, Michael. *Terra*. New York: Farrar, Strauss and Giroux, 2007.

Payne, Roger. *Among Whales*. New York: Dell, 1995.

Peattie, Donald Culross. *Flowering Earth*. New York: Putnam's Sons, 1939.

Pimm, Stuart. *A Scientist Audits the Earth*. Piscataway, NJ: Rutgers University Press, 2004.

Quammen, David. *The Song of the Dodo*. New York: Touchstone, 1996.

Raup, David M. *Extinction, Bad Genes or Bad Luck?* New York: W.W. Norton, 1991.

Rowe, Stan. *Home Place, Essays on Ecology*. Rev. ed. Edmonton: NeWest Press, 2002.

Skutch, Alexander F. *Life Ascending*. Austin: University of Texas Press, 1985.

———. *Origins of Nature's Beauty*. Austin: University of Texas Press, 1992.

Teale, Edwin Way. *Green Treasury*. New York: Dodd, Mead, 1952.

Tudge, Colin. *The Variety of Life*. Oxford: Oxford University Press, 2000.

Tyson, Peter. *The Eighth Continent*. New York: HarperCollins, 2000.

Wallace, Alfred Russel. *The Malay Archipelago*. New York: Dover, 1962. Reprint of 1922 edition.

Weiner, Jonathan. *The Beak of the Finch*. New York: Vintage Books, 1994.

Wernert, Susan, ed. *North American Wildlife*. Pleasantville, NY: Reader's Digest Association, 1982.

Wilson, E.O. *Biophilia*. Cambridge, MA: Harvard University Press, 1984.

———. *The Creation: An Appeal to Save Life on Earth*. New York: W.W. Norton, 2006.

———. *The Diversity of Life*. New York: W.W. Norton, 1992.

———. *The Future of Life*. New York: Alfred A. Knopf, 2002.

PHOTO CREDITS

Amsterdam albatross: Vincent Legendre/Wikimedia Creative Commons 2.5 attribution-ShareAlike 2.5 generic

Amur leopard: Silvain de Munck/Creative Commons 2.0 attribution-no derivatives Flickr

Arakan forest turtle: Wikimedia Commons public domain

Asiatic cheetah: Rob Qld/Creative Commons, attribution generic 2.0

Bali myna: Graham Racher/Wikimedia Commons, Creative Commons attribution-ShareAlike2.0

Black-footed ferret: Ryan Hagerty/USFWS

Blue iguana: Frederic J. Burton

Burmese roofed turtle: Rick Hudson

California condor: USFWS/Creative Commons attribution 2.0 generic

Campbell Island teal: Stomac/Wikimedia Commons public domain

Cat Ba langur: Jorg Adler/Cat Ba Langur Conservation Project

Chatham Island black robin: Frances Schmechel/Creative Commons attribution-ShareAlike 2.0 generic

Crested ibis: Andi Li/Creative Commons, attribution-no derivatives 2.0

Devils Hole pupfish: USFWS/public domain

Eastern North Pacific right whale: Scott Leslie

Echo parakeet: Christopher Sheehan

El lobo (Mexican wolf): USFWS/Jim Clark Creative Commons attribution 2.0

Greater Bamboo Lemur: Dede Randrianarista

Guam rail ko'ko': courtesy of Guam Department of Agriculture

Hainan gibbon: Patrick Barry/Flickr Creative Commons attribution-ShareAlike

He-cabbage tree: Rebecca Cairns-Wicks

Iberian lynx: Programa de Conservacion ex-situ del Lince Iberico/Wikimedia Commons, Creative Commons, attribution 2.5

Iranian Gorgan mountain salamander: Mehregan Ebrahimi/Wikimedia Commons Creative Commons attribution-shareAlike 2.5

Irrawaddy river shark: Bill Harrison/Wikimedia Commons Creative Commons attribution 2.0 generic

Kakapo: belgianchocolate/Creative Commons attribution 2.0 generic

Lord Howe Island giant stick insect: Peter Halasz/Wikimedia Commons Creative Commons attribution-shareAlike 2.5

Mangrove finch: Michael Dvorak/Wikimedia Commons Creative Commons attribution-generic 2.5

Milu (Père David's Deer): Wouter de Bruijn/Creative Commons attribution generic 2.0

Miss Waldron's red colobus monkey: Fanny Schertzer/Wikimedia Commons Creative Commons attribution ShareAlike3.0

Mountain bongo: Lazurite/Creative Commons attribution-no derivatives

Nene (Hawaiian goose): Jose Felipe Ortega/Creative Commons attribution-ShareAlike2.0 generic

Northern hairy-nosed wombat: Jason Pratt/Flickr Creative Commons attribution 2.0 generic

Northern sportive lemur: Leonora Enking

Northern white rhinoceros: Sheep81/Wikimedia Commons Creative Commons public domain

Pink pigeon: Christopher Sheehan

Pinta Island Galapagos giant tortoise: Putneymark/Creative Commons attribution-ShareAlike 2.0 generic

Przewalski's horse: Christopher Sheehan

Puerto Rican amazon: USFWS/public domain

Rabb's fringe-limbed tree frog: Dr. Bradley Wilson

Seychelles magpie robin: Jon Hornbuckle

Seychelles sheath-tailed bat: Gaetan Hoareau/Nature Seychelles

Short-tailed albatross: USFWS/Wikimedia Commons public domain

South China tiger: ltansey/Creative Commons attribution 2.0

St. Helena ebony: Rebecca Cairns-Wicks

Sulu hornbill: Wikimedia Commons public domain

Vancouver Island marmot: Oli Gardener/courtesy of Marmot Recovery Foundation

Virginia round-leaf birch: Vicky Somma

Whooping crane: USFWS/Steve Hillebrand

Wisent (European bison): Michael Berlin/Creative Commons attribution-ShareAlike2.0 generic

Wollemi pine: W.L. Cutler/Creative Commons attribution 2.0 generic

Yunnan box turtle: courtesy of Turtle Survival Alliance

INDEX